COUNTRY BOY

COUNTRY BOY

Growing Up In Norfolk
1940–60

COLIN MILLER

ISIS
LARGE PRINT
Oxford

First published in Great Britain 2005
by
Sutton Publishing Limited

Published in Large Print 2006 by ISIS Publishing Ltd.,
7 Centremead, Osney Mead, Oxford OX2 0ES
by arrangement with
Sutton Publishing Limited

The moral right of the author has been asserted

British Library Cataloguing in Publication Data
Miller, Colin, 1940–
    Country boy : growing up in Norfolk, 1940–60.
    – Large print ed. – (Isis reminiscence series)
    1. Miller, Colin, 1940– – Childhood and youth
    2. Country life – England – Norfolk
    3. Large type books
    4. Norfolk (England) – Social life and customs
    – 20th century
    I. Title
    942.6'1084'092

ISBN 0–7531–9358–2 (hb)
ISBN 0–7531–9359–0 (pb)

Printed and bound in Great Britain by
T. J. International Ltd., Padstow, Cornwall

Contents

Acknowledgements

Writing this book has given me immense pleasure but it would not have been possible without the encouragement and help I received from many individuals and organisations. I wish to thank my dear wife, Dr Celia Miller, for her patience, encouragement and practical assistance; my mother-in-law Edna Bushell, my cousin Stephanie Gallant and my friend Richard Tacon for reading and evaluating the manuscript. I am most grateful for the help given during my research by the staff of the Great Yarmouth Central Library and the Norfolk and Norwich Millennium Library. I must thank my editor, Simon Fletcher, at Sutton Publishing for his valuable assistance and advice. My thanks go also to the individuals and organisations that have permitted me to reproduce photographs and illustrations from their collections. Where possible, I have made every effort to identify and trace all current copyright owners for their permission to reproduce these photographs and illustrations. If I have failed or omitted any person or organisation from the following list, I apologise and suggest that they contact me immediately. My thanks go to Mrs S. Gallant, Mr Cecil Miller, Mr R. Tacon, Mrs G. Tooke, Mrs Sheila Allen, Mr and Mrs J. White, Mr Eddie Bates, Mr M. Teun; Regent Photographics on behalf of D.R. Nobbs & Son of Great Yarmouth; Archant Norfolk Limited for the

Great Yarmouth Mercury and *Eastern Daily Press*, in particular Jenny Sheldrake of Front Office Photosales; Norfolk County Council Libraries and Information Service, especially Aimee Lawrance, Picture Norfolk Administrator; and Mrs E. Ward, local history librarian at the Great Yarmouth Central Library.

Introduction

The following is an account of my early life in Rollesby, a small Broadland village in the county of Norfolk, during the years 1940 to 1959 based mainly on my memories of that time. My recollections cover the period when Britain was at war with Germany, through post-war austerity until, eventually, Harold Macmillan allegedly proclaimed "You've never had it so good"; through the period of nationalisation, the creation of the National Health Service and growing working-class expectations arising from the 1944 Education Act; through a time when Communism was in its ascendancy and war with Russia was a distinct possibility, and when the British Empire painfully evolved to become a Commonwealth of equals. Not that I was aware of these developments, although some undoubtedly directly or indirectly affected my early years. My memories are simply recollections of life in a small rural community as seen through the eyes of a child. Although I can remember wartime and its immediate aftermath, my clearest memories are of the late 1940s and the 1950s, a period when my mother, father and I lived as a family in a modest, rented semi-detached house on the Martham Road in Rollesby.

In this account I have tried to describe my memories as accurately as possible without recourse to any additional embellishments or fabrications in order to produce a good story. Neither have I attempted to analyse or pass judgement upon my recollections; this I leave to my reader. If possible I have substantiated my memories by referring to friends, relatives and a careful trawl of contemporary local newspapers, particularly the weekly *Great Yarmouth Mercury*. Where appropriate I have supported my descriptions with extracts from newspaper reports.

During a period of almost twenty years it is inevitable that many changes will have occurred, not only nationally but within a small village community. Nevertheless change was slow in a country recovering from the effects of a World War, much slower than those that have taken place during the last twenty years. Yet change did occur and in my text I have tried to identify those changes that affected family and village life during my childhood. To this end I have organised my memories thematically describing in turn the village, my family and my home, local employment, village facilities, education, health, entertainment and leisure. In the text I have referred to some individuals by name, but have done so only where I am sure that no embarrassment or offence will be incurred by those identified or by their friends and descendants. I also refer to my parents as Mother and Father when, in reality, I addressed them by the more familiar titles of Mum and Dad. Finally I have included a chapter exploring my recollections relating to manners, beliefs and the emergent teenage culture of the late 1950s.

The result, I believe, gives a glimpse of village and

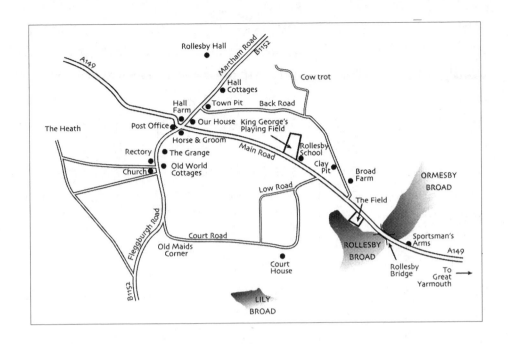

The village of Rollesby, 1940–60.

family life in the 1940s and 1950s, of the joys and difficulties of growing up in a rural community and of a way of living that has long disappeared. It was a time when television sets were a rarity and most people relied on public transport rather that the motor car, a time before supermarkets, out-of-town shopping malls, computers, e-mails and cheap continental holidays. Although my memories of childhood are mostly pleasurable, it is not my intention to suggest that these were the "good old days" or to compare them unfavourably with village or family life in the twenty-first century.

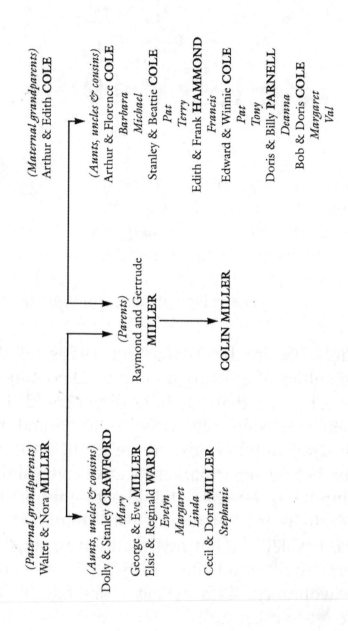

FAMILY TREE OF THE MILLER AND COLE FAMILIES 1940–60

(Paternal grandparents)
Walter & Nora MILLER

(Maternal grandparents)
Arthur & Edith COLE

(Aunts, uncles & cousins)
Dolly & Stanley CRAWFORD
Mary
George & Eve MILLER
Elsie & Reginald WARD
Evelyn
Margaret
Linda
Cecil & Doris MILLER
Stephanie

(Parents)
Raymond and Gerrude MILLER

COLIN MILLER

(Aunts, uncles & cousins)
Arthur & Florence COLE
Barbara
Michael
Stanley & Beattie COLE
Pat
Terry
Edith & Frank HAMMOND
Francis
Edward & Winnie COLE
Pat
Tony
Doris & Billy PARNELL
Deanna
Bob & Doris COLE
Margaret
Val

CHAPTER ONE

Rollesby 1940–59

I was born on 5 August 1940 in the village of Rollesby, 8 miles north-west of Great Yarmouth, in the centre of Broadland Norfolk. To be precise, I was born in the back bedroom of an historic thatched house opposite Rollesby Church known locally as Old World Cottage. According to an inscription on its gabled end the cottage was built in 1583 and had clearly seen better days, as during the 1940s it was divided into two small semi-detached residences. The roadside half, where my mother was staying, had been enlarged by the addition of a corrugated iron roofed single storey kitchen extension. Local folklore suggests that, in 1600, the cottage was also the birthplace of Rollesby's most famous inhabitant, Thomas Goodwin, a puritan clergyman who was at one time both chaplain and friend to Oliver Cromwell.

My mother's account of my birth acknowledges that it was not any easy one as she insists that her labour began in the evening of 3 August and continued until the early hours of Monday 5 August, a Bank Holiday Monday when the August holiday was taken at the start of the month rather than the end as now. Some of her difficulties were undoubtedly caused by my apparent insistence on arriving feet first and that I needed to be turned many times before eventually acceding to arrive in the conventional manner. The forceps' scars that can still be seen at the front and back of my head indicate that even then I needed some persuasion to be born. At the time of my birth, England was at war with Germany and the Battle of Britain had yet to be won. My mother often recalled that part of that battle was being conducted overhead as I was being born and that she was praying that a bomb would land on the cottage to put an end to her misery. Ultimately we were both pleased that no bomb fell. When I had been tidied up the midwife, appropriately named Mrs Nurse, announced that "In later life this child will be bald", a prediction that, inevitably, proved to be all too accurate.

Whether or not it was a consequence of my extended arrival, I was destined to be an only child. Not that this was a problem, as I received far more love and attention from my parents, particularly my mother, than I could have expected as a member of a larger family. Nor was I in any way indulged — I did not have many or expensive toys, for times were hard just after the war and money was scarce. However, I did not want for company, although I did learn to enjoy and sometimes crave being on my own. As well as many village friends, I was fortunate in having a large extended family. On my father's side, my Rollesby grandparents, Walter and Nora Miller, had had six children, four boys and two girls: Dorothy (Dolly), George, Elsie, Cecil, Raymond (my father) and Kenneth. Kenneth unfortunately died of diphtheria in 1924 while still an infant. My maternal grandparents, Arthur and Edith Cole, lived at 12 North Market Road in Great Yarmouth and had also produced a large family consisting of four boys and three girls: Arthur, Stanley, Edith, Edward, Doris, Gertrude (my mother) and Bob. By the 1940s, all my aunts and uncles were married and had children of a similar age to myself. Apart from Grandfather Cole who died when I was two years old, my surviving grandparents and many of my aunts and uncles continued to live locally. Consequently the benefits derived from being a member of two large and close families, and the company and friendship of many young cousins, compensated greatly for the lack of brothers or sisters.

At the time of my birth, my mother was staying at Old World Cottage with two of my aunts, Doris Miller and Elsie Ward. Both uncles, Cecil Miller and Reginald Ward, had already been called up for army service while my father, being a bricklayer and in an exempted occupation, was employed by the RAF as part of a construction gang that travelled around the country building airfields. Before the war my parents had moved to Birmingham in search of work and remained there until the outbreak of hostilities when my father moved back to Rollesby so that my mother could be supported by his family while he did his bit for the Royal Air Force. Soon after my birth, we moved into a rented property on Martham Road in Rollesby which became my home for the next nineteen years. My father continued his travels around the country eventually joining the Royal Engineers in 1942 and seeing action during the Italian campaign. At the end of the war he remained in service with the army for a further two years, attached to the British occupation force in Austria. It was 1947 before he was finally demobilised and we were able to become a whole family once again. My early life in Rollesby continued until Tuesday 6 October 1959, when I loaded my new red trunk, filled with all my possessions, into the goods van of the 9.20 a.m. steam train from Great Yarmouth's South Town station. Making sure that I was unobserved by any of my contemporaries, I kissed my mother goodbye, shook hands with my father and boarded the train for Leicester, university and the next phase of my life.

THE VILLAGE

The village of Rollesby lies between Ormesby and Repps on the A149, approximately 8 miles north-west of Great Yarmouth and 17 miles north-east of Norwich. Rollesby's "by" ending suggests that the village was established in the ninth or tenth century during the Danish settlement of East Anglia when Rollesby would have been located on an island, the Isle of Flegg, surrounded by the water and marshland of a great shallow inland estuary situated behind the sandbank on which Great Yarmouth now stands. Although the word Flegg derives from an Old Norse word meaning flat, the Rollesby landscape of the 1940s and 1950s was a gently undulating agricultural patchwork of hedged fields, woods, scattered farms and homesteads. Most of the village population lived either side of a 1 mile stretch of the A149, the Main Road, between the bridge — a narrow humpbacked bridge that crossed a short cut joining the Ormesby Broad to the Rollesby and Filby Broads — and the Horse & Groom crossroads where the A149 was crossed by the B1152 which linked Acle and Fleggburgh, to the south-west, with Martham, Hemsby and the coast to the north-east. Located on one corner of the crossing was the Post Office and Stores belonging to my grandparents, while a mere 50 yards along the B1152 towards Martham, the stretch known appropriately as Martham Road, was the small semi-detached house that became our home. Two other narrow lanes, the Back Road and Court Road, linked the A149 from close by the bridge to the B1152 either side of the Horse & Groom. Further short lanes and tracks led to numerous isolated farmsteads and houses.

The primary form of employment within the village was in agriculture, a combination of mixed farming, market gardening and fruit growing. Rollesby had three large farms of 150 acres or more, together with a number of smaller council owned holdings of 40 to 50 acres. Rollesby did not have an easily identifiable centre. Small groups of farms and houses were scattered throughout the village, each group identified by a place name such as Cowtrot, Old Maid's Corner or "Up the Heath". Most private housing had been built close to the A149 with two major concentrations at the opposite ends of the village, one between the school and the bridge, and the other around the Horse & Groom crossroads. Most accommodation was rented, either as council housing, privately owned lets, or houses tied to agricultural occupations, the latter mostly associated with the larger farms or with the Rollesby Hall estate. Apart from a few bungalows near to the Horse & Groom, little new housing was built in the village during the 1940s for the most part because of the lack of a mains water supply. In the early 1950s, two small housing developments were built along the Main Road, a private estate of ten houses for rent opposite Belle Vue terrace and, in 1952, a small council estate near to the school appropriately named Coronation Avenue. Little other new building took place until the bungalow boom of the 1960s. Consequently the village population was relatively static and changed little during the years 1940 to 1959. In 1931, the village had a population of 456; in 1951, 524 and in 1961, 533. Until the 1960s newcomers were a rarity and those that did move into the village mostly came from adjoining villages. The dominant accent was Broadland Norfolk. Those few incomers with an accent from outside East Anglia were treated with curiosity and, occasionally, suspicion.

The nearest we had to a community centre was the recreation field, known officially as King George V's Playing Field. Rollesby had no functional village hall and most communal indoor activities — wedding receptions, whist drives, dances and socials — were held in the school next to the recreation field or at a hall in the adjoining village of Little Ormesby. A "Church Room" donated to the village in 1929 for use as a community hall had been badly damaged by fire during the war and was little used thereafter. From the early 1950s, efforts were made to gain funding for a replacement facility and, as a result, in 1959 a new village hall was erected on a piece of waste ground immediately behind the bowling green of the Horse & Groom public house.

> . . . there is the Church room, which Rollesby used to do duty as a parish hall. This caught fire when troops were billeted there during the war and has been untenable ever since. As a result, social activities in the village are on a very reduced scale as there is just nowhere to hold meetings or social gatherings except the unsuitable hut on the playing field — the only King George V Memorial playing field in a village for miles around.
>
> "Portrait of Rollesby",
> *Yarmouth Mercury*, 7 July 1950

Three of Rollesby's most historic buildings, Rollesby Hall, the Old Rectory and Rollesby Courthouse, were requisitioned by the government during the war to house troops or evacuees from London and, by the end of hostilities, all were in a state of disrepair and mostly empty. Rollesby Hall, dating from the seventeenth century and owned by Colonel and Mrs Benn, was in such a derelict state that it was never reoccupied and was eventually demolished in 1950 to be replaced by a modern building in a Norwegian style. I visited the old Hall a number of times with my grandfather but can only vaguely remember a decaying building, surrounded by rhododendron bushes, which contained large, dark, damp, empty rooms with wood panelling on the walls. Having ceased to be the residence of Rollesby's vicars, the Old Rectory with the attached Church Room remained empty until 1950 when it was sold for redevelopment as private housing. Rollesby Courthouse, originally the Union Workhouse and Magistrates Court for East and West Flegg, was also sold to become a private house in 1946.

However important these buildings may have been, they feature very little in my recollections of Rollesby. My memories are related to family, our house on Martham Road, my grandparents at Rollesby post office, the farms and homes of my friends, Rollesby Broad, the church, the primary school and the recreation field, the Horse & Groom and the Eels Foot in Ormesby, the football and cricket clubs. As a young child the village was my world and, along with all the other local children, I was allowed to roam unrestricted anywhere within its bounds. There was not a road, track, farm, field, meadow or wood that I had not explored. Personal safety was not a serious consideration in days when local transport was more likely to be a bicycle than a car, a time when most residents worked in the village and strangers were rare. There were very few places that I could go without my presence being noted by some adult and, occasionally, reported back to my parents. My mother and father frequently seemed to know where I had spent my day even before I had time to tell them. In a quieter world we were able to communicate among ourselves over reasonable distances by means of various finger-assisted whistles or yodels. Many parents were exceptionally skilled at throwing their voices and could call their children home for tea from relatively long distances.

ROLLESBY BROAD

The 600-acre lake formed by the Rollesby, Ormesby and Filby Broads, known collectively as the Trinity Broad, is now acknowledged to be the result of peat digging during the Middle Ages and not, as I was taught, left over puddles from the last Ice Age. Being separate from the larger Broads' navigation system they were, for the most part, unaffected by the pre- and post-war growth in tourism and, for this reason, they had become a source of drinking water supplying Great Yarmouth and surrounding districts. A large waterworks had been built adjoining Ormesby Broad to extract and purify the murky Broads' water. As a result, in the 1940s and 1950s, the Trinity Broad was free from the motorboats and yachts associated with the holiday industry and provided a tranquil and picturesque location for fishermen, birdwatchers and local villagers to use and enjoy. At weekends and evenings during the fishing season, the bridge was usually crammed full of small boys dangling fishing rods over its parapets. From time to time a float would disappear under the water and, accompanied by a whoop of delight, a line would be reeled in usually to reveal a small, wriggling, silver fish attached to the end, barely worth the time, effort and enthusiasm expended in catching it. If lucky, the fish would be quickly detached from the line and returned to the water from which it came. If unlucky, it would be taken home as a treat for the household cat. I, too, had a fishing rod and occasionally took my place with the other small boys on the parapets of the bridge. My fishing rod was bought for me by Grandfather Miller and consisted of four varnished bamboo sections with a cork handle all contained in a purpose-made cloth bag. A reel was attached to the rod by two ornamented metal rings. My colourful spare floats, lines, hooks and lead weights were all contained in an old biscuit tin. I was extremely proud of my rod as most of the other boys' rods only had three sections. I was, however, unaware that the rod was for sea fishing and not particularly suitable for the freshwater Broads. I mostly enjoyed casting the line, taking great pride from landing the float on top of a predetermined point in the water. I frequently practised this art from out of my upstairs bedroom window to the annoyance of my mother. I actually disliked fishing, and I felt very sorry for any fish that finished up on the end of my line. My earnest hope was that I could detach the unfortunate creature from my hook without causing too much damage to its mouth. Regrettably, this was not always possible.

Most adults preferred to fish from small boats that they rowed out into the centre of the Broad well away from the jostle and noise of the shoreline rabble. Boats could be hired from two nearby jetties, one close to the bridge behind a public house called The Sportsman's Arms, now delicensed and a private house, and the other at the curiously named Eel's Foot Inn in Little Ormesby. At weekends, particularly during the summer, boats were in great demand by fishermen, families intent on a recreational row around the Broad and young couples seeking a private place in the reeds to do their courting. I was lucky in that Grandfather had his own private landing stage at the bottom of a field adjacent to Rollesby Broad that he hired from the waterworks' company for use as a market garden. The landing stage consisted of a small channel cut through the reeds together with a fairly rickety wooden jetty constructed from three pairs of upright stakes driven into the soft mud of the water bottom. Each pair of stakes was connected by a horizontal bar a foot or so above the waterline on to which planks were laid to form a walkway. As a small boy, I was never totally confident when walking on to this jetty as it seemed to be most precarious. However, it was extremely unlikely that I would have come to any harm if I had fallen off, as the water was very shallow at that point. Attached to the jetty was Grandfather's rowing boat — a rather cumbersome and heavy vessel that he insisted had at one time seen service as a lifeboat. Before it could be used it was frequently necessary to bail out all the rainwater that had collected inside since its last trip. Often, after heavy rain, the boat was barely afloat.

11

Despite my indifference to angling, I regularly accompanied my uncles, Cecil and George Miller, on fishing trips in grandfather's boat. Once settled on the Broad, my uncles would have a competition to see who caught the most fish, each keeping their catches in nets which they hung from the stern of the boat. In the quiet times between catches they would quaff whisky or brandy from large hip flasks while I would pig out on a pile of jam sandwiches made for me by my mother. We would often sit in silence listening to the calls of moorhens, coots and great crested grebes echoing across the Broad, our eyes glued to the small colourful floats that bobbed continuously on the surface of the water. I quickly learnt to distinguish between the different types of fish that we caught and could easily recognise if they were perch, rudd, roach, bream or some other variety. Eels were common and disliked intensely by all freshwater fishermen as, if caught, they would tangle themselves around the line or in the mesh of the landing nets. It was almost impossible to detach an eel from a fishing line without damaging it or incurring harm to oneself. In the winter, my uncles would fish for pike. Grown large with the easy pickings of a well-stocked Broad, these fishy predators were a prized catch, the largest of which usually ended up stuffed and displayed in a glass case at a local public house. I can remember pike-fishing expeditions on mornings so cold that ice had formed on the surface of the water. On one particularly cold trip we spent all day fishing without any sign of a catch when, to my surprise, as we reeled in our rods for the last time, hooked on to the end of my line was the one and only pike that I ever caught. Perhaps I can understand the pleasure gained from fishing for such game as, with encouragement and advice from my uncles, I battled with the fish for at least fifteen minutes before it was at last landed into the boat and dispatched. After proudly displaying my catch to my family and friends it was given to a local resident who considered pike to be an edible delicacy. None of our family ate pike, considering it to be tasteless and with too many bones.

As small boys we also learnt to swim in the Broad, although this was another activity I did not particularly enjoy. On warm summer days, gangs of boys and girls made their way through the woods behind the allotments on Court Road to a shallow part of the Broad, called Lily Broad, where they could swim and splash about in relative safety. My reluctance to join in undoubtedly resulted from the fact that, being small for my age, I was always the one to be thrown in or ducked. I preferred to swim alone when I would breaststroke at my own pace across a narrow part of Lily Broad, my head held well above the surface of the water. In the harsh winters of the late 1940s and early 1950s the Broads regularly froze and many adults were able to enjoy a period when they could skate on the iced-over water. My father was a keen skater and I well remember accompanying him on to the Broad where I was left standing, cold and rather apprehensive, as he glided and twirled at breakneck speed over the ice. My fear of being on the ice was worsened by his habit of testing its strength by jumping up and down, often causing cracking sounds to rifle across the surface, seemingly for miles, something that he always seemed to ignore.

Skating on the Broads — Ice 12 inches thick at Rollesby

The Norfolk broads, world famed summer holiday attraction, has since that great freeze became a winter sporting centre. Skaters have been travelling from neighbouring towns and villages during the last two weeks to the Rollesby Filby Ormesby Broads where the ice is 12 inches thick. It is possible to walk from Rollesby to Filby Bridge. Otters have been seen at Eels Foot where there is a small stretch of open water. The stretch, too, is covered by wild fowl seeking food. Many wild birds, particularly water hens, are being found dead.

Yarmouth Mercury, 1 March 1947

THE PLAYING FIELDS

Most outdoor activities within the village, official and unofficial, took place on the playing field. On weekdays during term time the village school used the field for PE and games activities, at weekends it was home to the village football and cricket teams. In summer it hosted the village fete and on 5 November a massive bonfire.

In a corner of the field close to the Main Road were three swings, a see-saw and a sandpit. Erected just after the war as a facility for village children, they were a potential source of injury as well as enjoyment as no soft safety surface was provided under the swings and many children were injured, albeit none seriously, through falling on to the ground underneath, which often had been baked as hard as concrete by the sun. My own enthusiasm for swinging was seriously dented after I fell backwards off one of the swings and lay on the ground for some time, stunned and winded. The sandpit became a convenient toilet for every cat within a radius of about a mile.

Fete and Show

Rollesby's annual fete and horticultural show was held on the playing field on Saturday. The show was opened by Mrs I B H Benn and the children's new amusement corner was opened by Mr J Gaze, chairman of the King George's Playing Field trustees. Children's sports, competitions and side shows were well patronised and Mr H Marsden Smith auctioned the show exhibits on behalf of the Playing Field Fund for which the effort was organised.

Yarmouth Mercury, 2 August 1947

In another corner, at the far end of the field and away from the road, was the men's toilet. This consisted of a

15

square enclosure, fenced with corrugated iron sheets and surrounded by firs for additional privacy. Men and boys would normally pee against the sheets or into a long strip of guttering conveniently attached to one side of the enclosure. At each end of the gutter was a hole. When in use, the contents of the gutter would empty through these holes on to the ground or, more often than not, over the shoes of some inattentive individual. For a while there was no facility for women; then, to the relief of the ladies, a lavatory for women was sited on the opposite corner of the field consisting of a lockable wooden shed containing a cylindrical chemical toilet. A large, green, wooden hut had been erected adjacent to the school for use as a changing room and for any other purpose as needed by the various playing-field users. These facilities were improved in 1948 when an electricity supply was installed. As far as I remember, the internal fittings of the hut consisted of a sink, one cold tap and one electric socket, a small counter at one end opposite the only door, and six or more collapsible wooden benches and tables. Despite this simplicity, it was a great improvement on what had gone before and provided a location for cricket teas, refreshments for village fetes and sports days, and a meeting place for the Ladies' Club as well as a room for teams to change in.

New club for women

To fill a long felt want the sports pavilion has been adapted to provide a clubroom for women. It will be officially opened next Tuesday at 2.30p.m. A whist drive (was held) in aid of the Playing Field Fund on Friday, £10 was raised.

"Village News: Rollesby",
Yarmouth Mercury, 18 March 1949

A veranda with a long bench seat was eventually attached to one side of the hut, financed from funds collected to celebrate the coronation of Queen Elizabeth, to be used as a shelter from which spectators could watch sporting activities on wet days. However, this veranda became the main meeting place for the young people of the village, particularly Rollesby's teenagers. At evenings and weekends, in winter as well as summer, the veranda would be full of children and teenagers discussing and doing what children and teenagers discuss and do when they get together, their bicycles littering the grass in front of the hut. On dark winter evenings many teenagers would contrive a convenient excuse to get out of their houses to join the multitude huddled together on the veranda seat. Luckily, I had aunts, uncles and grandparents in the village that I could visit. The visit normally lasted only five minutes, sufficient for a good alibi, before I cycled full pelt to the playing field. On the veranda, the very

17

young made a lot of noise but were usually just onlookers, learning the art of growing up, while the eleven and twelve year olds lit up cigarettes "borrowed" from packets left unattended by their parents. By thirteen the girls were discovering boys, by fourteen the boys caught up. We discovered the strange excitement to be had by sitting close to a girl, holding hands or engaging in nervous silly conversations and, sometimes, pairs ended up cuddling and kissing, always under the careful scrutiny of the very young. Occasionally, a pair would leave the shelter of the veranda to "go down to the bottom of the field", shadowed silently but remorselessly in the dark by the young observers who spied on them from behind tufts of grass or the ladies' toilet. I never really discovered why others found it so exciting to venture down to the bottom of the field as my trips in that direction were uneventful and never as described to me by others who had gone before.

On Saturday and Sunday mornings, the veranda was usually occupied by numerous boys of all ages waiting for someone to arrive with a football. My arrival was always greeted with enthusiasm as my Grandmother Miller was very generous and had bought me a full-sized leather football. A tennis ball had to suffice if there were no footballs to hand. Once the team captains had been selected, the remaining boys, and occasionally a girl or two, formed a line from which these captains, in turn, selected the members of their team. Usually the youngest or the most inept were picked last. On good days teams could be a dozen or more on each side, one team playing as shirts and the other as pullovers. Mostly we played in our everyday clothes as few children owned a proper football kit. Some, like me, had football boots: stiff, brown, ankle-high leather boots with a hard toecap and tied up by long white laces. Underneath each boot were six cylindrical leather studs, each stud being attached by three small metal pins. Periodically these pins protruded through the bottom of the boots and gouged holes in the soles of our feet while we played. Those without boots played in plimsolls or their ordinary shoes. We were lucky that, for the duration of the football season, the playing field boasted a marked out football pitch with permanent goalposts at each end. For young boys a full sized pitch was often too demanding and, consequently, our second goal was normally located on the halfway line, marked out by two piles of coats. The resulting additional wear and tear to the pitch became evident by the end of the football season when the goal area of the end most used became totally devoid of grass and resembled a mud bath when it rained, and, as a result, goal chances were often missed in the Saturday afternoon adult games when the ball became stuck in the mud. Sometimes, when neither a football nor a tennis ball was available, we cycled mob-handed to the Martham Recreation Field, where a similar game was usually underway, to deliver an inter-village challenge. The resulting match frequently degenerated into a game resembling more a cross between rugby and boxing than classic football.

The Horse and Groom

Dominating the crossroads, the Horse & Groom public house, tied to Lacon's Brewery of Great Yarmouth and managed by Mr and Mrs "Buster" Curtis, was the centre for many village activities. The solid square building was constructed in dark brick and had a large entrance porch supported by four upright wooden columns framing the main entrance. To the right of the porch, two wooden hatch doors led down to the cellar. A 3-foot tarred border ran around the base of the building and in summer this often bubbled in the sun, becoming subject to frequent prodding by the fingers of inquisitive little boys. From the porch, the front door opened into a poorly lit through passage which gave access to the public bar on the left, and a small narrow lounge on the right. Although I was very familiar with the outside, the interior remained a mystery until I was eighteen as the village policeman from Fleggburgh was so diligent in performing his duty that our area of the Fleggs was frequently commended by the licensing court for the lack of prosecutions for drunkenness. However boys will always find a way to be boys, particularly teenage boys, and to that end we developed an interest in bowls. To the back of the public house was the bowling green, a popular summer venue for teenagers as well as for the serious bowls player, which consisted of a perfectly tended green playing square adjoining the pub garden and enclosed by a high fence made from Broadland reeds. A small summerhouse, also made from reed and containing a wooden bench seat, stood halfway along one side. During opening hours we were able to borrow a set of bowls from Mrs Curtis at the back door of the pub and, in the summer months, we became very proficient bowls players — although that clearly was not the main purpose of the exercise. Whether or not Mrs Curtis was aware of our ages, it was usually possible to obtain a half-pint of Lacon's bitter, or shandy for the less adventurous, at the same back door. If challenged, we would pretend to be purchasing drinks for an adult playing on an adjacent lane. The location of the green gave adequate time for illegal drinks to be well hidden should the Fleggburgh policeman make a call. Not that we imbibed alcohol to excess as limited funds ensured that we remained relatively sober.

To the front and along one side of the building was the pub car park which also served as a stop for the red number 5 Eastern Counties bus that travelled through the village on its way from Norwich to Great Yarmouth and back. Passengers often made use of the wooden bench seats along the front wall of the pub to rest their feet while waiting for the bus to arrive. On Saturday winter evenings a crowd gathered for the arrival of the 8.30 p.m. service from Norwich which delivered copies of the *Pink 'Un*, a Saturday only evening newspaper that reported on the major national and local sporting activities of the day, including the football league and, in particular, the fortunes of Norwich City Football Club, then in Division 3 South. Once delivered, the *Pink 'Un* could be purchased from the Horse & Groom

21

car park and my father regularly sent me there to obtain a copy so that he could recheck his football pools coupon, as he was always concerned that he might have misheard the results declared on the radio at the tea time edition of Sports Report and could, after all, be this week's winner of the £75,000 Vernon's Pools' jackpot. A mobile van selling fish and chips usually arrived just before the bus and did a good trade with the waiting villagers and the customers inside the pub.

The car park was also home to a bright red telephone box that was in almost constant use, as very few people owned a personal telephone. Queues often formed outside as users waited impatiently for their turn. At weekends and on early weekday evenings, it was mainly used by teenagers and single men and women arranging dates with similar teenagers and singles at other boxes in neighbouring villages. Occasionally confrontations occurred between those waiting and those inside the box, particularly if their conversations were overlong, and I can remember one incident when a person using the telephone was locked in the kiosk by some impatient youths who had secured the door with wire. Sometimes personalities arrived at the pub, no doubt hoping for some anonymity and a quiet relaxing drink in the depths of rural Norfolk, well away from the holiday resort of Great Yarmouth. I can clearly recollect my grandfather frantically knocking on our back door to inform us that the popular entertainer George Formby was drinking at the Horse & Groom. Along with most of the other residents from our part of the village, we formed an excited but uninvited audience, adults inside and children outside standing on benches to peer through the window, while, to enthusiastic cheers, a thin-faced man with protruding teeth was persuaded to pick up a ukulele and perform a number of songs accompanied word for word by most of the assembled villagers.

St George's Church

From Fleggburgh the B1152 to Martham meandered into Rollesby, passing the junction with Court Road, Church Farm with its magnificent thatched barns, and on to St George's church, situated opposite to Old World Cottage where I was born. Built from stone and flint with an octagonal tower on a round Norman base, St George's church is situated on the top of a small rise and, undoubtedly, identifies the location of the original village centre. However, it is clear that sometime in the past this centre moved as, in the 1940s, only the Rectory, the Grange, Old World Cottage and Church Farm remained in close association with the church.

Although my parents were not regular worshippers, I was encouraged to take part in many church activities. In her younger days my mother had been a Sunday school teacher but, somewhere along the line, had lost her enthusiasm for organised religion — perhaps the experience of war had challenged her beliefs. As a family we rarely discussed heady issues such as religion, so I was surprised when, one summer's evening, mother suddenly confessed to me that she had difficulty in believing in God or that we went to Heaven after death. "If there is a Heaven, it has to be right here on Earth, and if you don't believe me then look at that," she said, pointing to a marvellous Norfolk sunset occurring in front of our eyes. My mother was a lovely lively person who always saw the best in everybody and everything. My father had twin passions: my mother, who we both adored, and sport, particularly football. These two passions, together with his commitments to work and the home, gave him little time for Sunday services. Like many others, my parents only maintained an appearance of religious observance by attending church for christenings, weddings, funerals and other special occasions.

It was my Grandfather Miller, a Church of England enthusiast, who was the prime mover in encouraging me to attend at church. Like his father before him, he was both parish clerk and churchwarden and attended Sunday services on a regular basis. Grandfather enjoyed church and sang the hymns of the day at the top of his voice, providing his own adaptations to both tune and words. To me, Sunday service was an unintelligible ritual and I perceived God as an all-seeing Father Christmas-like figure who would grant wishes as a reward for good behaviour. My occasional bedtime prayers were usually a lengthy list of requests relating to issues of importance to a small boy. "Please God, let me not wet the bed tonight", "Please God, let me live forever, or at least until I am one hundred years old", "Please God, let Rollesby win the football match on Saturday". I enjoyed going to church not for any religious reason but for the activities that took place there. On Sunday afternoons, along with a dozen or more other village children, I attended Sunday school which took place in a side aisle of the church in front of a small altar table and underneath a stained glass window. The window, depicting an old man carrying a lantern and based, no doubt, on Holman Hunt's *Light of the World*, strangely fascinated me, particularly in the way that its colours changed and glowed in the sunlight. I happily blanked out the boring bits of Sunday school and the Sunday morning sermon by gazing intently at this amazing window or staring fixedly upwards at the blue ceiling covered in gold stars. At Sunday school we listened to stories from the Bible, learned to say the Lord's Prayer and sang inharmonious versions of favourite children's hymns like "All Things Bright and Beautiful". At various times during the year and always at Christmas and Easter, we would perform religious plays in front of invited parents and relatives. In various Christmastime Nativity plays I progressed from a brief appearance as third shepherd to, eventually, the part of Joseph. At the end of Sunday school all the children were given a small pictorial stamp depicting some event from the Bible with an appropriate moralising caption, which I stuck into a scrapbook as a record of my attendance.

Mothering Day Service

A special service for Mothering Sunday was held at Rollesby church last Sunday. Presents taken by the Sunday School children and bunches of violets and primroses were presented to the mothers. The service was conducted by Mr Carpenter of Filby. The children taking part included G. Evans, J. Hewett, G. Gilbert, C. Miller, R. Wymer, T. Tubby, K. Knight and C. Ransome.

"Village News: Rollesby",
Yarmouth Mercury, 24 March 1950

The Sunday morning service became less of a bore when the vicar, Mr Grundy, invited me to join the choir, which I enjoyed not for the singing but for the dressing up. At best, the choir consisted of no more than five or six persons, normally three adults and three boys, all dressed in red gowns with white surplices. At the beginning of the service, we proudly marched in procession along the central aisle from the tower room to the choir stalls. Leading the procession would be one member of the choir carrying a large brass cross, followed by the rest of the choir in two columns and, bringing up the rear, the vicar in his finery. At the end of the service, we marched back again. For me the singing was a chore, particularly as I didn't possess a very good singing voice and was incapable of remembering the words to even the most regularly sung hymns. As hymnbooks were frequently unavailable in the choir stalls I did a great deal of humming, which didn't matter too much as my grandfather's weekly vocal virtuosity hid many of the shortcomings of the choir.

The most enjoyable task allocated to the choir was to ring the church bells for the half hour prior to morning service. St George's had three bells which we rang one after the other in sequence, without attempting any complicated variations. For the last five minutes before the service a single bell was rung, usually the largest and loudest, to inform those late for worship that the service was about to start. Choir attendance was variable, particularly in winter or at harvest, and there were times when I was the only member of the choir present. Then I rang the bells by myself. Ringing three bells was possible by standing on one leg with a rope in each hand and the third looped on to the end of my other foot. This often proved too much for a small boy and I was regularly lifted off my feet by the upswing of one of the ropes, upsetting the rhythm of the ring and resulting in a chaotic cacophony from the belfry. Occasionally, a boy from the choir would be asked to pump the bellows that supplied air to the organ. St George's church organ was situated to the right of the main aisle, just below the pulpit. Next to the organ and reaching almost to the roof was a three-deep bank of pipes, activated by air from the bellows located in a small room behind the organ seat. At a preordained signal, usually a withering glance from the organist, an ancient lady in a hat and long coat who arrived at church on a tricycle, the selected choirboy dived into the cubicle and began energetically pumping, although often too late to avoid the first notes sounding like a badly played bagpipe. My interest in church activities eventually waned at about the age of eleven when a combination of school homework, sport — football in winter and cricket in summer — and, eventually, the pursuit of girls occupied most of my weekend hours.

After the church, the road wound its way past the Old Rectory and the Grange, before eventually reaching the Horse & Groom crossroads. The road from the church to the crossroads was lined on both sides with trees and to a small boy, on dark winter nights without the benefit of streetlights, their silhouettes made eerie and frightening shapes against the night sky. Frequently I ran all the way from the church, chased home by imaginary demons, until the lights of the Horse & Groom provided a welcome haven of safety.

EMPLOYMENT

The majority of the adult population found employment within the village either in occupations associated with agriculture — as labourers on the farms, market gardens and smallholdings of Rollesby and surrounding district, or as blacksmiths, millers and hauliers — or in servicing the community as grocers, hairdressers, electricians, builders, milkmen or village based council workmen. A small minority commuted from the village to work in the schools, banks, shops and factories of Great Yarmouth. Although agricultural practice changed during the period 1940 to 1959, farming remained the primary employer within the village. In the 1940s, farming was powered by horses, large lumbering docile beasts with immense strength, and I clearly remember sitting astride a large Clydesdale horse that worked on the Fleggburgh farm of my great-aunt Nellie, my legs barely able to span the width of its back. By the early 1950s most of the village horses had been replaced by tractors and by the end of the 1950s the tractor, too, was being replaced in some tasks by specialised machinery such as the combine harvester. To a child, these subtle changes were not apparent; farms and farming were just a part of my normal daily life, particularly in the summer months. As the long summer holidays were originally planned to allow children to work on the harvest, it is not surprising that there was plenty to occupy a young boy in the six-week break from school. Along with many other village children, I spent long hours in the fields during the early 1950s watching or doing my bit particularly during harvest time, not for money, as there was never any chance of payment, but out of tradition and because it was interesting.

Harvest was an exciting time. Before the reaping could begin, the edges of the fields were cut using a scythe. Once this was completed, the reaper-binder, pulled by a tractor, could begin its work. Two men were required to operate these machines, one driving and the other sitting on the back of the reaper-binder controlling its operations. Together, tractor and reaper-binder clanked around the field with the reaper's rotating sails easing the corn on to the cutting teeth where a moving belt funnelled the cut corn into the binding mechanism. There, batches of corn would be bound together with twine into sheaves and thrown out sideways on to the ground. The air would be thick with dust and the smell of oil and cut straw. Bands of men, women and children followed behind the binder collecting up pairs of sheaves, one under each arm, which were then stood on end to dry. Four or more pairs were placed together to make a tent-like structure called a stook. Making, or shocking, the stooks was hard work but frequently we children were allowed to lend a hand as, with the most experienced men driving the machines, any help was welcome. The corn, usually wheat or barley, being quite stiff would chafe or nick the skin on our forearms as we collected up the sheaves. By the end of a day our arms burned with soreness particularly if, through a lack of foresight, we were wearing short sleeved shirts or had our sleeves rolled up instead of down. Often thistles were bound up in the sheaves, their sharp prickly leaves cruelly scratching any unprotected flesh. Many children preferred to be hunters instead of collectors and armed with a large stick, they waited as the area of uncut corn was reduced under the action of the reaper-binder. Eventually, terrified rabbits, trapped by the harvesting, bolted for their burrows from the cover of the uncut corn. Many, chased energetically by yelling youngsters, failed to make safety and were unfortunately dispatched by blows from the flailing sticks of their pursuers. At the end of the day, the farmer separated the best of the rabbit catch for sale to a local butcher, and divided the remainder among the men and boys as a bonus for their efforts with the harvest. I can remember taking home such a bonus only to meet with a tirade from my mother about the cruelty involved in catching these poor unfortunate creatures. The carcass was then consigned to an undignified end in the dustbin. I can also remember that, during wartime, Mother and Grandmother gratefully skinned and cleaned wild rabbits for the stew pot. Her rejection of my 1950s offering clearly demonstrated how things had changed in that intervening period. Unfortunately, soon afterwards, myxomatosis removed the spectacle of a rabbit chase from the harvest scene.

Once dry, the stooks of corn were transferred by cart to a stack in the farmyard. My friend Richard, a gentleman farmer's son, was expected to work at harvest time and in my teens I often helped on his farm with carting the corn to the stack yard. Richard and I took turns to drive the grey Ferguson tractor as the farm workers loaded sheaves from the stooks on to the cart that it was pulling. Our control of the clutch was not always of the best, especially when our boots were muddy or wet, and consequently the man working on top of the load was regularly thrown over because of our jerky driving. Inevitably we were regularly bombarded by frequent and unrepeatable oaths.

Occasionally we took up a pitchfork and helped with the loading although, as the height of the load got higher, it became more difficult for us to pitch the sheaves on to its top. Frequently, falling sheaves from a failed pitch would burst open as the twine broke when it hit the ground. Too valuable to be left, the broken sheaves were rebound using twisted strands of straw in place of the twine, usually accompanied by further irritable mutterings from the farm workers.

During the autumn, contract thrashers arrived at the local farms to process the corn. In the 1940s, work trains consisting of a thrashing machine, escalator and workman's hut would trundle slowly from farm to farm pulled by a massive steam traction engine, watched by scores of open mouthed children. Once these were set up, the stacks of corn were dismantled for the thrashing machine to separate the corn from the straw. Before this began, the farm workers tied twine tightly around the bottoms of their trousers and erected a ring of wire netting around the base of the stack to prevent the many rats and mice that had made their homes inside the stack from escaping. Inside the wire-netting ring, terriers would do their best to terminate the rats by shaking them in their mouths until their necks broke. Outside the ring, boys and men armed with sticks would beat at the mice or squash them under their hobnailed boots. The twine tied around the trouser bottoms was there to prevent a rat or a mouse from attempting to escape up a convenient trouser leg. Eventually the farm tractor replaced the steam engine as the driving force for the threshing machine.

The change from horses to tractors undoubtedly resulted in the demise of the village blacksmith. Rollesby's last blacksmith's shop was located opposite to King George's playing field, between the council houses and the flint and thatched residence of Mr Laxon, the miller. The blacksmith's shop, a rectangular wooden sided building with a red tiled roof and an arched window, was in regular use until the early 1950s. Often, after school, I would peer through the open door and watch Mr Bloom, the blacksmith, hammering at a piece of glowing metal and transforming it into a shoe for a waiting horse or a tool ordered by a local tradesman. The shop ceased to function as a smithy soon after Mr Bloom died in 1951.

This was my village, remembered through the eyes of a child, my eyes. A small self-contained Broadland farming village with a well-developed sense of community.

CHAPTER
TWO

A Working Family

MILLERS AND COLES

It is clear to me that "the family" played an important role in my early life. As well as my parents, my aunts, uncles, grandparents and cousins are all ever present in my memories of the 1940s and 1950s. Perhaps it was because I came from two large families, or maybe the uncertainties of wartime had strengthened family bonds as, with most adult males employed in some form of war service, it is conceivable that those left at home strove to make the lives of their children as full as possible. Whatever the reason, my childhood, especially during and soon after the war, was a delightful experience that I look back on with great affection and all of my family, not just my parents, made that possible.

With my father away on war service, the main man in my early life was my grandfather, Walter Miller. To me he was a big man and life was interesting in his company. Grandfather Miller was a man of many parts. Originally trained as a carpenter and wheelwright, he became a professional soldier, serving in the army

34

through the First World War and after, until ill health eventually forced him to leave the services in the early 1920s. With what money he had accumulated he hired a small market garden near to Rollesby Broad that we affectionately referred to as "The Field". Here, in addition to producing flowers, fruit and vegetables, he established a base from which to set up and run a small building firm, a notice on the gate proudly advertising "W.J. Miller, Builder". Together we would spend days at his market garden, visiting his building sites or driving around on various errands in his car. To him I was his "little man" and nothing was too much trouble.

My grandmother, Nora Miller, was everything a grandmother should be. A cuddly, rosy-faced woman with boundless energy, she was the great facilitator of the family. Parties at Grandmother's house, a frequent occurrence, were a non-stop round of games, competitions and sumptuous teas. Her home was neat, well-organised, and spotlessly clean. Every tabletop, corner and well-polished cupboard was filled with her collections of porcelain and ornamental brasses. Her village activities were many, including managing the Remembrance and Alexander Rose Day collections, organising theatre visits, whist drives for St Dunstan's and activities and outings for the Women's Social Club and the WVS. From her home on the Horse & Groom crossroads she ran a village post office and grocery store, yet always had time to spare for her various grandchildren. Living, as they did, only fifty or so yards from our house on Martham Road, my Rollesby grandparents played a full and active role in my upbringing even after my father returned from the war. Often Mother and I would stay with them at the post office, rather than turn out on a cold night to make the short journey back to our home, as the bed in their back bedroom was always left ready for any family visitors to use.

To have one close family would have been sufficient, but I was lucky enough to have two. My mother's family, the Coles from Great Yarmouth, was equally child orientated. My mother visited my other grandmother, Edith Cole, every Wednesday and Saturday without fail, especially after Grandfather Cole died in 1942. Throughout most of my childhood, Saturday mornings at Grandma Cole's small terraced house on North Market Road were a continual round of family visitors and cups of tea or lemonade. Mother and I regularly lunched with Grandma Cole on a pint of shrimps with brown bread, or fish and chips wrapped in paper, bought from stalls at the nearby Yarmouth market or Nichols' restaurant on the Theatre Plain. Grandma Cole's house was small and narrow with two reception rooms and a kitchen downstairs, and four tiny bedrooms upstairs. Attached to the front and occupying half of the garden was a small shop which, as I remember, was mostly unused in the 1940s and 1950s. The house was entered through a lobby barely large enough to accommodate the electric and gas meters on the wall and a large pink conch shell on the floor. I was always convinced that when I held this shell to my ear I could hear the sea. With no room for a passage, the two reception rooms and the kitchen connected one into the other from the front to the back. From the lobby a door opened into a modest sized front room which was fully filled by a large rectangular dining table, an out-of-tune old piano with yellow keys, a horsehair chaise longue and numerous stick backed chairs. In winter the room was warmed by an open coal fire set in a hearth surrounded by a blackleaded metal fireplace. In front, the fire surround had two metal boxes in each corner on which her grandchildren often sat to warm themselves on cold days. The back room was extremely small with much of its space taken up by the staircase and understairs cupboard. Along one side were a small table and two dining chairs, and opposite to these was yet another chaise longue and a fireside armchair. A door led into the kitchen which had a tiled floor, a large Belfast sink under the single window, numerous cupboards and a gas cooker. The kitchen smelt always of gas. As soon as a visitor arrived, Grandma would boil a kettle for tea, a steam-activated whistle attached to the spout indicating noisily when it was ready. As a small child, I enjoyed playing in her kitchen as Grandma had fixed a long rubber nozzle on to the single cold water tap which enabled me to squirt water accurately at designated targets, some outside the sink area. In the back yard, a concrete path gave access to the toilet and coal shed. Grandma had a flushing toilet which I considered quite a novelty, coming from the country and being unused to such luxury. However, the toilet was not in the best of repair, the plastered walls were flaking owing to damp, the roof leaked and the cistern had become

37

detached from its fittings. As a result, when the chain was pulled the whole toilet rocked and wobbled as the cistern flushed. Immediately at the top of the stairs leading up from the small back room were doors opening into two bedrooms each furnished with a brass bedstead. From both of these, further doors led into two more small bedrooms, one over the shop and the other over the kitchen. As there was no bathroom, Grandma had to wash in the kitchen sink.

Visiting the homes of my aunts and uncles was a regular and frequent occurrence, particularly my mother's two sisters, both of whom lived near Beach station, Aunt Edith Hammond on Tottenham Road and Aunt Doris Parnell at 22 Audley Street. Three of my uncles moved away from East Anglia in search of work: George Miller, from Rollesby, moved to London, while Arthur and Stanley Cole, from Great Yarmouth, spent most of their working years in Birmingham. However, all three continually referred to Norfolk as home and spent most of their holidays at Rollesby or Great Yarmouth, their arrival anticipated with great excitement and their presence an excuse for a family party. Like me, all three eventually returned to live in East Anglia. Although there is still a family presence in Rollesby and Great Yarmouth, my cousins and their children are scattered not only throughout England and Wales but also in Australia, Canada and the United States of America. It seems unlikely that many, if any of them, will ultimately feel compelled to return to their ancestral home.

Social historians would undoubtedly classify both my parents' families as working class, although my two grandfathers and most of my uncles were tradesmen rather than labourers and had served and completed apprenticeships in occupations related mainly to the engineering and building trades. Some of my uncles even managed to break away from tradition and gained employment in other fields. George Miller was fortunate to have had a grammar school education during the 1920s, an experience not common among working-class children, and eventually became a bank manager in London. Bob Cole, a working-class entrepreneur, left the building trade to initiate various ventures associated with Great Yarmouth's holiday industry, eventually opening a coffee bar and restaurant on the seafront at Gorleston. Cecil Miller was an insurance agent until he took over the running of Rollesby Post Office when Grandmother Miller retired. My mother and most of my aunts were in full-time employment as single women but, on marriage, most found difficulty in continuing to work owing to the time consuming demands of running a home and bringing up children. A few managed to remain in full time employment, as other family members took over the care of their children. During the war this was common practice and some managed to continue with this arrangement after the war. Aunt Edith Hammond worked as a machinist at Johnson's clothing factory in Great Yarmouth until her retirement. Others were able to supplement their household finances by working from home or assisting with a family business.

Most of Rollesby's village shops were family run businesses, attached to the home and tended for most of the time by the womenfolk, as was the case with Grandmother Miller. The income from Grandmother's shop enabled her to employ a young female school leaver to help with the household chores. One of Joyce's unofficial tasks was to entertain the grandchildren and I can remember happy days playing in the garden or attempting to assist her with the housework. When my Uncle Cecil Miller took over the business in 1950, Doris, his wife, did most of the serving in the post office and shop. In Rollesby most married women, like my mother, found some part time work on the local farms and market gardens or in nearby holiday centres. Grandma Cole did not go to work; at least I have no recollection of her in any paid occupation. As a widow and probably over sixty years old, I presume that she was in receipt of a pension. However, I can recollect that she occasionally took in lodgers during the summer season, the most memorable being two members of a crazy band called Doctor Crock and his Crackpots who were performing at the Regal Theatre. Two doors away from Grandma Cole's house, her friend Mrs Mulley spent most daylight hours sitting in the bay window of her home working at a sewing machine, making, repairing and altering clothes for a small charge.

ROLLESBY POST OFFICE AND STORES

Rollesby Post Office and Stores occupied one corner of the crossroads opposite the Horse & Groom public house, while Hall Farm and Violet Villa were sited in the other two corners. The cottage that housed Rollesby post office was originally built in the nineteenth century as two dwellings under a single thatched roof, but was subsequently converted into a single property consisting of two downstairs reception rooms, a large kitchen and three bedrooms. Attached to the house was a rectangular building originally a smithy. Initially, the post office was run from a counter across the front door of the house. When my grandfather bought the property in 1920 he converted the smithy into a shop to house grandmother's post office and grocery businesses.

Grandmother Miller's shop, like her home, was neat, tidy and meticulously cleaned. The shop door was approached from the outside down a concrete slope bounded by a wood paling fence. The front of the shop consisted of a large central window filled with cardboard adverts for various products sold inside, and posters and notices promoting village activities. To the left of the window and set into the wall was a red post office letterbox and, to the right, the shop door. When the door was opened, a brass bell attached to the top of the door would ring, informing my grandmother that a customer had arrived. The shop itself was a long rectangular building with a single window, mud splattered from passing traffic, set into the right-hand wall looking out on to the Main Road, and two doors on the left, one to a sitting room where my grandmother drank tea and waited for customers, and the other to a storeroom. Immediately on the left was a long heavily polished counter, half of which was given over to the post office located behind a large brass grille through which customers were served. Behind the grille, neatly arranged in folders, files and boxes were all the stamps, postal orders, forms and other items associated with the post office part of her business. A large heavy money drawer slid under the counter and was securely locked with a brass key when not in use. Being open at the top and sides, the grille would have been totally ineffective for preventing a robbery had one occurred; it merely served to give an official look to the post office section and distinguish it from the rest of the shop.

On the far end of the counter, beyond the post office grille, my grandmother served her groceries. Served being the correct term as, in those days, customers did not help themselves to goods from the shelves but expected the shopkeeper to do it for them. Many would leave weekly orders, lists of goods that they either picked up later, or which were delivered by Grandfather in his car for a small charge. My grandmother made up the orders in the evening or during slack times in the day, usually in the afternoon, after which the goods were boxed up or placed into a basket or bag provided by the customer. When completed, the order would be copied into a book, with prices added and totalled, and a carbon copy placed with the goods inside the basket or bag. Grandmother always kept a second carbon copy for her records, as customers often delayed the payment of their bills until the end of the week or until cash became available. She needed to be good at arithmetic as there were no mechanical aids to assist her calculations and errors were quickly spotted as customers always checked their bills.

Few goods were sold already packed. Many items were bought in bulk and were weighed and packaged by Grandmother. For this purpose there were various sets of scales on the counter, some with their weights arranged in order, either in rows or piled one on top of another. A black set with a large brass bucket was used to weigh heavy goods such as potatoes and vegetables, while another smaller set was used for loose items such as biscuits, sugar or flour, and a balance scale with two flat marble pans for butter and cheese. A different model with a single chromium pan and a movable circular scale was used to weigh sweets and other lighter items. Potatoes and vegetables were delivered to the shop in sacks and had to be scooped out with the brass bucket for weighing. Sweets came unwrapped in large bottles and toffee in slabs that my grandmother broke up with a small hammer. Once all the sweets had been sold, I was frequently given a long handled spoon to scrape off all the chips from the sweets that had fallen and stuck to the bottom of the empty bottle, a special treat at a time when sweets were rationed. Biscuits were packaged in large cube-shaped tins with corrugated paper between the layers of biscuits to prevent them breaking. Any biscuits broken in transit were sold separately at a cheaper price. Butter came in large pats that Grandmother cut to size with a large flat knife. Cheeses were cut into wedges using a board with a wire cutter. A slicing machine, turned by a handle, was used to cut thin slices of ham, bacon or luncheon meat. Under the counter were bags of various sizes and piles of different paper squares that Grandmother was most proficient at folding into various containers to hold the different goods that she sold. Sweets were put into cone shaped packets, greaseproof paper was used to wrap up the wedges of cheese and cubes of butter, while thick blue paper was folded to make bags to hold one or two pounds of sugar or flour. Some packages were tied securely with string as Sellotape had yet to be invented. Potatoes and vegetables were wrapped in newspaper and eggs were carefully placed into white paper bags, the top folded over and secured with a twist at each end as egg-boxes did not appear until the 1960s. Most of the available wall space was covered in shelving, where tins, bottles and other containers of all shapes and sizes were arranged in orderly rows. Oval Colman's mustard tins, tapering tins of spam and corned beef, and flat tins of salmon, sardines and pilchards opened with a key. For a small boy the shop was an Aladdin's Cave, a delight for the curious and a marvellous source of information and knowledge.

At work, whether in the house or the shop, Grandmother always wore a floral overall over her everyday clothes, and sometimes she also wore a headscarf tied into a turban, particularly when she had just had her hair done. When Grandfather was unable to take me with him on his travels I spent many hours sitting on the counter of Grandmother's shop talking with and, no doubt, entertaining her customers. In those days, people never seemed to be in a hurry and many of them would read stories to me while they waited their turn to be served, or added their pictures in my drawing books. I remember clearly being taught how to draw a pig using two circles and some dots, and an aeroplane from a series of straight lines.

The Field

Grandfather's Field was a 2-acre site near to Rollesby Bridge, sandwiched between the Main Road and the Broad. Access to the Field was through a central five-bar gate set into a 10-foot high holly hedge. A cinder drive led from the gate to the centre of the Field where a space existed wide enough for a lorry to turn with ease. On either side of this drive Grandfather had constructed a number of sheds from where he conducted his building and market garden businesses and where he stored his ladders, scaffolding, wheelbarrows and other building materials. Against each shed were a number of water butts for collecting rainwater from the guttering running around their roof lines. This rainwater, together with buckets of water collected laboriously from the Broad, was the only source of water for use on the Field. In the centre of one of the sheds was a large table on which the produce of the Field was sorted or bunched before being sent to market, the Thursday Acle sale or to Bracey's of Martham for jamming. Once every week, or more frequently during the height of the growing season, Grandfather would employ three or four women to pick the fruit and flowers, and prepare them to be collected by vans belonging to various florists, market stall owners and fruit and vegetable merchants. The sorting shed was always a hive of activity, the tedium enlivened by long choruses of the popular songs of the day as the women cut and bunched flowers, or placed washed fruit into punnets, baskets and trays. On wet days, the rain would drum on its corrugated iron roof. Mother worked regularly for Grandfather at the Field and, as a consequence, I spent many hours roaming around and playing in its sheds and pathways.

To the left of the drive was a more sturdily built wooden building with large windows which was used by another of my uncles, Stanley Crawford, as a carpentry workshop. In one corner a metal wood-burning stove not only warmed the workshop in winter but also provided a source of heat for boiling glue. Uncle Stanley's workshop always smelt of wood and glue. Inside the workshop were two long workbenches, one in the centre of the shop and the other against the longest wall, each with numerous vices for holding wood for Uncle Stanley to work on. When not in use his carpenter's planes were left upturned in the central gully of the bench, and around the walls his other tools were placed into convenient holders or suspended from wooden pegs. Saws of all sizes, chisels, hammers, screwdrivers, files, and many other tools were neatly arranged and always carefully cleaned and sharpened after use. A wooden cabinet contained his supply of nails and screws, each organised in order of size and packed into small labelled cardboard boxes, as well as bottles of varnish, tins of polish and sandpaper squares. A chest held smaller items such as doorknobs, window latches, hinges and door locks. The floor between the two benches was covered in sawdust and curls of wood shavings, and I greatly enjoyed wading, often knee deep, through this sea of wooden curls to visit Uncle Stanley in his workshop. Dressed in navy blue dungarees, flat hat and black shiny shoes, he could always be found there, busy at his carpentry, marking lines on wood with oval shaped pencils, sawing, chiselling, smoothing edges with his planes or boiling up glue. Ever since he had hurt his back falling off a ladder, he rarely left the workshop. Every Friday, weather permitting, he would sweep out and burn his wood debris on a bonfire.

At the end of the cinder drive was a large shed housing Grandfather's flock of a hundred or more chickens. From the shed, a chicken run surrounded by a 6-foot high wire netting fence stretched from the centre of the Field down to the edge of Rollesby Broad. A small brick building inside the run contained a coal fired boiler in which Grandfather brewed up his own chicken feed from a mixture of potatoes, corn and cod liver oil, that was served to the birds in long feeders situated at various points in the run. Grandfather banging the pail of food was a signal for an avalanche of bobbing brown feathered heads to descend noisily on to the feeders. The brick building also contained sacks of maize and corn that he cast with a metal scoop on to areas of dry ground. These were not too easy to find, particularly in wet weather when the ground was churned to a mush by hundreds of triple-toed footprints. Inside the main shed there were three perches down the centre of the building and two rows of nesting boxes, one on top of the other, fixed to the walls. I often accompanied Grandfather when he collected the eggs from the nesting boxes, carefully placing them in a metal pail. Often, birds would still be sitting in the boxes and then he would feel under their bodies for any eggs that they were hiding. I was never too sure about putting my hand under one of these birds as it frequently resulted in a sharp peck from the hen simply trying to protect her eggs. Occasionally we would tour the inside of the run, particularly around the water's edge, in case some of the birds had made nests of their own or laid their eggs in the reeds. When collected, all the eggs were tested to see if they were fresh by shining a light through them, especially those gathered from the waterside. The eggs were then washed and placed into square grey cardboard trays which were then stacked one on top of another and put ready for collection by a van, presumably from a licensed egg-buyer.

The sheds were also home to a small colony of cats, far friendlier and in better shape than the conventional farmyard rat-catchers although they were kept for the same purpose. Grandfather unfortunately ensured that the colony was never too large by disposing of any new born litters that he found, usually in a bucket of water. His cat colony was fed daily with bowls of bread and milk, often fortified by any cracked or soft-shelled eggs discovered during egg collections. Grandfather spent a lot of time at the Field fussing over or being followed around by these cats. On cold days a cat or two could often be found curled up in front of the stove in the carpenter's shop. Although almost everyone visiting the Field was able to approach these animals, they seemed to have a definite aversion to a noisy child and would flee any time I attempted to approach them. Occasionally a litter would survive undetected by Grandfather and those that were not given away as pets were allowed to join the colony. One such young black and white male, called Herbert, unfortunately acquired a taste for chicken and was discovered by my father inside the run enjoying a lunch of four-month-old hen. Had it been Grandfather that discovered him, his fate would have been well and truly sealed. Luckily for Herbert, my father took pity on him and brought him home to Martham Road to join our other cat, Granny, as another family pet. After neutering, Herbert was transformed into a delightfully affectionate, overweight and overindulged animal, and spent many years living a life of luxury far different from his non-chicken-killing siblings that had remained at the Field.

Behind the sheds to the right of the drive was an area of about half an acre given over mostly to growing flowers and some vegetables, particularly salad vegetables — lettuce, radish, onions and carrots. Rows of daffodils and tulips flowered in the spring and, later on, carnations, chrysanthemum and dahlias. Among the flowers, Grandfather placed flowerpots filled with straw turned upside down on the tops of wooden stakes. Periodically he would remove these flowerpots and shake out and squash the earwigs that made their homes inside. I frequently accompanied him through the rows of flowers on earwig, caterpillar, snail and slug squashing expeditions. To the rear of the sheds was a bank of maidenhair fern and other evergreen plants used in making up bunches of flowers. Grandfather could provide flowers for all special occasions: carnations for wedding buttonholes, bridal bouquets, holly wreaths for Christmas and mourning wreaths for remembrance and funerals, for which sad occasions Uncle Stanley could also make the coffin.

To the left of the drive, behind the carpenter's shop was an orchard consisting of five or more rows of apple, pear and Victoria plum trees. Under and between the trees were different fruit bushes growing black, red and white currants and various types of gooseberries together with long wire supported rows of raspberry canes. The Field was ideal for long games of hide and seek with the children of Grandfather's other flower ladies. We spent many happy hours playing there or picking and eating ripe or, occasionally, not so ripe fruit straight from the tree or bush, usually followed by even longer hours suffering from a stomach ache: strings of juicy white currants, large reddish gooseberries that were extremely sweet tasting not sour like the green cooking gooseberries, and purple Victoria plums were all sampled. As the Victoria plum is also a favourite fruit of the wasp, the latter had to be gathered from the ground or picked from the tree with great care.

Late in the afternoon the Field would become a hive of activity as the men from grandfather's building firm returned from where they had been working. After reporting to grandfather on their day's progress, they retrieved their cycles from one of the sheds and set off home, many in old khaki army greatcoats with backpacks containing the remnants of their lunches. Often I travelled with Grandfather in his black Wolseley car to visit his building sites where I got to know many of the men who worked for him. A special favourite of mine was Harry and, under his supervision, I was often allowed to climb up ladders on to the scaffolding surrounding a part-built property. No doubt modern health and safety rules would not permit such activities. Also, if I could fearlessly do it then I wonder why I am now unable to climb more than 6 feet up a ladder without being terrified.

WORKING PARENTS

When my father returned from war service he resumed working in the building trade. At fifteen years old he had been apprenticed to Grandfather's firm, first as a painter and then as a bricklayer. In 1936, at the age of twenty, he had joined my mother's brothers, Arthur, Stanley and Bob, in search of employment in the manufacturing industry and on the building sites of Birmingham. If war had not broken out in 1939, he would most likely have stayed in Birmingham and I would have been a "Brummie", not a Norfolk boy.

In common with many serving soldiers, he was deprived of family life for nearly seven years and was not able to play a father's role during my infant years. I was six and a half years old when he returned, almost a stranger in my world where the important rules and relationships had already been established. I certainly found it difficult to accommodate another adult in my life, particularly one who insisted on sharing my mother's affection. With hindsight, knowing the ways of young children, I have no doubt that I made things very difficult for him. It took some time before an appropriate father–son bonding took place and even then we both found it hard to communicate our feelings for each other. I always sought his approval and can still clearly remember small tokens of his affection: a treasured tin of coloured pencils that he brought back for me from Weymouth, where he had been engaged in army Z-reserve training, and a brown and cream wireless he bought for my room when I was ill in bed with influenza.

After the war, my father rejoined Grandfather's firm in Rollesby where he became a builder's foreman. When Grandfather retired in the early 1950s, he joined another local builder, Holmes and Son of Great Yarmouth, before becoming self-employed as a contract bricklayer and plasterer, finally retiring in 1980 at the age of 63. My father was an old-fashioned tradesman who produced work of quality, enjoyed what he did and was proud of the result of his labours. As a child I was not entirely sure what he did do. I understood that he "went to work" and that this involved leaving home every weekday at 7.30a.m. and returning at 5.30p.m., or later in the summer. On Saturdays he often worked until 12.30p.m., when mother would have dinner ready for his return so that he was able to enjoy an afternoon of football or cricket. Every morning, after washing in the scullery sink, he dressed for work in grey trousers, shirt and tie, a pullover — two in the winter — and black hobnailed boots, all covered and protected by a pair of navy blue dungarees with numerous pockets in which he would keep his collapsible yard rule, string, a plumb line and many other useful items. Over this he wore an old grey jacket which he removed when working. On his head he wore a flat cap with numerous pencils tucked into its peak. All his clothing was liberally spotted with cement and plaster.

While he was eating his breakfast, usually two shredded wheat biscuits in warm milk, Mother prepared his lunch box containing sandwiches, cake and a screw topped bottle filled with strong tea. The bottle was eventually replaced by a vacuum flask, giving him the pleasure of hot tea with his lunch rather than cold. These she placed inside an old army knapsack together with a copy of yesterday's newspaper. After a farewell kiss for my mother, he climbed into his car that was parked outside the house and set off for work. As one of Grandfather's foremen, he regularly provided transport for those employees who had no car of their own. At one time he used a small green covered lorry that we affectionately called Amy after the letters on the registration plate, and this was also parked outside our house. On Saturday afternoons he occasionally used it to transport the cricket and football teams to their matches. As a treat, after lunch every Sunday he often took my grandparents, mother and me for a drive in the car, frequently visiting his latest workplace so that we could gaze in admiration at his most recent brickwork. When a car was unavailable we were driven around in Amy, adults in the front and me bouncing around in the back.

To supplement his income my father tried a number of ventures, with varying degrees of success. On his return from war service he rented a Nissen hut in the grounds of Rollesby Hall, a relic of wartime, where he made fireplace surrounds in the evenings and at weekends. When Grandfather retired, Father took over the running of the market garden at the Field, continuing to produce fruit, flowers and eggs as Grandfather had done before him. In the summer he brought home buckets full of flowers for Mother to bunch for market, and I can remember one evening when Grandma Cole was staying with us, she tried to help my mother by making us all a cup of tea. Unfortunately, she used the water from the wrong bucket and halfway through our drink we discovered that our tea was flavoured with chrysanthemum leaves.

Another venture involved using apples from the Field to make toffee apples for Uncle Bob to sell in his café on the seafront at Gorleston. Despite many evenings of practice boiling saucepans of brown sugar on our stove, my parents never managed to produce toffee of the right consistency. Instead of a hard, clear, shiny, brown coating of toffee, their apples were usually covered in a soft, opaque, light-brown coat of sugary crystals. Quality control featured little in their production, as even bruised and insect-eaten apples were all covered in this sticky home brewed concoction. Holidaymakers of the 1950s must have been easy to please as Uncle Bob managed to sell most of the sweets that my parents produced although, after a tactful period of time, he wound up the toffee apple part of his business. In the late 1950s, in response to an advert from the Birds Eye factory in Great Yarmouth and in common with many of the other small market gardeners in the district, my father removed all the trees and bushes and ploughed up the Field in order to grow beans for Birds Eye to freeze, and, for a time, this proved to be a much more profitable activity for less effort.

Like most married women of the 1940s and 1950s, Mother's work was primarily housework and consisted of long hours for no pay. Before the advent of modern labour saving devices, activities that now take hours could take a whole day of hard monotonous work. Monday was traditionally washing day, Tuesday ironing, Wednesday shopping, Thursday cleaning and Friday baking. Saturday morning would be spent shopping again at Great Yarmouth. Main meals also had to be produced every day without the benefit of modern convenience foods. With the exception of shop produced fish and chips once or twice a week, all our meals were home made. Indian, Chinese and pizza takeaway meals or frozen ready-made dinners were unheard of, not that she would have used them, as she dismissed any food other than "good old English home cooking" as being unhealthy or too spicy. On top of all that she had a family to look after, a family of two rather old-fashioned males who found it difficult to look after themselves. It was a wonder that she found any time for herself, let alone undertaking paid work to supplement the family income.

During the war and just after, Mother worked part-time for my grandparents delivering newspapers and the daily letter post, serving in the shop and helping at the Field. After they retired she joined the gangs of village women who did seasonal casual work for local farmers, setting and harvesting crops of potatoes, runner beans, French beans and sprouts, picking fruit for jamming or singling rows of sugar beet with a hoe. From the late 1950s, every Saturday during the summer she cycled to Martham Staithe where she cleaned boats hired out for holidays on the Broads. Mother's domestic responsibilities took up so much of her time that it would have been impossible for her to pursue a full-time paid career of her own even if she had wished for one.

My parents followed the normal pattern for the time in allocating their personal domestic responsibilities. Mother looked after everything in and to do with the house, including managing all the household finances. Major building work or the decorating, however, was totally the responsibility of my father. Often our decoration depended upon what paint was available at his current place of employment. Normally wood surfaces were painted cream, green or dark brown; white gloss was rarely used inside the house. On the walls he pasted thick wallpaper in an attempt to cover up the cracks in the plaster, usually heavily patterned with an elaborate flower design and hung with the repeats not always perfectly matched. A 6-inch frieze, often in a different flower design, was pasted over the tops of the wallpaper strips just below the curtain rail to cover any imperfections at the join between the wall and the rail. Only once can I remember him using emulsion on the walls, when he chose an aggressive raspberry colour that matched nothing in the room including the cream-coloured window frames and doors. In addition to the decorating, my father was in charge of everything outside the house, mainly the garden. Working long hours meant that domestically he was limited to tasks that could be completed at weekends. In summer, managing a productive garden in addition to long hours at work and at his other "commercial ventures" was a strain on his time and could not have been achieved without some help from Mother and myself, albeit reluctantly on my part. Gardening was not my favourite occupation.

My grandmother at the post office took her domestic responsibilities to the extreme and had a reputation for being exceedingly house-proud. Grandfather was virtually banned from any task inside the house other than eating, sitting and sleeping. His outside coats and shoes had to be left in a lobby and the latter replaced by slippers. He was not even allowed to do the paperwork for his building firm inside the house. For this he built a shed in the garden, fitted with an electric light and a power socket for his electric fire, which everybody called "his office". The sole exception to my grandmother's strict regime occurred during the early morning, usually around 6.30 a.m., when the kitchen table would be used to sort the incoming mail for the postman and newspapers for grandfather to deliver, and which would be all completed and tidied up before breakfast time. However, as these tasks were associated with her role as postmistress and shopkeeper, possibly that was why they were permitted.

My parents worked hardest during the summer months and, as a result, I cannot ever remember going away for a summer holiday. My father regularly took his holiday entitlement during the winter in order to avoid being laid off from the building trade in bad weather. We did not need to go far to enjoy a holiday area as the Broads, Great Yarmouth and the east coast were all within a few miles of where we lived. On the other hand, my Miller grandparents always took a one week long holiday in the summer. Every year they hired a chalet on the coast at Hemsby, a mere 6 miles distant. Apart from the occasional nights that she spent with us in Rollesby, I have no recollection of Grandma Cole spending any time away from her home on North Market Road.

WORK EXPERIENCE

In the 1950s, as now, money, or the lack of it, was a constant problem for teenagers. There never seemed to be enough of it to finance the need for clothes, general entertainment and, eventually, cigarettes and alcohol. Being in full time education until the age of nineteen, I relied heavily on my parents for a basic weekly allowance to provide me with some element of independence. Regular weekly pocket money was not forthcoming until after the age of thirteen, an age undoubtedly heralding the transition between childhood and adulthood and worthy of some form of recognition. As far as I can remember, at thirteen I was given an allowance of one shilling a week. Not that I needed much more as we mostly went out as a family and my father paid any expenses involved. My sweets and comics came with the groceries and newspapers, and were paid for from Mother's housekeeping. On Sundays Grandmother Miller paid me sixpence to clean all her and Grandfather's shoes. One shilling and sixpence easily covered most of the expenses incurred by a thirteen-year-old in the early 1950s. At each subsequent birthday my allowance increased in line with my growing need for independence and entertainment separate from my parents, until at eighteen I was receiving the handsome sum of ten shillings a week. This may not seem a great amount until it is compared to my father's earnings at the time which were under £15 a week. Ten shillings certainly provided for my basic needs and was easily supplemented by occasional and seasonal earnings.

Work for teenagers still at school was usually limited to the vacations, as part-time work during term time was discouraged. Some children were beginning to find employment by delivering the morning newspapers, although this was generally frowned upon. However, the opportunity for such work was limited to urban districts.

The question whether part-time paid employment is a good thing for a pupil at a grammar
school was discussed by Mr A. H. G. Palmer,
the headmaster, at the annual prize day of
Yarmouth Grammar School held at the Town
Hall on Tuesday . . .

. . . in itself, I should definitely say "no". The
experience gained from delivering newspapers
or groceries is not of value as a preparation for
the sort of career which a boy educated at a
grammar school is likely to enter. An intelligent
boy should be able to find far better ways of
spending his time.

Yarmouth Mercury, 19 November 1954

Before the age of thirteen, pocket money was irregular
and usually given for a specific purpose: to spend at
Great Yarmouth's Easter Fair or at the village fete.
However, there were other ways in which money could
be accumulated and saved in my moneybox, a yellow
lockable box in the shape of a book with three prongs
inside the slot to prevent any illegal extractions with a
knife. Aunts and uncles were always extremely generous
and when encountered would slip a sixpenny piece or
even a shilling into my hand, especially if we had not
met for a while; at Christmas and birthdays their
generosity was even greater. Mother was keen that not
all of my wealth was frittered on trivial items and
insisted that I saved a proportion of any money that I

was given in a post office savings account that she had opened in my name. By the time I left home for university the balance on this account had grown to the impressive sum of £12, unfortunately reducing very quickly to zero once I was away from Mother's controlling supervision. Seasonal paid work was also readily available especially during the long summer holidays.

My first experience of working for money was fruit picking, specifically picking blackcurrants for Bracey's of Martham. Almost all of the fields between Martham and Hemsby were owned by Bracey's and filled with row upon row of bushes growing blackcurrants for jamming. For two to three weeks at the end of July and the beginning of August, men, women and children, although mostly women and children, were employed to gather ripe blackcurrants on a piecework basis, everyone being paid a set amount per pound of fruit that they picked. From the age of six during the school holidays I regularly accompanied Mother on summer fruit picking expeditions. Once my father had left for work Mother packed a picnic lunch of jam or potted-meat sandwiches and a bottle of fizzy lemonade before we set off on our bicycles for the blackcurrant fields. Once there, we reported to the field foreman at the weigh station, which was normally positioned close to the field entrance. The weigh station consisted of a bench with a chair behind for the foreman to sit on, and was protected by a tarpaulin in case of rain. To one side of the bench were piles of baskets and punnets for the pickers to use and on the other large flat trays into which the fruit was emptied. Close to the bench was a set of scales for weighing the gathered fruit. Periodically a tractor with a trailer brought more trays to the weigh station and took away the filled ones. On our arrival, the foreman entered our names into a ledger and provided us with two or more baskets or punnets, usually baskets for Mother and punnets for me, before directing us to a row that needed picking. Picking blackcurrants was a back-breaking activity, especially in the mid-summer sun. The bushes were usually about 3 to 4 feet high with six or more branches arranged around a central stem. The fruit hung in strings from below each branch, often hidden by its lush foliage, and it was normally necessary to get down almost to ground level in order to see the fruit that needed to be picked. Some pickers bent over, others sat on a stool, while some, like me, knelt on the ground. No matter what method was employed, by the end of the day our backs ached and our arms, knees and clothes were stained purple by squashed fruit. If it had rained we were soaked through reaching under the leaves for the fruit. However, by the age of sixteen, I had become an expert at gathering blackcurrants and spent all my time during the picking season at the fields where, thanks to one of my cousins, I earned the nickname "scrabber". Nevertheless, the earnings were welcome and provided an essential fund for clothes and entertainment.

Outside the long summer break from school, paid work was hard to come by and my only source of income during the autumn and winter was as a beater for the pheasant shoot. Three or four times during the shooting season, Sidney Tooke, gamekeeper to the Rollesby Hall Estate, employed men and boys from the village as beaters for the shooting parties that he organised on behalf of Colonel Benn, usually on a Saturday. Although this was hard work, the pay was good and from the age of fifteen I was happy to take part. Early on the morning of the shoot, usually around 8.30 a.m., beaters from around the village were collected by an open-topped Land Rover and transported to the shooting area, normally the woods and farmland adjoining Back Road and the northern shore of Ormesby Broad. Beating at that time of year, in all weathers, was a cold and wet occupation as our routes took us through field, marsh and woodland, so it was essential to prepare accordingly. I usually set out dressed for warmth and protection in a thick vest, shirt, pullover, jacket and long trousers or denim jeans. Two pairs of socks were worn under my knee-length water boots, a short pair inside a long, with my trouser bottoms tucked inside the longer pair. This outfit was then covered by an old raincoat, while on my head I wore a leather airman's helmet, an old wartime souvenir. Beating did not lend itself to wearing good clothes and those that I wore had normally seen better days. As a group we must have resembled a tramp's convention, dressed as we were in pullovers with holes and jackets and raincoats without buttons, held together by belts of twine.

The day consisted of a number of sweeps which aimed to drive pheasants, other game birds and, occasionally, rabbits and hares towards the shooting party that, prior to the start of the sweep, had each been allocated a static firing position a few hundred yards ahead. The shooters were mainly local farmers, landowners and VIPs, most of whom would have paid a fee for their day's entertainment. At the start of a sweep the beaters spread out in a straight line, each beater about 10 yards from the next. On a signal from Mr Tooke everyone moved forward, calling out or banging sticks on their water boots, driving any poor unfortunate birds and animals towards the shooters. Driving across fields was easy, although if it had rained and the crop was wet our legs and trousers were quickly soaked in the process and our boots covered with mud. Driving through woodland was a different matter, particularly woodland close to the edge of the Broad as, in order to progress in an orderly manner, we were expected to walk in a straight line maintaining an equal distance between each other. This meant that we had to walk through or over rather than around pools, bushes, brambles or any other obstacle that appeared in our path. By the end of the day we were exhausted, wet, covered in mud, bruised and scratched, yet to a relatively fit teenager it was exciting. When birds or animals were disturbed by the beat we shouted out "pheasant", "duck", "woodcock", or whatever to identify and warn the shooters of the targets about to arrive over their gun positions and, at the end of each sweep, we collected up the catch and carried it to a waiting trailer. Dogs, usually spaniels or Labradors, retrieved any dead or wounded game that had fallen into distant or inaccessible places away from the shoot.

If any of the shot birds were still alive and fluttering we were expected to put them out of their misery by breaking their necks or knocking them on the head with our sticks. When everything had been cleared the beaters and guns were transported to their respective positions for the next sweep. At lunchtime, we were taken to an old thatched gamekeeper's hut close to the Broad where we rested and ate our sandwiches. The shooters, on the other hand, were transported to a sit-down lunch provided by their host and served from hampers, often accompanied by a bottle of wine or a tot or two. The day ended at dusk when the catch was counted and the beaters were paid their dues. Regularly the catch of pheasants alone was in three figures.

By the 1950s, Great Yarmouth had resumed its pre-war popularity as a seaside holiday resort. Cheap continental holidays had yet to make any impact on the holiday habits of most British workers. Many people from the Midlands returned year after year to Great Yarmouth for their holidays, content and secure in the familiarity frequent visits had given them. The holiday season provided many income opportunities for local teenagers and students. Most holidaymakers of the 1950s arrived in Yarmouth by train rather than by car, as they do now. Every Saturday morning throughout the summer, bands of children arrived outside Great Yarmouth's three stations, Beach, Vauxhall and South Town, pushing or pulling a set of pram wheels, a wheelbarrow or a trolley, to compete with one another in an attempt to carry the suitcases of the newly arrived holidaymakers from the station to their hotels or digs. For this service they expected a substantial tip, particularly if they could direct first timers to the location of their holiday address.

At the age of fifteen, my first job associated with Great Yarmouth's holiday trade was when Uncle Bob employed my services for a few hours every Saturday morning, almost certainly as a favour to my mother. "Money doesn't grow on trees, money has to be earned through hard work" was one of her many and often repeated mottoes, and my Saturday morning job was undoubtedly her attempt to instil in me the concept of working for pay. Weekly pocket money was a reward for working hard at school; anything else had to be earned through personal effort. Uncle Bob always had an eye for any moneymaking opportunity, especially during the summer season, and one such opportunity occurred when he rented a courtyard site in a prime position at the seafront end of Regent Road, the main route between the town centre and the seaside promenade. There he installed a number of carousels that he filled with cheap paperback novels of dubious quality and postcards of a saucy nature. Dressed in a white coat, with a money pouch over my shoulder, my job every Saturday morning was to encourage passing holidaymakers to purchase these goods. In any quiet times, I avidly perused both postcards and novels, guffawing at the risqué humour of the cards and wondering why many chapters in some of the novels ended in a line of dots.

> ## Ban on Objectionable Postcards Sought
>
> The sale of objectionable postcards in the borough has been referred to in a report presented to Yarmouth Education Committee at its monthly meeting on Tuesday. The Youth Committee reported that its chairman, Mr H.J. Shorten, had referred to the display in local shops during the summer season of many objectionable postcards and their possible adverse effect on the morals of young people.
>
> *Yarmouth Mercury*, 27 November 1953

In 1959, I spent my final summer before leaving for Leicester University working in the kitchens of Caister Holiday Camp. Established in 1906 by a socialist visionary, Fletcher Dodd, and one of the first of its kind in the country, the camp occupied a hill top site between the Caister water tower and the beach, bisected by the then main A149 from Caister village to Ormesby a mile or so distant. Holiday accommodation was provided in row upon row of wooden chalets. The site was also crossed, near to the beach, by the main railway route from the Midlands and, before Dr Beeching axed this line in 1959, most holidaymakers arrived by train, disembarking conveniently at the camp's own private halt. Once installed, it was barely ever necessary for any of the campers to leave the site as all their food and entertainment was provided by this

Butlin's style holiday camp, and access to the sands and sea was merely a short walk away. In the main hall, dances and cabaret entertainment took place continuously throughout the day, and competitions, both the serious and the not so serious, were held on the sports field: tug of war, knobbly knees, bathing beauty and beautiful baby competitions to name but a few. Cricket and football matches, three-legged, sack, and egg-and-spoon races, as well as proper competitive sprints, were all supported enthusiastically by everyone intent on having a good time. Indoor activities such as painting, whist and beetle drives, or games of darts, table tennis, billiards and snooker, provided entertainment even in the wettest of weather. In the evening, adults relaxed in the numerous bars while many chalet walkers listened for restless youngsters, recalling their parents through the camp Tannoy system if their presence was felt necessary. For the adventurous, the surrounding countryside could be explored on one of the camp's unusual cycles made for two, a Heath Robinson contraption resembling a bench on wheels. For the less energetic, coach trips were arranged visiting all the popular destinations in the Broads, Great Yarmouth and the Norfolk countryside, usually stopping at a convenient public house before returning to the camp.

From the completion of my A level examinations in June until the beginning of September, I worked in the camp kitchens for five and a half days every week, Mondays to Saturdays. Working hours were long — six in the morning until seven to seven-thirty in the evening and to midday on Saturday — but the pay was very good. In addition, my days were made even longer by a 30-minute cycle ride each way between Rollesby and Caister before and after work, a necessary journey as six in the morning was well before the first available bus. However, the midday Saturday finish provided me with the opportunity to continue playing cricket on Saturday and Sunday afternoons, an important consideration for a sport-mad teenager. In addition, a two-hour break in the middle of the day gave plenty of opportunity for me to join in with activities on the camp, to fraternise with teenage holidaymakers of the opposite sex, or merely to read and rest in the staff facilities. The dining complex was located on the water tower side of the road and consisted of six restaurants, three each side of a central service corridor leading off from the kitchens. This complex was responsible for providing the campers with a sit-down breakfast and an evening meal. Campers were allocated to a particular restaurant and were expected not only to use it exclusively throughout their stay but also to sit at the same table. Mealtimes were fixed and everyone was served together. The menus offered no choice although, in exceptional circumstances, special diets would be catered for but were considered to be a bit of a nuisance. In my first week I alternated between washing-up and peeling potatoes, both dirty activities and exceedingly boring but considered to be an appropriate initiation for kitchen newcomer. In my second week I graduated to assistant cook, although in name only. As I remember, my breakfast responsibility was porridge and, at dinner times, any odd and usually messy task that the head chef required me to do.

To their credit, the kitchen managers quickly realised that my capabilities as a cook were very limited and by the third week I had been transferred to the post of restaurant attendant. One attendant was designated for each of the six restaurants, responsible for transporting all the meals for that restaurant from the kitchen to a counter where the waitresses would be waiting to serve them to their allocated tables. As their tip at the end of the week very much depended upon the efficiency of their service, the waitresses demanded quick and personal attention from their kitchen go-betweens. If we were successful in providing them with an efficient service, they rewarded us with a proportion of their tip. I enjoyed this job and became expert at providing a slick service to the waitresses in my designated restaurant. At dinner time I arrived early to make sure that I had the requisite number of meals, all pre-plated and kept warm in an electric hot trolley, which was then trundled up the central corridor and plugged in at the restaurant waiting for the waitresses to descend on it. I discovered that the secret to a good meal was hot gravy and potatoes straight from the steamer, although providing both these requirements, particularly the hot potatoes, involved some personal risk. Potatoes were placed in metal trays and cooked in a steamer at the far end of the kitchen. Immediately after they had finished cooking,

71

protected by gloves and a thick blanket around our necks, we pulled the metal trays out of the steamer and on to our shoulders. We then ran as fast as we could up to the restaurant where hot melted butter was poured over them before they were ladled into tureens for collection by the waitresses who had, by that time, distributed the plated meals. Occasionally someone would slip on the wet kitchen floor, causing everyone to scatter rapidly in front of a descending tray of hot potatoes. My worst experience occurred when the protecting blanket fell off my shoulders at the precise moment that I pulled the tray from out of the steamer. My only course of action was to get the tray to the restaurant as quickly as I could, which I did in record time. Nevertheless, I received a severe burn to my right shoulder and a large blister that remained with me for the rest of my time at the camp, a sore reminder that there was some truth behind the saying "more haste, less speed".

Working in the kitchens was not particularly enjoyable because heat and steam made them an extremely uncomfortable working environment. The kitchen and restaurant personnel were a curious mixture of professional catering staff, itinerant or seasonal workers and students. Mostly we all got on very well, some better than others, although the differing backgrounds of the staff, together with the stifling atmosphere in the kitchen, occasionally led to arguments and, sometimes, even to violence. In one memorable disturbance, the kitchen was evacuated hurriedly as we all attempted to avoid the pots, pans and other implements being hurled about by two of the senior kitchen staff engaged in a particularly noisy and acrimonious confrontation about the usual subject of violent disagreements, relationships with the opposite sex or, more accurately, their conflicting relationships with the same woman.

CHAPTER
THREE

Our House

MARTHAM ROAD

Of all the places in Rollesby that I knew well, I knew Martham Road the best. From the Horse & Groom crossroads to Hall Cottages, Martham Road was my backyard and my playground. I knew every tree, house and blade of grass, I knew all the residents by name and their children were my friends. The road was so familiar to me that I could walk from the post office to our back gate with my eyes shut, a feat that was a necessary skill on dark winter nights in a village without street lighting.

On the left of Martham Road, just after the crossroads, was Hall Farm, managed by Mr Arthur Tooke and his family. The farmhouse was a long thatched building with two upper floors fronting on to the Main Road but with a working entrance to the rear on Martham Road. Attached to one side of the house was a dairy and behind it various barns, cattle pens and sheds housing the farm carts and other machinery. The house featured little in my life except for the few occasions when I was invited to attend a birthday party there and, consequently, I remember little about its interior. However, the farmyard and its barns were a regular playground for small gangs of children. While we were not discouraged from roaming the farmyard we were continually warned of the dangers from the animals and machinery, and were, for the most part, sensible in what we did. The barns and sheds were marvellous for long games of hide and seek, and the animals, particularly the young animals, were a great source of interest and amusement. The farm was managed as a traditional mix of arable and dairy, producing wheat, barley and milk. Most of the local children found themselves involved in some way with the routine and annual events of the farming year, even if only as a spectator. Ploughing, sowing, reaping and thrashing were usually accompanied by willing gangs of interested and perhaps annoyingly noisy children. Watching milking, the bull performing or helping to bottle-feed young orphaned calves, gave us all an education beyond that contained in any school curriculum.

Some impressions remain clear in my mind and, where Hall Farm is concerned, my first thoughts are of cats, for it was home to many cats of all shapes and sizes — not friendly household cats but nervous, unkempt, semi-wild animals whose primary function was to catch the rats and mice that plagued the barns and outbuildings. Every evening these cats emerged from the barns and sheds and gathered outside the dairy for their daily feed of bread and milk, served up in numerous chipped enamel bowls. None of the cats was neutered and, consequently, quiet evenings were frequently shattered by the sound of confrontations between the males and the seemingly painful but certainly noisy process of cats mating. Kittens were a regular occurrence although few made it to adulthood owing to endemic disease and frequent population culls. My father was a soft touch when it came to cats and he would patiently endeavour to entice some of these animals to abandon their wild ways, especially those with a brood of kittens. One of his successes was our cat, Granny, a Hall Farm cat who had sought shelter with two kittens in a tree stump opposite our house. His persistence was rewarded as, although both kittens died, Granny moved in and remained with my mother and father for the next fifteen years.

Early mornings and late afternoons were milking time at Hall Farm. During wartime I recollect that this was done by hand, but milking machines were installed soon after, and then the rhythmic pulsating hum emanating from the cattle sheds, morning and evening, indicated that milking time had started. The milk was pumped from the milking sheds to the dairy through an overhead pipe. One of the farmer's daughters, Elsie, was in overall charge of the dairy and its associated activities, and when my mother ran out of milk — a regular occurrence — I was often sent over to the farm with a jug to purchase milk from her. The dairy, entered through a stable door, was a square room with whitewashed ceiling and walls and a concrete floor that appeared to be permanently wet. Elsie seemed always to be engaged in emptying buckets of milk into a cylindrical metal tank on top of the milk cooler. The milk then ran down over a corrugated cooling surface into a trough below, thence into a churn standing on the floor underneath. At the end of the day these churns, full of milk, were rolled to a stand at the farm gate where they were collected by tankers, presumably belonging to local milk distributors. Elsie served the milk direct from a churn using a long, cylindrical milk measure that was usually hooked on to its top. In my early days, a pair of immense shire horses was used to provide the motive power on the farm, housed in stables whose walls were hung with various harnesses and collars stuffed with straw. At the end of the 1940s, these magnificent beasts were replaced by two or more large blue Fordson-Major tractors.

From the crossroads to Hall Cottages, Martham Road was a straight tree-lined stretch of about 500 yards. The road was narrow, but wide enough for two cars travelling in opposite directions to pass with ease. On the farm side of the road there was a narrow tarmac footpath edged on both sides by a grass border. On the other side there was a grass verge about 3 feet wide in front of a bank topped by a mature hedge. Periodically, Mr Hodds, the village roadman, cleared all the dust, dirt and sand that gathered along the roadside, collecting it up with his stiff bristled brush and shovelling it into heaps all along this verge. He also ensured that the drainage channels either side of the road remained clear of obstructions. On the farm side, any excess rainwater drained through metal pipes laid under the footpath into a small pond in the farmyard opposite to our house. On the other side, channels were cut into the bank allowing rainwater to escape into a ditch that ran along the opposite side of the hedge. These measures were not totally successful and during heavy downpours rainwater ran the length of the road to the Town Pit, a large pond at the far end by the junction with Back Road. Small rivers of water rushed through the dirt and sand at the edge of the road on their way to the Pit, providing great entertainment for the children who would race matchsticks, twigs or matchbox boats down these flowing streams. The road surface consisted of a tar skim covered with loose stone chipping. On hot summer days, the tar bubbled into soft puddles, adhering to the soles of shoes and little boys' knees. My knees were regularly subjected to a vigorous scrubbing or mother's butter treatment in an attempt to remove the resulting tarry black stains. When it was soft, we engraved our names into the tar with a convenient twig. Providing they were not immediately deleted by car tyres, these road graffiti were legible for quite a while.

Motor traffic was extremely light and, consequently, the road itself became a playground for the Martham Road children. Football matches were regularly played up and down the road with our coats laid out as goalposts, and during the Wimbledon fortnight, our own tennis tournament was played out on the street with a chalk line denoting the net. Test matches were played with a tennis ball and frequent sixes were hastily retrieved from neighbouring gardens, while numerous hopscotch squares were permanently chalked on to the surface, the stones used in the game left on the road for the next player. During spring and summer the grass verges grew tall with wild flowers: primroses first, followed by blood-red poppies, purple mallow, white flat topped cow parsley and swathes of yellow dandelions. A series of telegraph poles lined one side of the road heading towards the Martham telephone exchange. Hanging between the poles were a dozen or more telephone wires, frequently making humming sounds in the wind which, in September, provided a resting place for hundreds of swallows and martins gathering in preparation for their winter migration to Africa. Our section of the road was also the main thoroughfare for Hall Farm's herd of thirty or more cows plodding, usually unattended, before and after milking between the sheds and the meadows near to the Town Pit and, as a result, its surface was regularly covered in circular pats of cow dung. In dry weather, the tops of the pats solidified and were sometimes used as a 1950s version of a frisbee while, in wet weather, the road was frequently awash with light brown slurry. The fact that our road was persistently used as a bovine toilet did not deter us in any way from continuing to use it as a playground.

Immediately on the right of Martham Road just down from the crossroads was a pair of semi-detached houses, one half occupied by Mr Holt, the village postman, and his wife, and the other was our home. Next along the road was a small, single-storeyed thatched cottage occupied by Miss Julia who, in her retirement, had become an enthusiastic bowls player and regularly travelled to Great Yarmouth to play on the many perfectly tended bowling greens that lined the seafront. She eventually persuaded my Grandmother Miller to join her and throughout the early 1950s they played competitive ladies bowls at venues all over Norfolk. Whether Miss Julia moved or died I cannot remember, but Elsie from the farm dairy and her husband Harry had taken residence in the cottage by the time I left Rollesby in 1959. Next to Miss Julia's cottage was a large house, originally a farmstead, called the White House. During the 1940s this was home to Rollesby's vicar, the Revd Mr Grundy who, not surprisingly, was nicknamed Solomon by the local children. The grounds of the White House contained two features that were a great attraction to young boys: a large ornamental pool with a small island at its centre and a tall oak tree in the meadow. When he was in a good mood, Mr Grundy allowed children to row a small boat around the pool and over to the island. The oak tree was a challenge to the intrepid tree climbers among us, as the lower branches were quite easy to manage. The tree was regularly full of children until, inevitably, Clifford Attew fell off and broke his leg. When Mr Grundy died, the Taylor family moved into the White House and so began my first teenage crush. However, despite my hopes and fantasies, Linda only had eyes for others and, at the age of fourteen, I suffered for the first time the agony of rejection. Not that Linda knew of my infatuation, because even if my hopes were high, my courage was non-existent and I never got beyond yearning at a distance.

At the junction of Martham Road with Back Road was the large pond, fringed by a row of willow trees, called the Town Pit. To one side of the pond was a level grassy bank with a large oak tree growing from its centre. Every morning a tractor-drawn water tanker belonging to Hall Farm rumbled along the road to the pond, where it was filled to provide drinking water for the cattle in the fields. As a result of this activity, the pond was deep and clear along the roadside, a magnet for children with jam jars intent on fishing for newts or collecting frogspawn from among the pond's weeds. In the harsh winters of the late 1940s and early 1950s the pond regularly froze over and became a convenient ice rink for sliding and skating competitions.

Opposite to the Town Pit was a long thatched cottage belonging to Mr and Mrs Marsden-Smith. Mr Marsden-Smith was a short, well-dressed, elderly man, white haired but bald on top, his baldness usually covered by an expensive-looking trilby hat. A well-liked and successful businessman who owned a number of factories in Great Yarmouth, he supported and sponsored many village activities and societies, in particular the bowls, cricket and football clubs. I remember clearly that he possessed two or more large chauffeur driven cars which he parked on the green by the Town Pit, where they were regularly washed by his driver using water from the pond. In a village where few people owned cars, both adults and children alike constantly admired Mr Marsden-Smith's vehicles. Children used various observation points on the green or in the tree to peer at, under or into the car interiors. It seems remarkable that these cars were left unattended in a public place without any fear of them being stolen or vandalised.

When my grandparents retired in 1950 they transferred ownership of the post office to my Uncle Cecil and moved to Hall Cottages, a few hundred yards further on from the Town Pit, a pair of semi-detached, mock-Tudor, thatched cottages owned by the Rollesby Hall Estate and constructed by Grandfather's building firm in the early 1930s. Mr Sid Tooke, the Hall Estate gamekeeper, lived in the other cottage. In his back garden there were two large sheds, each with an enclosed run. In one he kept his black Labrador gun dog and in the other three or four ferrets. These deceptively friendly looking animals would frequently bite chunks off fingers poked at them through the wire of their cages.

Facing Hall Cottages was the entrance gate to the driveway of Rollesby Hall. On either side of this entrance were two immense horse chestnut trees. Every autumn numerous boys, including myself, congregated under these trees intent on obtaining the champion conker of the district. Not content with those lying on the ground, we hurled sticks into the upper branches to dislodge more chestnuts in the hope of finding a prime example. The fall was usually sufficient to break open the prickly green outer shell to reveal the prized shiny brown conker inside. Ignoring the herds of bullocks grazing on the grass, the more adventurous boys among us would venture into the parkland of the Hall to collect conkers from an even larger horse chestnut tree growing there. Every boy collected as many as he could find and took them home to apply his own secret recipe for producing a hardened champion. At various times I tried baking my conkers in the oven, soaking them in vinegar or knocking them in as I would a cricket bat. Using mother's best meat skewer I bored a hole through each conker in order to attach it to a foot long piece of string. Equipped with a pocket full of similarly stringed conkers I entered the school's unofficial playtime conker championship, along with most of the other boys of the village. Each boy matched his conker against that of another boy. Using "paper, scissors and stone" to decide who went first, each boy in turn tried to hit the other boy's conker with his own. The target conker was dangled at arm's length for the striker to hit as hard as he could with his own. This continued strike for strike until one of the conkers broke or was knocked off its string, thus deciding the match. A conker that had won one of these competitions was called a one-er, the winner of two competitions a two-er and so on. A champion conker was the one that had won the most competitions and a twelve-er or even a twenty-er was not unheard of. Needless to say none of my conkers ever got beyond being a five-er or six-er. Disputes frequently occurred when the boy holding out his conker wiggled his arm at a crucial moment, apparently accidentally, causing the striker to miss. Or when the striker, also apparently, missed wildly and hit the child holding the conker instead, usually on the hand. From personal experience, I can assure you that this is extremely painful. These disputes were usually settled by a playground scuffle.

OUR HOUSE

Access to our house from Martham Road was through a wooden gate set into the privet hedge that surrounded the property. It had neither garage nor drive and, consequently, my father had to park his car on the grass roadside verge in front of the house. A short concrete path led to the front door, which was rarely used during the time we lived there and apparently existed merely to fulfil the requirement that a house should have at least two exits in case of fire. Entry was normally through the back door that was approached from the front of the house by a shingle path winding around the side. Everyone, including family, friends, neighbours and tradesmen, would automatically call at the back door rather than the front, their arrival announced by the click of the garden gate and the crunch of their feet on the shingle. Anyone who called at the front door would immediately be classified as a stranger and astutely ignored. My recollection is that most front doors in our village were frequently unused and often considered to be a nuisance, as they were a prime source of draughts in houses that often suffered badly from such afflictions. In many houses it was impossible to use the front door as it was often taped up or draped in blankets to prevent these draughts from the bitter easterly winter winds. Although defended by a substantial lock and two sturdy bolts, our back door was rarely locked except at night, although my mother insisted on locking it when she made her twice-weekly shopping trips to Great Yarmouth. However, the key was always left in an obvious location just in case someone wanted to get in, normally on the seat of the outside toilet. Visitors could, and often did, walk straight in announcing their presence by rattling the knocker that covered the letterbox or calling out to anyone inside. The postman and the newspaperman rarely used the letterbox and preferred to deliver their packages by opening the door and throwing them on to the scullery floor, at the same time calling out "post" or "papers". Post inadvertently delivered through the letterbox of the front door could lie undiscovered for weeks, even months.

Our house had three bedrooms, two double and one single, two reception rooms and a single storey wash house or scullery with adjoining coalhouse and an outside toilet. There was no bathroom, indoor toilet or any form of central heating. The house was rented from "old" Mr Tooke who lived in Violet Villa, a large house immediately behind our property, which fronted on to the Main Road through Rollesby and is now The Windmill, a care home for the elderly. In 1940s Rollesby, our house was considered modern and up to date, but in twenty-first-century terms it would be considered primitive. Mains water was not installed until early 1952, when it consisted solely of a single cold water tap in the scullery. Until then, our drinking water was collected in an enamelled pail from a pump by the back door of Violet Villa, a round trip of 100 yards or more, undertaken twice daily no matter what the weather. Neither did we have the benefit of mains drainage, as the small drain outside the back door, into which almost everything liquid was emptied, led merely to a soakaway, while the downpipes from the gutter either poured rainwater straight on to the ground or into three large water butts positioned at various points round the house. But at least we had electricity and the benefits of electric light, although some more remote parts of the village were without an electric supply until the late 1940s. A few households even refused to be connected, fearing that the brilliance of electric light would damage their eyesight. I can recall a number of houses "up the heath" and in the neighbouring village of Fleggburgh that were still illuminated by paraffin lamps well into the 1950s. Our four larger rooms had fireplaces, although those in the two bedrooms were rarely lit and their flues were stuffed with paper to prevent heat loss or cold draughts from coming down the chimney. When needed, a single bar electric fire was used to heat the other rooms or the main rooms when it was uneconomical to light a coal fire — central heating was non-existent in working-class housing. Generally our house was cold, draughty and damp, but it was home and we loved it.

The Ground Floor Rooms

The three downstairs rooms were the living room, front room and scullery. Although it was the largest room in the house and had the best furniture, the front room was only used on special occasions. For everyday purposes we used the living room and the scullery, and inevitably it was these rooms that changed the most during the time that I lived there, while the rest of the house remained very much the same as it must have been when it was first occupied. During the 1940s, we cooked, ate, sat, played and rested in the living room which was a dining room, sitting room and kitchen all rolled into one; on Friday nights it was even a bathroom. At one end, set into the chimney wall, was a blackleaded kitchen range. As well as cooking our food and heating up water, it provided warmth on cold days and nights, not always effectively. On the coldest nights we huddled as close as possible to the small open fire door of the range, often burning our hands and legs while the rest of our bodies froze. When my father was eventually demobilised from the army in 1947, the range was replaced by a more efficient open coal fire surrounded by a beige-tiled fireplace that he made himself. To my mother's delight, a new electric cooker was installed in the scullery. Small amounts of water for tea and other purposes were boiled in a copper-coloured electric kettle.

To one side of the range were two cupboards, one above the other. The top cupboard was used for linen and the bottom cupboard held all my toys and books. On the other side of the range was a small alcove which, at various times, held a small table, my child's desk and finally a cabinet that contained grandfather's birds' egg collection. The living room was simply furnished. There were three armchairs, one each for my parents and one for me. My father always had the largest and most comfortable chair. In his absence, there was always a keen contest between Mother and me to sit in it. The first armchairs I remember were more functional than comfortable, with solid wooden backs, arms and seats, and several cushions were needed to provide some semblance of comfort. Eventually, these were replaced by a contemporary three-piece suite of the latest 1950s design with open sides, wooden arms and latex-filled cushions supported by tension sprung seats and backs.

Pushed against the wall under the window was an extendable brown dining table with four chairs. It also served as an ironing board, a surface for pasting wallpaper when decorating time came round, and a games table, particularly for playing various card games or highly competitive ping-pong tournaments. It also served as the base for our portable billiard table. During the war it was even used as an air raid shelter. I can remember numerous occasions when I was hidden under the table while, from the back door, my mother watched the Acle and Yarmouth anti-aircraft guns, assisted by two or more searchlights, try in vain to down unseen enemy aircraft droning overhead. Our table had a perfect iron shape burnt into its top, the result of an unexpected visitor while mother was doing the weekly ironing.

When not in use it was covered by a brown tablecloth and a vase of flowers.

Opposite to the table there was a large dark brown sideboard and on the opposite wall to the range a small ornamental table on which sat the radio, or the wireless as it was usually called, the most important item in the room. The wireless retained this prime position until 1957 when it was replaced by a black-and-white television set and relegated to a lesser position on the sideboard. A square carpet covered the central part of the floor and the gap between the carpet and the wall was filled in by strips of linoleum, an ideal skating surface for a small boy in socks. A rag mat in front of the fire protected the carpet from the sparks and hot coals that often flew from or dropped out of the fire grate. Sparks often went unnoticed until a smell of burning indicated their presence. We were all very good at wetting our fingers with spit in order to quench small sparks or to return larger pieces to the fire. A small brass shovel and brush, the latter having most of its bristles shortened by burning, were used to sweep up and return hot coals. These hung from a matching brass holder that stood beside the hearth, together with a poker and toast fork. A well-secured fireguard was usually placed in front of the fireplace at bedtimes or when the house was left unattended. Sparks from fires were always a concern and a potential cause of household accidents. Chimney fires were quite common, particularly in flues that were irregularly swept. We had our share of chimney fires but these were dealt with efficiently by my father in his own peculiar style, which usually involved either poking brushes up the chimney or stuffing it solid with wet sacks. Most of our fires were the result of my father's habit of drawing up a lazy fire by placing a newspaper over the fireplace to create a strong draught. Many houses in our neighbourhood had thatched roofs and were liable to catch fire from sparks coming from chimneys or neighbouring bonfires, particularly in dry summers. I can clearly recall joining a group of excited children to watch the Martham Fire Brigade dealing with a thatch fire at a pair of cottages on the Martham Road.

Five brigades fight cottage fire at Rollesby

Fighting against fierce flames fanned by a lively wind, five fire brigades on Sunday saved from total destruction a building divided into two cottages on Martham Road, Rollesby. The heavy thatch of the roof, however, was almost completely lost and some damage done to the upper storey . . .

. . . The firemen climbed on to the roof and pulled away the blazing thatch, while the families and neighbours stored furniture in the garden. One of the first on the scene was P.C. R. Jenkinson of Martham who helped to carry beds and tables from the burning houses.

"Village News: Rollesby",
Yarmouth Mercury, 3 February 1950

On top of the sideboard was a biscuit barrel that my father won at a local bowls tournament in 1936, a pink glass fruit bowl and a tin box in which Mother kept the rent book, insurance policies and shillings for the electric meter. On my birth, Mother had taken out a one-penny-a-week policy with the Prudential Insurance Company to cover funeral expenses in the event of my early death, a precaution that thankfully proved unnecessary. A large tray made by blind ex-servicemen leant against the wall behind the fruit bowl. Its main function was to carry up the Sunday morning tea-in-bed made as a treat by Father — a particularly inadequate reward for Mother who, on every other day of the week, even in the cold of winter, rose first so as to clean out and relight the fire, prepare breakfast and heat up the wash water for my father and myself. This task was made less onerous during the 1950s with the installation of an all night burner although, by the morning, there was very little heat left in the fire and it still required some encouragement to revive.

On the walls hung two untitled pictures of Mediterranean-type scenes, a large mirror, and a smaller mirror with two clothes brushes attached. On my father's return from army service, he brought back a large carved photograph frame proclaiming "souvenir of Rome, Italy 1944" which was also hung on the wall. For nearly sixty years this frame has held three photographs: one of my parents on their wedding day, my father in his army service uniform, and a studio portrait of mother and me on my fifth birthday. On top of the fireplace near to my father's armchair were two mugs that held numerous pens and pencils. Behind these he stacked any unanswered letters, bills and his

91

current copy of Vernon's football pools. In the centre was a clock, an essential item that governed our daily routine. When the main form of transport for most villagers was the bus, an accurate knowledge of time was essential. In the bouts of silence that frequently occurred in a house without television, stereophonic CD players or a perceived need for 24-hour radio broadcasting, its regular ticking was somewhat comforting. Last thing at night the clock would be wound up, a ritual that happened without fail whether it was needed or not.

On either side of the wireless table were two doors. The door to the right gave access to the stairs that led up to a small landing and the three bedrooms. There were fourteen steps on our staircase, an insignificant fact engraved for ever on my memory as, when I was a small boy, Mother and I counted them every night as she led me up the stairs to bed. By the age of four I knew all the number names in order up to fourteen, but I was always confused by the fact that our step counting always ended with "and through the Rory O More and into Uncle Ned's bed". I never did find out who or what a "Rory O More" was or why my bed belonged to Uncle Ned, who I had never even met. The left-hand door opened into a whitewashed understairs pantry. Tins and dry goods were placed on two deep shelves to the right of the door. Underneath these shelves mother stored lines of Kilner jars, full of bottled fruit: pears, plums and greengages, all picked from our garden or grandfather's small market garden, and jars of jam made from garden-produced strawberries, blackcurrants and raspberries, or blackberries gathered from the roadside. To the left was the meat safe, the 1940s version of a refrigerator which consisted of a wooden cabinet, about 3 feet high, on four short legs with a mesh door. The mesh was large enough to allow a good circulation of air over the contents of the safe but small enough to prevent most of the flies that infested our house from penetrating inside. Two interior marble shelves added to its cooling ability, although compared with a modern refrigerator and freezer it was not particularly efficient and perishable goods including meat and fish had a very short shelf life. On top of the safe was a large wooden cutlery tray and, above that, two shelves on which were stacked all our everyday crockery, with cups hanging from hooks along their edges. Permanently placed under the safe there was a mousetrap, as house mice were ever present and a constant problem. The household cat was not just a decorative pet but performed the essential function of pest control. Unfortunately the cat also brought with it another pest, fleas, which we were less able to control then than we can those on our cats today. Mother regularly stripped our beds, and even Father and me, in futile attempts to locate rogue fleas.

Two other doors led out from the living room, one into the scullery and the other to the front room. Although it was the largest room in the house, fitted with a relatively ornate red tiled fireplace, the front room was only used at Christmas, on special occasions and for other family gatherings. On a mantelshelf above the fireplace there was a clock and two ornamental porcelain Pekingese dogs. The latter were held together by copious amounts of glue, having been broken many times. Most of the breaks were the result of accidents that occurred while I practised my football skills with a balloon at Christmas. It was always my naive belief that my invisible mending was so good that my parents never noticed.

The front room furniture consisted of an imitation leather three-piece suite, the repair patch on the front of the sofa being the result of a very boisterous eighth birthday party. The recess of the bay window contained a gateleg table, on which stood a statue of an Alsatian dog with a chipped nose. Finally there was a piano. Most people owned a piano even though, frequently, nobody in the house could play it. We were no exception. When I was ten, my mother employed the services of Miss Dyball, a music teacher from Martham, to teach me how to play. As I remember, Miss Dyball was a short, thin, grey-haired lady with the hint of a moustache. She always arrived exactly at the allocated time for the lesson, 2.30 on Saturday afternoon, on an old black sit-up-and-beg bicycle. This she rode in a very sedate and pedestrian manner, to the extent that one felt it would be quicker for her to walk and that if she rode any slower she would be in danger of falling off. Unfortunately for Miss Dyball, Saturday afternoon music lessons were not as attractive to a young boy as the football match that I was missing. Most of my lessons were spent in persuading her to cut the session short so that I would not miss the second half. Truthfully, I must admit that I was incapable of making sense of musical notation and was totally uninspired by practice pieces such as "Home Sweet Home", "The British Grenadier" and other traditional compositions. Most of the pieces that I was able to play, albeit badly, were learned by watching Miss Dyball's finger movements or by experiment and ear. After three months, she informed Mother that I was a particularly ungifted child and that she saw no future in continuing with the lessons.

A door off the front room led to a walk-in cupboard where mother kept our cylindrical vacuum cleaner and other cleaning materials and, next to that, another door led to the front hall, empty save for the shilling electric meter on the wall. A man from the electricity board emptied the meter every quarter, carefully counting out the shillings on our living room table and putting them into neat piles of twenty. When he had finished, Mother would buy back as many of the shillings as she could afford and then refill the meter, a form of payment in advance.

The floor of the front room was covered by yet another square carpet and in front of the fire was a semicircular, sandy coloured, imitation fur rug. The uncovered floorboards around the edge of the room were stained dark brown and polished. A number of wood splinters in my feet quickly convinced me that this surface was not as good as linoleum for sliding over. Pride of place in the front room eventually went to an oak dresser given to me by Grandfather Miller when he retired. He had made it himself in the 1920s, mainly from old oak pews salvaged from a disused local church, incorporating some of the original fourteenth-century carvings in the design.

My earliest memories of the scullery are of a bare whitewashed room with an uncovered stone tiled floor. In the far corner, heated from underneath by a coal furnace, was a brick built copper in which my mother did her weekly wash, conventionally on a Monday. The washing water was heated in a hemispherical chamber sunk into the top of the copper and into which the washing was added when the water was at the right temperature. A circular wooden lid covered the chamber while the contents were boiled. During the washing session mother agitated the clothes with a well-worn and frayed dolly stick. A large white rectangular sink rested on top of two brick pillars, fixed to the wall under the scullery window. Large green squares of soap, boxes of soap flakes, canisters of Vim and other cleaning materials were stored underneath the sink behind a check curtain. Fixed to the wall on the right of the window was a green mirrored bathroom cabinet which contained Father's shaving kit, various toiletries, plasters and medicines. A woven wicker laundry basket and a 3-foot-long tin bath hung from pegs on the back wall. On Mondays the tin bath was used to soak and pre-wash dirty clothing which Mother did using a washboard. On Friday evenings it was placed in front of the living room fire for each of us in turn to take a stand up bath before retiring to bed. Modesty required that I should bath first and then depart upstairs. Father bathed next and Mother last, frequently using the dirty water of the previous bather.

A magnificent, large, ancient iron-framed mangle completed the scullery equipment. A circular metal cogwheel turned its two large frayed orange rollers, while a screw on the top of the mangle was used to adjust the pressure between them. I regularly turned the mangle to press my tie by running it to and fro between the rollers, often while still wearing it. In good weather, mangling was done outside, the water squeezed out of the wet washing emptying into the drain by means of a chute under the rollers. In bad weather, this was done inside when the tin bath deputised for the drain. Eventually, this was replaced by a gleaming white modern Acme wringer. Finished washing was hung to dry on a clothes line suspended between a metal post and a dead tree stump close to the back door. In wet weather Mother used a laundry rack suspended from the scullery ceiling. All our outdoor coats and hats were hung on the back of the scullery door and our boots and shoes were lined up on the floor.

Washing, drying and ironing were a major part of Mother's weekly household chores. This work was time consuming and laborious, particularly when all the water used in the process had to be carried from the pump by the back door of our landlord's house. During the 1940s and 1950s the increased availability of basic services such as electricity, a mains water supply and waste disposal, together with the purchase of labour-saving devices did much to improve Mother's lot by easing the burden of her domestic tasks. The advent of the cold water tap in 1952 saved much of the time and effort that was expended in collecting and transporting pails of water from the pump. A cylindrical metal electric boiler eventually replaced the old brick corner boiler, which was subsequently removed. This, too, was replaced in the mid-1950s by the introduction of a twin-tub washing machine. The washboard continued in service as one of my instruments in a local skiffle group together with a number of Mother's thimbles.

In the depths of winter, during quiet times in the building trade, my father did his bit to update the scullery fittings. The old-fashioned scullery sink was replaced by a "modern" aluminium kitchen sink with an attached drainer, although it still had only the one cold tap. A full-length enamelled bath was also installed, on to which my father added a wooden top, hinged at the wall, so that it could be dropped to form a table when the bath was not in use. Bath water could be quickly heated in the adjacent electric copper and conveyed into the bath by a pail. Consequently, we were able to bath more frequently without the need for any elaborate and lengthy preparation or concern for the bather's modesty. Following on from the installation of the electric cooker, these changes effectively transferred most household tasks from the living room to the scullery which was subsequently used for all the activities associated with the kitchen, dining room and bathroom. Only Sunday lunch and meals for special occasions continued to be taken at the living room table, all other meals were eaten at the bath-top table. The living room became a room for rest, relaxation and entertainment, and the front room became essentially redundant except at Christmas and for parties.

UPSTAIRS

Upstairs, the three bedrooms were simply and sparsely furnished. My parents' bedroom was the largest and looked out over the scullery roof to the back garden. Their furniture consisted of a large wooden bed covered by a yellow candlewick bedspread, a chest of drawers, a dressing table with mirror and four drawers, and a washstand. The washstand consisted of a marble topped table with a single drawer on which was placed a matching decorated wash bowl with jug and soap dish. Underneath the stand was a shelf on which stood a white enamelled pail, with a lid, intended for removing used washing water. The whole served little purpose and was only used when someone was ill and required bed-bathing. Two built-in cupboards served as wardrobes.

The spare bedroom, with front facing window, was similarly furnished but with an additional free-standing wardrobe. For a while, this room became home to an evacuee from the East End of London, Mrs Sally Pitchford, and her son Peter, with whom Mother formed a lifelong friendship. During the war, I shared the main bedroom with my mother, while the single bedroom, really no larger than a boxroom, was used to store the apples from our four apple trees. When it eventually became my bedroom it was barely large enough to hold my single bed, a chest of drawers and a washstand, the latter without jug and bowl as the survival rate of such articles in a child's bedroom was considered to be virtually nil.

All the upstairs floors were covered with linoleum that, although easy to clean, felt cold to bare feet on very chilly winter's mornings and warm slippers were a necessity rather than just a substitute for outdoor footwear. A few appropriately placed mats helped but were often dangerous in that they tended to slip over the smooth surface of the linoleum, not that this worried a small boy who was fixated on playing sliding games. An essential "potty" was located under all of the beds. First thing every morning we each carried our personal potty downstairs, emptying it into the drain by the back door before rinsing it in the nearby water butt and replacing it under our beds ready for the next night's use. The upstairs rooms were unheated and consequently freezing cold in winter, while our beds were normally preheated with a hot-water bottle. Grandma Cole frequently used a metal soldier's water bottle for this purpose, often scalding many unsuspecting visitors to her house who jumped into bed without noticing its presence. On cold nights, once upstairs, my aim was to get into the warm bed in the shortest possible time. Clothes tended to be tossed rather than laid on a bedside chair, as there was little incentive to fold them neatly when your hands were freezing, before hastily snuggling down into a bed heavy with blankets securely tucked in at the sides. On the coldest nights my dressing gown and overcoat were often added to the pile of blankets in an attempt to remain warm. Some winter mornings were so cold that I had to scrape away the frost from the inside of the bedroom window before I was able to look out.

OUTSIDE FACILITES

Outside and to the rear of the scullery were located the coal shed and toilet, both linked to the kitchen by a concrete path. Their doors made an excellent surface on which to practise my football and cricket skills. In the summer, I drew a wicket in chalk on one of the doors and spent many hours bowling at it with a tennis ball. In the winter, I drew numbers at different points on both doors, targeting each in turn as I practised my accuracy at penalty taking. Often a football smacking into the toilet door elicited a shout from inside as the concentration of the occupant was disturbed by the noise. Our coal was obtained from Mr Lown, a coal merchant from Martham who delivered on a regular basis, usually two to four one hundredweight bags a fortnight, depending upon our needs or how much mother could afford. At the end of the summer, the coal shed would be full although by the end of winter we would be down to the dust that had sunk to the bottom of the heap.

Inside the toilet, the operational part consisted of a large box across the back of the cubicle with a hinged top that served as a seat. An oval hole was cut into the top and covered by a wooden lid. Under the hole was placed a large bucket for the purpose of collecting human waste. On the back of the door was a nail on which, in hard times, hung newspaper squares for use as toilet paper. In better times, a toilet roll was placed on the loo seat although this usually had the consistency of stiff greaseproof paper and was barely an improvement on the newspaper. When full, the bucket had to be emptied and, during the war, this was the responsibility of the householder which, with my father away on active service, fell to Grandfather. While everyone else hid inside, he would carefully empty the contents of the bucket into a large trench that he had previously dug in the back garden. Undoubtedly the fertility of the garden and the quality of its produce owed much to this practice. Many of our relatives commented favourably about the good taste of our vegetables until they were acquainted with the growing medium.

Some toilets had more than one hole and, therefore, more than one bucket, thus reducing the number of times that the toilet needed emptying. My grandparents' outside toilet had two holes and two buckets and when one bucket was full, they merely moved over to the other. At Martham, Aunt Dolly and Uncle Stanley Crawford shared a water well and a communal toilet block with the residents of the five other houses in their terrace. To avoid our bucket filling too rapidly, Father and I were encouraged to pee against the hedge or into the scullery drain. Our potties were also emptied into the drain. By the 1950s, the responsibility for emptying our bucket toilets had passed to the local council. Every fortnight a tanker lorry, affectionately known by some as the honey cart and by others as the shit wagon, pulled up outside our house for the driver, dressed in blue overalls and hat, and wearing large black gauntlets to protect his hands and arms, to gingerly carry our bucket down the garden path to be emptied into its tank. While this was happening, all our windows and doors were firmly shut in a valiant attempt to keep out the ensuing stench. When the process was completed, Mother scuttled out to the toilet and poured half a bottle of Jeyes fluid into the empty bucket.

Periodically the toilet was thoroughly cleaned and a stiff yard brush was used to remove the cobwebs from the walls and under the seat. The concrete floor was scrubbed and also doused with copious quantities of Jeyes fluid. The walls were also frequently whitewashed and the seat painted. This could be particularly hazardous, especially when my father painted it on impulse, as he was often wont to do. I vividly remember one occasion when, on using the toilet after dark, I found the seat to be particularly sticky. On my return, I was informed that the seat had just been painted and, on inspection, I found that my bottom was perfectly framed in green paint which my mother attempted to remove by smearing it with butter. Up until the 1950s householders were also responsible for the disposal of their household waste, although there was much less of it than now and what there was contained virtually no plastic or cellophane. Glass bottles were mostly recycled: milk bottles were returned via the doorstep to the daily visiting milkman, lemonade and other soft-drink bottles were returned to the shop from which they had been bought, and beer bottles to the pub, sometimes encouraged by a refundable deposit. Organic matter was recycled through a compost heap. Clothes still useable were either passed down to younger siblings or sold at a jumble sale. Other rubbish was usually burned or buried and larger items were frequently dumped in a local landfill site, in our case the Clay Allotment. Every six months or so, a rag and bone merchant drove around the village with a horse and cart, calling out for "any old lumber". A household rubbish collection service was not established in Rollesby until the early 1950s.

Refuse carts for the Flegg villages

A scheme for the collection of household refuse employing five vehicles and 14 men and costing £6000 a year was approved at a meeting of the Blofield & Flegg Rural District Council on Tuesday . . .

. . . it was also decided that with the next notice of rates, householders should be asked to burn as much of their refuse as possible to keep down the cost of collection to a minimum.

Yarmouth Mercury, 31 March 1950

In the summer, flies and other insects were a problem to an extent hardly credible nowadays. Swarms of flies inhabited the toilet, their access eased by the ventilation gaps at the top and bottom of the door. Squadrons of flies flew through the house or circled round the living room light. Attempts to control their numbers were tried but usually found to be futile. Rolled up newspapers were used as fly swats and long sticky bands hung from every suitable point. In desperation my father would occasionally use a spray device filled with an insecticide called Flit. Sometimes cards, usually in the form of a parrot and impregnated with DDT, were hung from the light shade. The advent of readily available insecticides was considered a great boon and they were used liberally inside the house without any thought or concern for the potential hazard to human health. My personal favourite fly control method was the use of an elastic band gun that I had been given as a Christmas present. Elastic bands were stretched between a groove at the end of the barrel and a cog at the butt end. On pulling the trigger, the cog was released and the elastic band was ejected forwards at a considerable speed. It appeared that flies resting on the ceiling or on the walls were not nimble enough to avoid the elastic band. Unfortunately the band had the effect of squashing the smaller flies against the ceiling or wall, although luckily not the largest bluebottles. As a result, the walls and ceilings became spotted with dead fly corpses and my parents were forced to confiscate the gun.

During August and September, wasps became a nuisance. Mother attempted to control these by placing numerous jam jars partly filled with water at strategic points around the outside of the house. The wasps that were attracted to the residue of jam remaining in the jar then, hopefully, drowned in the water, although it appeared to me that these jars merely ended up attracting even more wasps. Boiling water was the usual treatment for ants' nests. I have had a healthy respect for ants' nests ever since a number of ants crawled into my trousers while I was sitting on our lawn and proceeded to bite me in places where you would not expect to be bitten. This experience was so painful that the memory of it still brings tears to my eyes. Gnats were also more abundant, buzzing in clouds over our rainwater butts and the stagnant water in the ditch. I spent many hours watching their larvae wiggling up and down inside the water butts although I was not always pleased to see them there, as we often washed ourselves in the water from these butts when it was considered too much of an effort to go up to the pump. At night, after lights out, gnats could frequently be heard buzzing through the bedrooms and were either ignored or pursued with a rolled up newspaper or comic. Woodlice were common inside the house, perhaps a confirmation that the property suffered considerably from damp. These trilobite-like creatures were great fun as they curled up into a ball when touched, an invitation for me to roll them around the floor.

The close proximity of the toilet and the kitchen, together with the abundance of flies, may account for the regularity with which I suffered from stomach upsets. Certainly the lack of a ready supply of water, particularly hot water, made basic hygiene difficult. I hated vomiting so much that I had the habit of noting when these bouts occurred and considered that six weeks or so between episodes was a good record. With flies came their predators, spiders. Our house had its fair share, especially in the toilet. Inside the house, cobwebs would appear overnight, usually attached to the light shade, and in parts of the house that were infrequently used, such as the front room and the spare bedroom, cobwebs colonised each and every corner. None of us was at all scared of spiders, not even the large, dark brown, long-legged spiders that could grow to 2 or more inches across. One spider, christened Fred by Mother, would cross from one corner of the living room to the other at about the same time every night. While she was staying with us, Grandma Cole was encouraged to look out for Fred, considered by us to be quite a novelty. Sure enough, at the allotted time, Fred appeared. With a yell, my grandmother leaped from her chair and brought her foot hard down on top of Fred, leaving a mangled mush of legs and body on the carpet, proclaiming, "There, now Fred is dead."

Spiders in the toilet were less appealing. Cobwebs hung from under the seat and from the ceiling, often vibrating with the buzzing of trapped flies, and I frequently ended up sitting on the toilet eyeballing a large brown spider clinging to the wall. Usually it remained motionless for the duration, but when these spiders moved, they moved suddenly and quickly, so it was advisable to be prepared so as to usher them in the opposite direction to where you were sitting. I can remember numerous occasions when aunts, uncles and cousins, unused to toilets with wildlife, ran shrieking from the loo, often in a state of partial undress, convinced that they were under attack from a giant poisonous arachnid. At night, it was an adventure for anyone to use the toilet as it had not been fitted with an electric light. Sometimes a torch was available in the kitchen which could be used to illuminate the visit or as a searchlight to explore the walls for spiders and other insects lurking in the dark. When a torch was not available, trips to the loo were often made by feel when you just sat and hoped.

THE GARDEN

The garden surrounded the house on three sides. Compared to modern gardens it was quite large, about a third of an acre in area, although this was by no means exceptional for a time when most rural housing, from the smallest cottage or council house to the larger homes of the better off, had big gardens. Usually ornamental gardens were only to be found in the grounds of the bigger houses. In houses like ours, gardens were functional rather than ornamental and used to provide fresh fruit and vegetables for the table. Frequently there was a small lawn for recreational purposes, often surrounded by flower borders although most of the garden was given over to growing food, a practice reinforced by the wartime call to "dig for victory". It amazes me that people who were normally working five and a half days or even six days a week found the time to tend their gardens. It may be that while men were committed to work for longer hours than at present, women, who were predominantly home-based, were able to find odd moments in their busy day for gardening activities. My father enjoyed gardening and gave as much attention to it as he could, but it was Mother who somehow found the time to do the routine jobs such as watering, weeding, gathering and general garden maintenance, often with my unenthusiastic assistance.

Our garden plan, if indeed it was planned, consisted of four distinct areas. On the right of the front path, in front of the bay window, was a small square lawn surrounded by a flower border in which were five or six standard roses as well as a few border plants. To the left of this path and stretching from the front hedge to the back end of the house was a fruit and vegetable area. Next, in front of the scullery was another small lawn that served as a sitting area for my parents and a play area for me. At the far end of this lawn my father had built a number of sheds and glasshouses, while along the near edge ran the clothes line. Finally, behind the house, another vegetable area stretched back a further 80 feet or so to the rear hedge. A cinder path ran alongside the party hedge of our semi-detached houses to the back gate that opened out into the garden of our landlord.

Our garden contained four mature apple trees, two in the front vegetable area and two in the rear, which were a legacy of the fact that our houses were built in what was originally the orchard of the landlord's large garden. Two of the trees produced cooking apples and the other two had eating apples which, when carefully stored, would last well into the winter. On Sundays we regularly had apple pie and custard or baked apple and sultanas for pudding. Mother also took great pride in serving our own home produced eating apples at Christmas. The left-hand boundary of the garden ran partly along the wall of Miss Julia's single-storey thatched cottage then to a rough hedge with a drainage ditch alongside. Close to the hedge was a greengage tree and set into it was a bullace tree, the latter about 20 feet high with thin branches and spindly twigs. In spring it produced a marvellous display of pink blossom and in late summer a crop of small yellow to orange plum-like fruits. Apparently the bullace is an ancient European plum variety from which the damson has evolved. Two rows of blackcurrant bushes ran close to and parallel with the front hedge, the second row also included a large gooseberry bush. A small strawberry bed nestled close to the cottage wall and a row of raspberry canes bordered the middle lawn, supported by wires strung between two sturdy wooden posts.

Father's motto was never waste anything and never buy anything new if you can get it for free. When involved in demolishing buildings, he had the annoying habit of bringing back home any salvaged material that "might come in useful someday". As a consequence, his garden buildings were always constructed from scrap and the result normally resembled a shanty town. A pile of bricks and two old windows could easily be

110

transformed into a cold frame. However, in the austere days immediately after the Second World War such ingenuity made a difference to the quality of our lives as we always had a greenhouse full of tomatoes and a cold frame crammed with cucumbers and marrows, never mind that they were both made from reclaimed windows. I also recall a number of home-made hutches lined up against the side hedge, in which he bred rabbits. One of my jobs was to feed these rabbits with dandelion leaves and cow parsley that I collected from the roadside verges. Periodically, apart from one breeding pair, all the rabbits would disappear, "off to a good home", according to father, and it was a long time before I realised that they would have gone, via the Acle livestock sale, to a fur factory or the butcher's slab.

The two vegetable areas were very productive and were cropped according to my father's version of a two-course rotation, where one half would be given over to bulk produce such as potatoes, cabbages, cauliflower and Brussels sprouts, while in the other he grew salad and root crops, lettuces, radish, celery, carrots, turnips and parsnips, together with beans and peas. The following year the contents of each plot would be reversed. Things changed slightly when he decided to keep chickens in the garden. To house the chickens a small run was set up in the garden surrounded by a wire netting fence supported by iron stakes and containing a home-made coop on wheels. The intention was that this arrangement would be mobile and moved periodically to different parts of the garden and, as well as providing eggs for the house, this would allow for the chickens to serve a useful function by cleaning and fertilising the ground. The run was eventually filled with two dozen Red Leghorns, which arrived by post as day-old chicks in an octagonal cardboard box with ventilation holes around the edge. A few extra chicks were always included to allow for losses during transport. Initially these were kept in an incubator placed in the alcove of our living room until they were old enough to fend for themselves in the chicken run. The incubator consisted of a square based tin box about a foot high with a pitched top, heated by a paraffin lamp placed in the centre and with a wire mesh around the heater to prevent the chicks from burning themselves. Small fluffy chicks are quite endearing but adult chickens are the most boring of birds, their only achievements being an ability to escape from their run on a regular basis and to get themselves stuck in the topmost branches of the apple trees. We spent many an hour chasing escapee chickens round the garden or retrieving them from neighbouring properties. For a time, at Mr Grundy's request, the chickens were moved into the orchard of the White House to help clear the ground of weeds. They were soon moved back into our garden when it became apparent that, for some inexplicable reason, they produced fewer eggs there than at home. The chicken experiment worked reasonably well for a few years, providing fresh eggs for the table, until the chickens had to be destroyed in 1951 during a major fowl pest outbreak. Mother and father, having become strangely attached to their chickens, took the loss badly and decided not to restock. The run was subsequently rolled up and the coop used as night quarters for our spaniel, Rover.

Fowl Pest

The government has made a welcome decision to stop all imports of poultry from countries where fowl pest is endemic. This ought to have been done sooner. It is now to be hoped that the ban will be enforced not just until the disease has been wiped out, but until such precautions have been devised as will prevent the infected countries for ever again sending to this country carcasses which could endanger the health of our flocks. The reputed origin of the outbreak in East Anglia shows how strict these precautions should be. It is all said to have started from the refuse from one infected carcass which an American soldier took out of camp to give to some friends. No doubt he meant it kindly, but not even Gambia has produced a fowl so expensive as that one. The Americans have agreed to stop bringing over poultry for their troops' rations . . .

Eastern Daily Press, 2 March 1951

My parents continued to live on Martham Road until 1964 when they bought a two-bedroom bungalow on a small housing development along the Back Road in

Rollesby. It was a struggle for Father to convince Mother of the wisdom of buying their own house, and of undertaking a 15-year mortgage at the age of fifty. Mother had a pathological fear of being in debt, having seen the effects that debt had had on families during the depression of the 1920s and 1930s. She often warned me to "never a borrower or lender be" and suggest that what I couldn't afford I shouldn't have. Mother saw a mortgage as an immense debt that would only be a constant worry. She eventually conceded that to move was a sensible decision when she realised that the mortgage repayments were almost exactly the same as the rent she was paying to her landlord, and agreed to the purchase on the understanding that the mortgage repayment was seen as a form of rent and not the settlement of a debt.

CHAPTER
FOUR

Village Services

ALL OUR DAILY NEEDS

Everywhere, village life gradually changed between 1940 and 1960, and Rollesby was no exception. People became better off as Britain recovered from the hardships of wartime and technological advances made daily tasks easier both at work and in the home. But change was slow, much slower than in the latter years of the twentieth century, and many things remained much the same as they were. Perhaps some things were all the better for remaining the same. During the whole of my childhood, almost all our everyday needs were provided for within Rollesby or its immediate neighbourhood. Most of life's necessities, our food and household goods, could be bought locally in the village shops or from travelling vans. More often than not, what was unavailable in Rollesby could be found in neighbouring villages, particularly the village of Martham a mere 1½ miles away. Furniture, electrical appliances and clothes could be bought from the shops and department stores of Great Yarmouth, 8 miles distant. Most children were educated at the local village school and our health needs were catered for by two surgeries, one in Fleggburgh and the other at Martham. Clubs and societies provided a variety of entertainments sufficient to satisfy the interests of every age range, including the teenage members of the village. Film shows, whist drives, dances and socials were regularly held in the school or in neighbouring village halls, and at the Horse & Groom the social drinker could compete at darts, bowls and cribbage. Immediately beyond Rollesby Bridge in the adjoining village of Little Ormesby, similar activities were also provided by two other public houses, the Sportsman's Arms — until it closed in the late 1940s — and the Eel's Foot Inn, while behind both were jetties where rowing boats could be hired for excursions on to the Trinity Broad.

The regular bus service gave access to the cinemas, dance halls and other attractions of Great Yarmouth, as well as to the shops. There was little need to travel beyond the confines of Rollesby, its neighbouring villages and Great Yarmouth for all the requirements of home, work and leisure. Occasionally my mother would accompany Grandmother Miller on a shopping trip to Norwich. As this involved a long and uncomfortable bus journey, such visits were not a regular occurrence. I hardly ever travelled to Norwich and can recollect only one or two trips to the theatre, a school visit to the Bridewell and Castle museums and a number of excursions to Carrow Road to watch Norwich City Football Club, mainly during their resurgence in the 1957-8 and 1958-9 seasons. I vividly remember one theatre trip to Norwich organised by my grandmother, as the entertainment turned out to be a Windmill style variety show and involved static nudes, much to her disgust. However, to a ten-year-old it was an interesting and eye-opening experience. Grandfather expressed suitable words of disapproval but made full use of his opera glasses. A passing familiarity with other areas of East Anglia, mostly within the counties of Norfolk and Suffolk, was derived either from outings with my parents, visits to family and friends, or through regular sporting trips, particularly to cricket and football matches.

Before starting my studies at Leicester University, I had travelled outside East Anglia on only three occasions. In 1945, I accompanied my mother on a visit to see Uncle Arthur Cole and his family in Birmingham. I assume it was 1945, as I can clearly recollect accompanying my Birmingham cousins to a Victory street party, where I sampled chocolate blancmange for the very first time. I had also been twice to London: the first time was in 1950 when my parents, grandparents and I spent Christmas with Uncle George and Aunt Eve Miller at their home in Bexleyheath; the second was a day excursion to Windsor Castle and Runnymede in 1952 organised by Mr Hogg, the history master at Yarmouth Grammar School.

Transport

Although there was little need or inclination on my part to travel away from Rollesby and its immediate locality, like most village residents I was limited by a lack of mobility. Today it is easy to take for granted the ease of travel that car ownership has provided but, back then, few people in the village owned cars and those working class people who had cars usually needed them for work. My father and grandfather both had cars of their own and used them for leisure activities as well as for work. Grandfather needed his car to deliver groceries, newspapers, produce from the Field, and materials to his various building sites, the latter carried in a brown wooden trailer that he attached to the rear. As a contract bricklayer, my father needed his car to travel to work which could be anywhere within a 20-mile radius. Most women did not drive, and of all the adult women in our family, only one aunt had a driving licence. My father tried briefly to teach Mother to drive but quickly abandoned the attempt, considering it hardly worth the resulting arguments and stress.

Teenagers rarely owned cars. At the age of eighteen I asked my father if he would give me driving lessons. His reply was to suggest that I waited until I could afford a car of my own before learning. He argued that as our car was necessary for his work, he could not take the risk of allowing me to drive it. As I was still at school I had no option but to wait. I actually waited until I was twenty-eight years old before I was able to meet his criteria and learned to drive. One or two of my better-off contemporary sixth formers did have access to motor transport, but they were a rarity. Occasionally they would cram as many school friends into their cars as they were able, in order to transport us to dances or other "important" social engagements. Some who had managed to accrue enough capital or had generous parents bought Lambretta or Vespa scooters. These had become a fashionable alternative to a motorcycle having been popularised by a series of films set in Italy, in particular *Roman Holiday* starring my then favourite screen actress, Audrey Hepburn. Two of my school sixth form friends, Tim and Roger, owned scooters and for a time went some way towards solving my transport difficulties, despite the fact that neither had passed a driving test. On one occasion Tim and I had a narrow escape when, while giving me a lift home, he skidded on black ice as we were passing through Caister. After a slide of apparently massive proportions, we — Tim, me and the scooter — landed in a heap on the steps of the Caister police station. Luckily, no one came to our assistance and we escaped unchallenged. Eventually my scooter lifts ceased when Roger and I were stopped close to Potter Heigham Bridge by two members of the Norfolk Constabulary, the end result being a £5 fine at the North Walsham Magistrates Court and a serious telling-off from my parents.

Apart from lifts, legal or otherwise, I had to rely on my legs, a bicycle, the bus or, occasionally, a train for transport to wherever I needed to go. I thought nothing of walking anywhere and everywhere within the village, making full use of the many well used footpaths that often provided convenient short cuts. I regularly walked to Martham, sometimes with my friend, Tony, to visit his grandmother who lived on the green, or to train-spot at the station, or to see if there was a football match at the Martham recreation ground. Every day from the age of five I walked, skipped or ran all the way to Rollesby School no matter what the weather. Sometimes in winter, despite being muffled in balaclava and scarf, the bitter east wind blowing in my face took my breath away — then I walked to school backwards. In the bad winters of 1948 and 1949 I walked to school on the tops of 6-foot-high snowdrifts.

Some villagers were great walkers and travelled long distances on their own two legs, sometimes for pleasure, other times for their daily shopping. Every morning "Old" Kelly Hodds, a short thin elderly man with a white moustache and a stoop, walked from his home in Cowtrot to the post office for a morning paper — a distance of over a mile — and he was totally blind. It never occurred to me at the time to wonder how a blind man could read a newspaper, let alone walk all that way without mishap. Presumably, the paper was read to him by the rest of his family. Nevertheless, at 8.30 a.m. as regular as clockwork Kelly would tap his white stick along the length of Martham Road, shouting hello to everyone he met, recognising us all by our voices. Better than an alarm clock, his appearance was the signal that it was time for me to leave for school. Going for a walk was a popular Sunday afternoon or summer's evening pastime and whole

120

families, often accompanied by panting dogs and whingeing children, courting couples holding hands, or the energetic countryman with a walking stick would circumnavigate the village, pausing for a while at the bridge or the playing field for a conversation with other fellow walkers.

Walking apart, the primary means of transportation within and between villages was the bicycle. Everybody had a cycle of some sort, some more than one, occasionally a tricycle, each with their personalised decorations and extras. As a toddler I was ferried around the village strapped into a wicker baby carrier fixed above the back wheel of my mother's bicycle, which also had a basket attached to the handlebars to carry her handbag and shopping. My father's had a flat platform over the back wheel with a spring grip for carrying boxes of goods and two leather straps on the crossbar for carrying spades and other tools.

My first cycle was bought for me from Acle sale, a regular venue for buying and selling cycles of all ages, conditions and styles. Although a child's bicycle, it was too large for a six year old and my legs were not long enough to comfortably reach the pedals. However, with the seat at its lowest setting, together with the addition of wood blocks to the pedals, I was able to ride sufficiently well to receive cycle tuition from my mother up and down Martham Road. For hour upon hour mother ran behind me holding on to the seat of the cycle to prevent me from falling while I yelled "Don't let go, don't let go." Eventually, the inevitable happened and a distant voice replied, "I let go a while back,"

121

causing me to instantly panic and crash into the hedge. Nevertheless, her tuition paid dividends and, in time, there was little that I couldn't do on a bicycle. We raced around the village roads and footpaths in gangs, often imitating motorbikes by attaching cardboard or cigarette packets to our brake blocks so that they sounded like an engine as they rubbed against the spokes.

Our world was defined by the distance that we could cycle. As teenagers, inspired by the thought of girls, we thought nothing of cycling 10 miles or so to a film show, dance or social. The village halls of Ormesby, Hemsby, Caister, Filby, Fleggburgh, Martham, Potter Heigham, Ludham and even distant Hoveton, were all regular Friday or Saturday night venues, our cycles propped against their walls often three or four deep. If the quest had been a success we cycled home in pairs, holding hands with our conquest of the evening. In winter evenings, travelling could be extremely hazardous as the way ahead was barely illuminated by the inadequate battery lit lamps attached to the front of most of our cycles. Some managed to afford lights powered by dynamos attached to the rear of the cycle frame, generating electricity through turning a cog by rubbing it against the back wheel. In order to create light, cycles had to be in motion; the faster you travelled, the better the beam. Some even risked travelling without lights, relying on moonlight or their own night vision to guide them. While walking home from Martham one dark evening, I was knocked over by a cyclist with no lights when, surprised, confused and shouting at an apparent unseen assailant, I finished up lying on the road surface pinned down under the rider and her cycle. Shocked, but unhurt, we picked ourselves up and both learned a valuable lesson from the experience.

My most stylish bicycle was one that Uncle Cecil and I put together at his workshop in the barn at Rollesby post office based around a cycle frame retrieved from a large excavated hole on the Back Road, commonly referred to as the Clay Allotment. In the past this hole was a source of clay for the village, whether for making bricks or for spreading over gardens and fields is not totally clear, although I have no evidence for any local brick manufacture. By the 1940s the hole merely served as an unofficial rubbish dump for larger items that were otherwise difficult to dispose of, as well as a combined rally and speedway track for numerous boys on bicycles. After months of slow, painstaking work I became the proud owner of a crimson-painted three-geared bike, with dropped handlebars and a racing seat. By way of decoration, a pendant was attached to the front mudguard, and two mirrors and a hooter to the handlebars. A small mileometer screwed to the front wheel recorded how far I had travelled. I proudly raced around the village on this bike, the mileometer clicking rhythmically and my backside higher than my head, frequently slipstreaming buses and vans for extra speed. At sixteen, I was sure that my new bicycle gave me an advantage in the competition for favours from the opposite sex.

When travelling to Great Yarmouth we would normally use the bus. By "we" I mean Mother and me, as my father rarely found the need to visit Yarmouth other than for family outings, football matches and the occasional Sunday drive along the seafront, when he used his car. Our daily service, the number 5 bus from the Eastern Counties Omnibus Company, travelled a winding route from Norwich to Great Yarmouth and back via Wroxham, Ludham, Potter Heigham, Rollesby, Ormesby and Caister. In the 1940s and 1950s most residents were dependent on the bus for transport out of the village and, as a consequence, we were provided with a red double-decker bus that could carry sixty or more passengers at a time. From the bus stop at the Horse & Groom crossroads, the journey to Yarmouth took 30 to 35 minutes and the journey to Norwich just over one hour. For most bus travellers from Rollesby their destination, whether for work, shopping or entertainment, was Great Yarmouth; the one hour journey made Norwich unattractive other than for a special need or event.

During peak times the bus service was hourly, and two-hourly during the rest of the day. Early morning and late afternoon services were filled with workers, mostly men and young women, commuting to and from work in Great Yarmouth's shops and factories. The 8.40a.m. service through Rollesby was full of noisy school children travelling from the many villages on the route to secondary schools at Great Yarmouth and Caister, returning home on the equally noisy 4.15p.m. bus. From September 1951, I too travelled every day to school in Great Yarmouth, my fare paid by the local education committee who issued me with a scholar's season ticket that had the added benefit that weekend trips were also free. In the busy early mornings a second double-decker was added to each service acting as a relief for the main bus, arriving from Great Yarmouth to wait and join in convoy with the main through service at the Horse & Groom car park. Together, the two buses often carried one hundred or more passengers from the villages to their destinations in Great Yarmouth, many standing in the downstairs aisle. The last bus from Great Yarmouth left at 10.45p.m., 9.05p.m. on Sundays, making it barely possible for villagers to use many of the late night facilities in the town. Each bus was manned by a driver and a conductor, both dressed in the uniform of an Eastern Counties employee, the latter fully occupied with collecting fares, issuing tickets and storing passengers' luggage in an understairs compartment. Many conductors became well known to regular travellers, particularly to the younger travellers: who was a good laugh, who was officious, who was likely to eject noisy young passengers from the bus. The latter event usually resulted in a long walk home, but had little effect in changing our behaviour. Upstairs passengers were allowed to smoke; downstairs was smoke free. The upper deck was normally the domain of the young — the very young preferring to sit in the front seats pretending to drive, while the teenagers congregated on the back seats, often boy with girl draped over one another. Many of these young

125

passengers smoked cigarettes, even some of the front seat drivers.

Two other less frequent services, the 6A and the 48, also passed through Rollesby. The 6A, a single-decker, travelled between Rollesby and Great Yarmouth via Martham, Hemsby, Scratby and Caister while, in the summer, the 48 provided a weekend link between Norwich and the small but popular seaside resort of Hemsby. Great Yarmouth had its own blue corporation buses, which I used occasionally to travel to the beach at Gorleston or to the nearby Floral Hall, a popular dance venue. Special late night blue buses were organised to take Saturday night dancers back from the Floral Hall to destinations in Great Yarmouth or Caister. Bensley's of Martham provided motor coaches for private hire which were regularly used by Rollesby's clubs and societies to carry their members on day trips to seaside resorts such as Cromer, Sheringham and Hunstanton, revellers to the theatre and club dinner-dances, or spectators to cricket and football matches. A Bensley's coach regularly toured around the village with the outing organiser in the front directing the driver and ticking off each passenger's name as they were collected. Occasionally the organisers enlivened the outing for their passengers by holding draws and competitions. On trips that she planned, my grandmother chalked each seat number around the rim of a wheel on the coach and awarded a prize to the person sitting in the seat whose number was at the top of the wheel when the coach arrived at its destination. Return journeys were always accompanied by raucous sing-songs, frequently made even more raucous by a refreshment stop at a convenient public house.

> On Thursday Rollesby Ladies Club had its annual outing to Norwich where members visited the Theatre Royal to see "Robinson Crusoe".
>
> "Village News: Rollesby",
> *Yarmouth Mercury*, 27 January 1956

Although Martham had a station, I rarely used the railway for travelling to Great Yarmouth except in an emergency. A few people from Rollesby preferred to travel by train, either leaving their bicycles propped up in racks outside the station building or taking them with them in the guard's van. Martham station lay on a branch of the Midland & Great Northern Joint Railway, affectionately known as the muddle and get nowhere railway, which linked Yarmouth Beach station with Birmingham and the East Midlands via North Walsham, Kings Lynn, Peterborough and Leicester. This single-track line crossed the road from Rollesby to Martham at a level crossing immediately after Martham recreation ground, the track splitting in two at the station to allow trains travelling in opposite directions to pass one another. To the right of the crossing was a signal box and to the left the main station, which consisted merely of two platforms on either side of the track with a small building containing

127

the ticket office and waiting room on the Rollesby side. The station area was enclosed by trellis fencing, the station sign announcing "Martham for Rollesby". A single siding allowed for the collection and delivery of goods and animals. Behind the station was a parking area, a loading dock, cattle pens and an immense mountain of coal.

Martham station was usually impeccably clean and tidy, and frequently achieved "Best Station" status on the North Walsham to Yarmouth section of the line. In my younger days I spent a lot of time at the station as Grandfather regularly used the railway to send and receive goods for his market garden and building businesses. Hurry was not in Grandfather's vocabulary and he lingered for hours talking with the stationmaster, railway staff and other users of the station's facilities while I was allowed to wander unhindered. As with most young children, I was both terrified and fascinated by the steam engines, leviathans with steam and smoke escaping from every orifice while pulling long passenger trains or seemingly endless strings of goods wagons. I was regularly lifted on to an engine's footplate by the stationmaster so that I could peer into the firebox or watch the fireman at work, no doubt breaking every rule of the railway company. I knew many of the drivers and guards by sight and they waved at me as they passed through the station. In the quiet of the night, from my bedroom I could hear the late evening and early morning trains as they rattled their way between Martham and Potter Heigham.

Despite my obvious fascination with trains I hardly ever had cause to use their services except for odd occasions such as when the Eastern Counties Omnibus staff joined a national bus strike, a few trips to North Walsham and for an interview at Leicester University. Any opportunity to use the train for local journeys ceased in February 1959, when the line was closed under a railway modernisation scheme and Beach station was turned into a coach park. For a while, mainline routes could still be accessed from Yarmouth's two remaining stations, Vauxhall and South Town, but this inevitably involved many changes from one train to another. Ultimately only Vauxhall survived, from where travellers were transported to connect with mainline routes at Thorpe station, in Norwich.

THE NECESSITIES OF LIFE

Most of Rollesby's employed population worked on the land or in trades associated with agriculture. A small minority commuted for their employment, mainly to work in Great Yarmouth. The rest were engaged in occupations that provided for the needs of a village community. Indeed, the lack of mobility in a predominantly carless society meant that all the necessary goods and services had to be provided for locally, or at least within a short cycle distance of our homes. My mother travelled regularly by bus to Great Yarmouth and made full use of its department stores, shops and market stalls. However, the main purpose of her journeys was to visit her family, the shopping was a bonus, and in any case she was not able to carry large amounts of shopping on the bus. Had she wished, she could have obtained most of her daily needs in Rollesby or Martham.

Rollesby had four grocery shops: grandmother's Post Office and Stores, Hayton's on Martham Road, Smith's Central Stores between the school and Court Road, and Houseago's on Belle Vue Terrace near to the bridge. Fifty yards beyond the bridge into Little Ormesby was another shop known as Ellis' Grocery Store. All four of Rollesby's shops offered goods of a similar nature yet managed to make a living, each having their own regular customers. Naturally, Mother shopped at the post office but if Grandmother had run out of something she needed, it was normally obtainable from one of the other three shops. Together with many of Rollesby's teenagers, I regularly used Ellis' shop to buy cigarettes as they could be bought there in ones or twos as well as in packets of ten or twenty. It was also the shop furthest away from where I lived and I was clearly unknown to the elderly lady who served behind the counter, an advantage when buying cigarettes.

The facilities at Martham, a much larger village, were far superior to those in Rollesby and were also regularly used by my mother. As well as the usual grocery shops there was a Co-operative store, two butchers, a hardware store, a garage and a branch of Barclay's bank. Mother regularly used the Co-op, saving her "dividend" for a Christmas purchase. The shop itself was memorable for the overhead pulley system by which counter staff dispatched payments to a central cashier. Money and bills were placed inside a brass container slung underneath a wire leading to the cashier's desk, a firing mechanism then projected the container and its contents along the wire to the cashier. Receipts and change were returned in a similar manner.

During the week, groceries and other goods could be purchased from visiting vans. The daily milk round was just one of a number of doorstep deliveries. Our milk was supplied by Cotton's Dairy, a Yarmouth based firm, and delivered to our doorstep by a local roundsman, Mr Wymer, who lived close to Rollesby School. My abiding memory of Mr Wymer is of a thin wiry man dressed in an army greatcoat, a proudly worn souvenir of the war. Whether true or not, Mr Wymer gained the admiration of many local youngsters because he was, according to legend, the only member of the Rollesby Home Guard to have used his rifle in anger, engaging a low flying Messerschmitt fighter aircraft from the safety of his back door. In the 1940s, our milk was delivered in glass pint bottles with a large opening at the top sealed by a round cardboard disc. In the centre of this disc was a smaller indented circle. To remove the cardboard disc the central circle was pushed in and a finger inserted, thus lifting it off from the bottle. The used discs were often saved and sent to the local school where they were turned into colourful wall decorations. The pupils covered the discs by winding wool of different colours around the cardboard

131

and through the central hole, and then joined them together to make hanging designs. During the 1950s, our milk was delivered in narrower topped glass bottles sealed by a thin silver metallic cap. In winter, these became the targets for blue tits that tore holes in them in an attempt to reach the cream on the top of the milk.

Our bread was delivered twice weekly by a van from Matthes' Bakery, also based in Yarmouth. The roundsman, dressed suitably in a long white coat and white hat, delivered orders to the back door in a large woven wicker basket. As well as loaves of bread, the van also held numerous trays of rolls, buns and cakes for sale to their customers. At weekends, mother often succumbed to temptation and bought three vanilla slices, chocolate éclairs or cream horns for a Sunday teatime treat. On Tuesdays and Fridays a small blue van belonging to Jeary's, a Martham butcher, would park outside our house, selling meat. The driver announced the arrival of the van by ringing a large brass handbell and honed his knives on a long sharpening stone while he waited for his customers to arrive. Meat was served from the back of the van, cut or chopped from larger joints by various knives, choppers or saws, and weighed on a scale that hung from the van's roof. On Tuesdays mother bought chops, liver or sausages, and, on Friday, a joint for the weekend. Orders were prewrapped in greaseproof paper on which was written the name of the recipient and the price. Chickens, rabbits and long strings of sausages hung from hooks also attached to the van's roof. The white interior perhaps provided a suggestion of hygiene, although the blood dripping on to the van's floor, together with the accompanying clouds of flies and wasps in summer, was sufficient to deter my natural curiosity and I usually left the meat purchases to my mother.

Fresh fish was also sold from touring vans, although Mother preferred to buy her fish from Yarmouth market believing, as she frequently said, that it was caught and landed that very morning. In the early 1950s a soft drinks firm, Corona, started a doorstep delivery and for a time we regularly ordered five or six bottles weekly, not just lemonade but other interesting flavours such as dandelion and burdock, cherryade and ginger beer. For a while a visiting grocery van set up in opposition to Rollesby's four shops, but the venture was clearly unsuccessful and lasted only a short time. Mother did some of her food shopping in Yarmouth, essentially for those food items generally unavailable in Rollesby or Martham. She occasionally bought fruit and vegetables from the greengrocery stalls on Yarmouth's market or from the nearby shops of Savory & Pordage and McCarthy's, particularly imported items such as bananas, oranges, lemons and cherries, or fruit and vegetables not yet available from our garden or the Field.

Immediately after the war, clothing was rationed and in short supply; consequently many of my clothes were either handed down or bought in village jumble sales. On his Christmas visits, Uncle George often brought the suits that he no longer wore to work as a bank manager for my father to wear. It was lucky that they were both the same size, so none of the clothes needed

133

altering. New clothes were stored until the old ones were no longer wearable. When possible, old clothes were repaired. Tears in my trousers were frequently mended and my school jacket had leather patches sewn on to its elbows. Holes in the toes and heels of my woollen socks were regularly darned using a mushroom shaped device with wool closely matched for colour. Mother had an ancient Singer sewing machine and frequently made dresses and skirts from complicated looking patterns consisting of numerous sheets of tissue paper that she pinned to material that she had bought from the department stores in Yarmouth. She also knitted, mainly in the winter, and most of my pullovers and jumpers were home produced. Old worn out knitwear was frequently unravelled and the wool used again. If the wool was too tired to be used for clothing, she used it to make cushion covers. Occasionally we received charity clothes and I can remember a distribution of clothing given as a goodwill gesture from "friends" in America. Mother attended the distribution at the hut on the playing field and I was given a colourful green and white patterned jumper that for a long time was a personal favourite, until holes appeared in the elbows and the jumper was unravelled. Like most boys, I wore short trousers until the age of 14 — undoubtedly the smaller amount of material needed was cheaper, and legs and knees were easier to clean. Life became especially difficult for Mother when I passed "the scholarship" and gained entry to Yarmouth Grammar School. As a consequence of my success she had to provide me with a school uniform, a major expense at the time. However, with some help from my grandparents, I was equipped with a brand new outfit to begin my schooling in Yarmouth. Thereafter, all my out-of-school clothes were worn-out and tight fitting school uniforms. Some less fortunate pupils were forced to wear second hand uniforms to school.

Handing down the old school uniform

Because of the difficulty of buying clothes for their sons, parents of the boys of Yarmouth Grammar School have decided on a scheme of mutual help. Those with school uniforms, shoes, football boots and overcoats which are still in good condition but have become too small for their boys will meet at the school on Saturday, February 21st for a sale. The scheme was suggested at the annual party for the Parents Association at the school at which about 90 members were present.

Yarmouth Mercury, 14 February 1948

By the mid-1950s, rationing had ceased and money for new clothes was more readily available. Then Mother bought our clothes from shops in Yarmouth, particularly those around the market or along King Street and Regent Road — department stores such as Arnolds, Palmers, British Home Stores and the Great Yarmouth Co-op, or specialist stockists such as Burton's and Hepworth's on the market and Bradley's down Broad

Row. My first suit was bought for me as a fifteenth birthday present from Grandmother Miller. As it was a birthday present I was allowed to choose both the style and material. Since I had very little colour sense and was particularly naive regarding fashion, the result was a tailor-made suit unique to me and one that I was particularly proud of. My choice of material was a bright light powder blue woollen cloth checked with red; the jacket was double-breasted with large pointed collars and the trousers had 24-inch bottoms with turn ups and were designed to be held up by a pair of braces. The whole I believe cost £15 from Burton's Tailoring Limited, a considerable expense at the time. Worn with a pair of black shoes, a white shirt and blue woollen tie I considered myself to be the height of elegance at local dances and socials. In my late teens I became more fashion conscious.

Like many of my generation, I was greatly influenced by the teenage rock and roll culture emerging from America. In Norfolk we were made even more conscious of this new alternative fashion by the large presence of American Forces. In my late teens, a goodly proportion of my holiday earnings was spent on clothes, mainly denim or corduroy jeans, baseball jackets, sweaters and patterned shirts. In accordance with fashion my trouser bottoms became narrower, complemented by black slip-on shoes and, occasionally, luminous lime green or pink socks. Mother frequently disapproved of my choice of clothes and often took them back to the shop whence they came, exchanging them for a more acceptable purchase. She always preferred to see me dressed in cavalry twill trousers, brown suede shoes, green shirt and tie with a green and brown check sports jacket. It was just such an outfit that she bought for me as a going away present when I left home for college. At college, the outfit was quickly replaced by blue jeans and a sloppy jumper, for fear of looking "square".

At college I was particularly ashamed of my underwear. Up to that time I had always worn vests and floppy underpants. In summer these would be made of cotton but in winter the cotton underwear was exchanged for warm wool vests and pants. These were exceedingly uncomfortable and itchy next to the skin and wearing them was a torment. Before the advent of long trousers, my floppy pants would often hang below the bottom of the legs of my shorts causing great amusement particularly among the girls. At college my underwear was the subject of concern among my more fashionable companions in Hall, until I was eventually taken in hand and encouraged to replace them with modern Y-fronts and T-shirts. Grandfather persisted in wearing long johns well into the 1960s.

Shoes were normally bought from Yarmouth, best shoes from the Co-op or Freeman, Hardy & Willis. At primary school I wore black boots in the winter and sandals in the summer, rubber wellingtons if it was raining. When not in school I preferred to wear black plimsolls or American style baseball boots, the latter a cloth boot with a thick rubber rim around the edge of the soles, rubber toecaps and circular rubber patches on each ankle, both of which could be obtained cheaply

137

from stalls on the market. At Yarmouth Grammar School sensible black lace-up shoes were the norm while fashionable slip-on shoes were acceptable for sixth form boys. In the 1940s, boots and shoes were a big expense and mother took every precaution to preserve them against wear and tear. Shoes were regularly soled and heeled and steel plates were added to the underside of my boots to protect the toe and heel. These plates made an impressive clanking sound as I walked to school and sparks often flew from underneath my boots as they scraped against a suitable stone. All our footwear was regularly cleaned and polished although, to my shame, this task usually fell to Mother. Shoe repairs were mostly carried out by the village cobbler, Mr Alexander, who ran a successful boot and shoe business from a wooden shed in his back garden.

For most other goods and services we relied on shops in Martham or Yarmouth. Mother's favourite shops were Yarmouth's two big department stores, Arnold's and Palmer's, where almost anything could be purchased from safety pins to furniture. Except for a new set of armchairs for our living room, purchased from Palmer's furniture department in the mid-1950s, our furniture changed little. A few small pieces were given to us by my various grandparents when they moved or retired. We did, however, keep up with advances in electrical goods. My father was fascinated by mechanical and electrical appliances and gadgets, and would try to keep abreast of new developments even if he could barely afford them. With Mother, he spent many hours looking at the displays of electrical goods in Bowers & Barr and the Electricity Board showrooms, including new labour-saving devices for the kitchen and scullery. However, he always knew where he could get them cheaper. Our television sets were annually changed for newer up-to-date models. Mother and I frequently held our breath when his sublime confidence allowed him to remove the back cover from our television set and to fiddle around inside in an attempt to improve the sound or to sharpen the picture without, I assume, any knowledge of the electrics or mechanics of a television's interior. He treated television sets in the same way as he treated clocks and watches. He often bought old and usually deceased clocks and watches from local sales and spent many happy hours taking them apart and reassembling their insides in an attempt to set them working again, usually unsuccessfully.

Father was also a compulsive car buyer. Not being able to afford a new or even a nearly new car he changed his model on a regular basis, usually at a local garage in Repps, on the assumption that the longer he kept them the more likely they were to break down. On these occasions he arrived home with a smile on his face asking "Would you like to see our new motor?" In my years at home we were driven around in cars of various makes, ages and sizes: Austin (7s and 10s), Wolseley, Morris, Singer, Humber and Ford, to name but a few. Records, television sets and other electrical goods we bought from Carr & Carr on Regent Street or Wolsey & Wolsey on King Street, linen and bedding from Plattens on Broad Row, hardware, ironmongery, wallpaper and paints from Francis' in Martham or from Coopers or Leach's in Yarmouth. All our gardening requirements came from Hollis', near the market. We had no need for mail order catalogues, as all our needs were catered for by local shops, travelling vans or the weekly Acle sale.

In an age when fewer people owned cars, out-of-town supermarkets and shopping malls were not a viable proposition. Small village stores and urban corner shops, catering for the immediate needs of a local clientele, provided a reasonable living for their owners. Other items were mostly bought at shops located at a nearby town centre. In the 1940s and 1950s, the area surrounding Great Yarmouth's market place was a busy and prosperous shopping precinct.

CHAPTER
FIVE

School Days

GREAT CHANGES

Perhaps the most important social changes directly affecting my early life came as a result of the 1944 Education Act and the establishment of a National Health Service in 1948. "Rab" Butler's 1944 Education Act aimed to provide every child with a relevant secondary education according to their skills and needs, and the National Health Service gave free medical treatment to everybody at point of need. As a child I neither appreciated nor understood the enormity of these great changes — although it is clear that the Education Act, in particular, provided me with the opportunity to receive an education that had been unattainable for the majority of my parents' generation. Not that these goals were achieved immediately as, in the Yarmouth region, facilities in both areas were inadequate and an urgent building programme was needed.

To accommodate the growing numbers of "scholarship" children, in 1957 the Great Yarmouth Grammar School for boys was extended by the addition of a modern, seven-classroom teaching block while a new school was built in Gorleston to rehouse the High School for girls. Technical secondary education, initially based in the Edward Worledge School, was enhanced when the Duke of Edinburgh opened a purpose built Technical High School in Great Yarmouth in 1954. Secondary education for all eventually became a reality as many new secondary modern schools were established throughout the region, including rural schools at Caister, Acle and Martham. Neither of my parents nor most of my aunts and uncles had benefited from a secondary education, most leaving their elementary schools at the earliest opportunity to become apprentices in various trades or to work in Yarmouth's clothing factories. Like Mother, some had passed selection scholarships, but were unable to take up a secondary education owing to the lack of available places or the inability of their parents to afford the expense involved. In the 1920s George Miller, Father's eldest brother, took a scholarship place at Great Yarmouth Grammar School, a privilege that my grandparents could not afford to extend to their other children. Despite the award of a Norfolk Major Scholarship, because of a lack of funds George was unable to continue his studies at university and moved to London to begin a career with the Bank of India.

ROLLESBY COUNTY PRIMARY SCHOOL

My first experience of school was not a particularly happy one. One Monday morning in September 1945, at just five years old, small for my age and unused to the company of other children, I was taken by my mother from our house on Martham Road to the gates of Rollesby Elementary School where we joined six or more other children and their parents waiting to be introduced to the infant teacher, Miss Deacon. To my embarrassment, mother often recalled that, on meeting Miss Deacon, my confidence deserted me and I informed her that, although I was pleased to see her, I would rather start school on another day. Certainly the constraints of school appeared less attractive to me than those enjoyable days I had spent with my grandparents at the post office and the Field. What happened next has become a well-told family legend, although, like most legends, it is undoubtedly a massive distortion of the truth. Apparently, after reason had failed to change my mind, I was dragged screaming and kicking through the school entrance by my mother and Miss Deacon, assisted by the head teacher, Miss King, and anyone else willing to help. When eventually I was forced unwillingly into the infant classroom, the legend states that I was tied to the fire surround while mother made a hasty escape and where I remained until my hysterics subsided. On reflection, I cannot believe that Miss Deacon would have ever considered tying me to the fender. Not that mother had any need to worry as Miss

143

Deacon was the kindest of teachers and, in no time at all, not only introduced me to the joys of learning but also became the fourth most important woman in my life after Mother and my two grandmothers. Indeed, to cause me further personal embarrassment, mother would regularly tell how I frequently informed Miss Deacon that I intended to marry her when I grew up.

Rollesby School, a solid rectangular red-brick building with a slate roof, was opened in 1923 to replace an older and smaller thatched school building located behind the Horse & Groom public house. This building was apparently destroyed by fire in the 1920s. The new school occupied a central village location on the Main Road next to King George's playing field. The main entrance to the school was through a double metal barred gate set into a low brick wall topped with green painted iron railings. Behind the wall and to both sides of the gate was a small plantation of trees and bushes, a popular place for games of chase and hide-and-seek. A high privet hedge formed the boundary along the other three sides of the school grounds. A wooden gate in the left-side hedge led on to the playing field and a gate in the rear hedge of the school led to a garden where the older boys learned how to grow fruit and seasonal vegetables. Periodically groups of younger children were taken into the garden for lessons on the principles of horticulture or to help with weeding and other manual tasks. As most of us could not tell the difference between a weed and an emerging flower or vegetable, these sessions caused more harm than good.

144

In front of the school building was the main playground, a rectangular asphalted area with a netball pitch marked on to its surface, complete with a netball post at each end. At break times, the playground was the scene of many varied and robust children's games that often resulted in grazes and cuts from falls on to the rough surface. We played many different forms of "catch", a chasing game. A girl or boy was declared to be "it" when their task was to chase and catch hold of another child in the playground who then became "it". Sometimes a touch was sufficient for the pursuer to catch their target; other times they had to hit them with a ball. Children shrieked and yelled as they ran from their pursuer, and in a crowded playground collisions were frequent and inevitable. The most terrifying game of this genre was chain catch. When a child was caught they had to hold hands with their pursuer and together, linked in this way, they continued the chase. Each time a child was caught they too linked on to this ever growing chain. Often when a long chain turned in pursuit of a victim, the children on the outer end of the revolving chain were often thrown off their feet by the speed of the turn. We also played a game called "statues". A selected individual would stand facing the school wall while the rest of us would line up about 20 yards away. The aim of the game was for each child to achieve safety by touching the wall without being seen to move by the individual who was "it". On the word "go" we began to creep forward towards the wall, stopping motionless when the "it" person turned round. If anyone was seen to be moving or failed to remain motionless, they were sent back to the start line. This process was repeated many times until everyone reached the safety of the school wall. The last person to reach safety suffered some form of forfeit, often being forced to kiss an unsuspecting victim, and then became "it" for the next game. Ball games were common; the girls played netball, practising their shooting around the two netball posts, and the boys played football with a tennis ball. Piggy-in-the-middle was one of my favourite games. Three or more children formed a line and the two at either end would throw a ball to one another which the children in the middle tried to intercept. If a child was successful in this quest, he or she changed places with the thrower on the end.

Periodically different games became the craze of the moment and I can remember when spinning tops became popular and the whole playground seemed to be filled with children whipping away at small revolving objects. Another time, hoops were fashionable and gangs of children ran around the playground propelling their hoops with a small stick. Wooden rigid hoops were the best and I quickly discovered that a bicycle tyre was not an appropriate substitute. Skipping was popular with the girls, most having their own personal skipping rope. Occasionally some of the girls joined their ropes together to make one long one. A girl at either end then turned this rope for as many children as possible to skip inside its circle, often accompanied by chants such as "salt, mustard, vinegar and pepper", helping to maintain the necessary rhythm of their jumps. Often, five or six children, girls and boys, skipped inside the rope, bobbing up and down in unison, with the boys' hobnailed boots crashing rhythmically on the tarmac. Occasionally a child left the skip only to be replaced immediately by a new skipper jumping inside the revolving rope. Anyone causing the skip to fail by tripping on the rope was met with howls of protest and banned from taking any further part in the proceedings. At other times the whole playground was covered in chalk-drawn hopscotch squares.

Many of the boys collected cigarette cards despite the fact that most brands had ceased to include cards in their packets by the 1940s. Aunt Muriel (not a proper aunt but a distant relative who lived near the Courthouse) was a heavy smoker of Turf cigarettes which still included cigarette cards as part of their packaging and these she saved for my collection. I regularly visited and even pestered her in my quest to collect one particular series that depicted famous British sportsmen and contained illustrations of most of my favourite sporting heroes: Stanley Matthews, Tom Finney, Len Hutton, Denis Compton, Godfrey Evans, Bruce Woodcock and Gordon Richards to name but a few. Periodically boys risked their spare cards in a playground game of chance in which, in turn, they flicked their cards at a target area drawn on the ground. If a card landed on another card then the latter was considered to be captured and taken as a prize by the thrower. Sometimes more than one card was covered, and then they were all taken as a prize. A game continued until all the cards were captured or break time finished. Cards thought to be special were never risked in such a game. A similar game was played with marbles when the target was a small chalk circle or a depression in the ground. Throwers could win marbles from their opponents by knocking them into the circle or the depression with their own marble.

To the rear of the school were the bicycle sheds and the toilets. Many of the older children cycled to school, storing their cycles in the racks inside the sheds. For a time I also rode my bicycle to school but was banned by my mother after she heard that I had nearly collided with a car while having a race with some other children on my way home. During the race, my front wheel was knocked by another cyclist which caused me to lose control of my bicycle and to career across the road at the precise time that the one and only car for miles was about to overtake. As I lay in the hedge I was subjected to such a severe telling off by the driver of the car that I unfortunately wet myself, much to the amusement of the other children who had gathered to watch. As a consequence, I was forbidden to ride my cycle on the main road.

Along the rear boundary hedge was the brick-built toilet block. The boys' toilet was a square, walled enclosure with a gulley running around the bottom, in which the boys peed against the wall, their liquid waste running down the wall, along the gulley and disappearing into a small drain in one corner. The boys regularly had competitions to see how high they could pee up the wall, each attempt being carefully measured with a ruler. Next to the boys' toilet was a block of six lockable cubicles which were used by the girls and, occasionally, any boy who desired something more than just a pee. These were regularly patrolled by the older girls to prevent curious boys attempting to peer inside through any gaps in the doors. Not that they would have seen much as these cubicles had no electric lights and their interiors were in almost complete darkness once the doors were closed. Inside each cubicle was a seat with an oval hole which, when not in use, was covered by a wooden lid. Under the hole was a sloping wall descending down into a black empty space below the toilet, and down which liquid and solid deposits would run, where to we were not at all sure as we could not see to the bottom of the slope. The smell was unpleasant and I hated these toilets so much that I resisted even the most urgent desires until I could get home. At least I knew where I was with a bucket beneath me.

THE CLASSROOMS

Inside, the school building was divided into three classrooms leading off from an L-shaped corridor. Entering through the main door, Miss Deacon's infant classroom was on the right with the infant cloakroom to the left. Ahead, where the corridor turned to the left, were two doors; the one on the right opened into Miss King's senior classroom and the other into Mrs Bates' junior classroom. These two rooms were separated by a wooden partition that, when required, could be folded back to create one big room suitable for accommodating large-scale social and educational activities, and which compensated in part for our lack of a school hall. A small door in the partition connected these two classrooms and every morning and afternoon, at the start and finish of the school day, this was thrown open with great gusto by Miss King who would then straddle the doorstep, one foot in the juniors and one in the seniors, to conduct prayers and make special announcements. Further down the corridor and to the left were the staff room and a second cloakroom, before the corridor ended at another door that opened to the outside opposite the gate to the playing field. A kitchen suite was eventually added to the side of the school blocking this entrance. Without the convenience of a school hall, lunches were eaten in the classrooms on collapsible tables which were stored in the corridor.

About sixty to seventy pupils between the ages of five and fifteen attended Rollesby School, divided among the three classes. Despite the Education Act, most of the village children spent all their schooldays at Rollesby until the early 1950s, when pupils aged fourteen and above were then transferred to a secondary modern school in Caister. There was no regular school uniform although most of the boys wore shirts, ties and jackets, short trousers and caps, long trousers for the senior boys, and the girls mostly wore gymslips.

All three classrooms were of a similar design — square with a large window along one side and heated by a central open fireplace. In the winter, particularly in the early mornings, the rooms were freezing and we were often allowed to keep on our overcoats, scarves and gloves as protection against the cold. Pupils sat in desks designed to accommodate two or more children, usually with well-engraved and ink-stained lids, that were neatly arranged in rows and columns and in which we kept our texts and exercise books. Along the top of each desk was a groove in which we placed our pens and pencils, and to the right-hand side of this groove was a circular hole which contained a porcelain inkwell. Every morning the designated ink-monitor filled all the inkwells with ink from a large enamelled jug. In front of and facing the pupils' desks were the teacher's desk and a blackboard and easel.

The teaching style was formal with an emphasis on the three Rs: reading, writing and arithmetic. Every morning commenced with a spelling or tables test before we began working from our textbooks. We learned many facts by frequently repeating them aloud as a class: spellings, multiplication tables and lists of weights and measures. We were competently familiar with everyday factual knowledge and knew by heart that 12 inches make a foot, 3 feet make a yard, 22 yards make a chain, 10 chains make a furlong, 8 furlongs make a mile, and other such relevant information. Good clear handwriting was encouraged, and we practised with chalk on a slate or with a pencil into a ruled exercise book in the infant class, and with a pen and nib in the junior and senior classes. At the end of the day our fingers were stained blue by the ink from our pens. Teaching aids were few, although Miss Deacon used seashells contained in old metal cocoa tins to help with our counting and arithmetic sums. Then, as now, money for equipment was short and I can remember taking part in a school concert for parents and friends, put on for the purpose of raising money to buy a wireless set for each classroom. I can remember few details of the concert except for the fact that I was a rook and my costume consisted of a yellow beak made from cardboard that was sewn to the peak of my school cap.

Pantomime Visit

The children of Rollesby School were the guests of the Parish Entertainments Committee at the pantomime "Mother Goose" at the Wellington Pier, Yarmouth. At a subsequent whist drive in the school to raise money for the treat, over £17 was realised.

Ambition realised

The children of Rollesby School, under their headmistress Miss A. T. King and the assistant mistresses Mrs M. Bates and Miss W. Deacon, presented a very good concert and reached their ambition of providing a wireless and sewing machine for the school.

"Village News: Rollesby",
Yarmouth Mercury, 17 January 1948

The curriculum for English and mathematics was organised into seven or eight blocks of work called "standards", each intended as the work for one year and based on a series of workbooks which we worked through at our own pace. When the work for one standard was successfully completed we then proceeded to the next. A few children were able to complete a standard in less than a year and, as a consequence, some children as young as 9 years old were being taught alongside the older children in the senior classroom.

During the morning, each class in turn took a session of physical exercise in the playground, commonly referred to as "drill". After a warm-up run around the playground, the class lined up in four columns facing the teacher who then took us through a series of exercises on the spot. "Knees bend, arms stretch, arms to the front, arms to the side. Jumping on the spot — go." For fifteen minutes, no matter what the weather, we performed our exercises with military precision before lining up in order of height and returning to our tasks in the classroom. In the afternoon we studied various topics of interest, many to do with our local neighbourhood, learned singing and folk dancing, played games on the playing field, did painting and drawing, read books and wrote stories and poems.

The Christmas period was always a special time at Rollesby School. Towards the end of the autumn term all our work was focused on the Nativity and Christmas celebrations. We made paper chains from coloured strips of paper, gluing each link with thick white paste applied with a paint brush. The windows were covered in cotton wool snow and cardboard boxes were decorated to become snowmen. In the afternoons, we painted Christmas cards for our parents and every year made a calendar as a present. A square of cardboard was covered with wallpaper and on to this we stuck a drawing, usually of a robin in the snow. The teachers then attached a small booklet showing the days and months for the coming year. On the last day before the holiday we always had a party where we played games, sang carols and enjoyed a Christmas tea. My first

Christmas party at Rollesby School was special as it celebrated not only the Nativity but also the end of wartime hostilities. The party, which was well attended, was held in the junior and senior classrooms with the partition opened. In the seniors' end we had a sit down tea followed by various entertainments that we watched while sitting on the floor. In the junior end was a large decorated Christmas tree from which hung presents for all the children, to be distributed by a jovial Father Christmas. I was given a set of multicoloured building bricks in a wheeled container.

V-J Christmas Party

The village V-J thanksgiving celebration took the form of a Christmas party at the school on Saturday arranged by the Rollesby Peace Celebrations Committee under the chairmanship of Capt. D. G. Tacon. Nearly 100 children were provided with tea; the catering arrangements being in the hands of Mrs L. E. Smith. A large Christmas tree with coloured lights was laden with presents and every child in the village from the age of four to fifteen years received two gifts from Father Christmas (Mr H. Marsden-Smith). Community singing was led by the Rector (Rev. G. R. Grundy) and prizes were awarded for the best home made paper hats. Other entertainment was supplied

---

by a conjuror and illusionist, a troupe of girl
singers and dancers and a Punch and Judy
show. During the evening a presentation was
made to the secretary and school mistress,
Miss A. T. King.
"Village News: Rollesby",
Yarmouth Mercury, 5 January 1946

THE ELEVEN-PLUS EXAMINATION

The climax of my primary education was an
examination known as the Common Entrance Examination or, simply, the eleven-plus. One day late in the
spring term of 1951, along with all the other ten- and
eleven-year-old pupils attending Rollesby School, I was
invited to sit this examination while the rest of the
school enjoyed a day's holiday. We were all left in no
doubt by our parents and teachers of the importance
attached to these examinations, as for weeks we had
practised on pages of sums, spellings and missing words,
number or shape puzzles. Our general knowledge had
been honed by endless quiz sheets. "What is the name
of this?", "What is the meaning of that?", "Who won
the battle of so-and-so?", "Who invented this?", "Who
discovered that?", until our brains could take no more.
Occasionally we would invent answers to liven up
proceedings. I remember Miss King asking me, "Colin,
if an Indian man is called a brave and his wife is a

squaw, what is their baby called?" "A squawker, miss", was my imaginative reply, much to the delight of my fellow students and a resigned sigh from Miss King who was, no doubt, as tired of this endless practice as we were. Unfortunately this reply branded me with the nickname "Squawker" for the rest of my stay at Rollesby School and for a long time thereafter.

My parents and grandparents attempted to instil in me the importance of what I was about to do by a combination of bribery and veiled threats. "If you work hard and pass we will buy you a new football", "If you fail the test you will end up being a dustman, and you wouldn't like that would you?", "Your Uncle George did it so you should be able to do it as well". By the time of the examination, I was in a state of nervous tension not particularly conducive to performing at my best. The day of the examination I remember as being sunny and warm, a day when a holiday would have been preferable to answering questions about the children of Native Americans. As I joined the small group of examinees waiting in the playground, the strain told and I was stricken by a bout of diarrhoea that sent me scuttling to those outside toilets that I hated so much. Not that I was alone; a number of my co-examinees were similarly afflicted. Eventually, we were summoned to the senior classroom by Miss King and seated in desks well apart from each other. Jean, Rita and I, and some others whom I have forgotten, waited nervously as Miss King distributed question papers and answer books, wound up the classroom clock and announced that we could start the examination. The examination papers were not a problem as my days in Grandmother Miller's shop had done wonders for my arithmetic — money and measure sums did not worry me one bit. I loved doing puzzles so I had little difficulty with the "sequence", "what comes next" and "find the connection" problems in the IQ test. Spelling was my only weakness but somehow I managed as, a few weeks later, a letter arrived informing my parents that I had passed the first part of the selection procedure and that I was required to attend for an interview at the Art School on Trafalgar Road in Great Yarmouth.

The interview I remember clearly. At the Art School, Mother and I were directed to sit on some seats that were lined up against the wall of a long corridor where, together with a number of other children and their parents, we waited to be called into the interview room. Eventually, it was our turn and we were ushered into a large square room with a round table in the middle where Mother was asked to sit on a seat by the door while I was led to a chair at the table. Around the table were three men and a woman who, after enquiring who I was and where I came from, began asking me questions about various topics and some items that had been placed on the table. I remember clearly being shown a photograph of an urban street scene with lots of cyclists and a few cars, and being asked what I could see in it. "Why are the cyclists wearing white shirts?", "What is the purpose of the different overhead wires?", "Where in the world do you think the photograph was taken?" I went to town on that photograph and answered all of their questions in detail, finally concluding that the photograph had been taken in Singapore or Hong Kong. My answers must have been acceptable as a few weeks later my parents received another letter stating that I had passed the examination and had been accepted for a grammar school education. As a rural candidate I could choose to attend at Paston Grammar School in North Walsham or the Great Yarmouth Grammar School for boys. According to Mother, I was also offered a scholarship to Gresham's, a public boarding school in Norfolk, which would have been a very attractive proposition had I been born into the right social class, but she correctly deduced that Great Yarmouth Grammar School would be less intimidating for a working-class country boy.

Examination Successes

In the Norfolk Secondary Schools' Examination, Colin Miller has been accepted for Yarmouth Grammar School and Rita Lucas for Wymondham College. In a handwriting test organised by "The Children's Newspaper" Josephine Hewitt has been awarded a geographical globe.

"Village News: Rollesby",
Yarmouth Mercury, 29 June 1951

My success in the eleven-plus was a mixed blessing in that it caused many changes in my life, not all for the good. Instead of walking to the village school with the children of our neighbours, I joined a small band of pupils who travelled on the number 5 bus from the surrounding villages to various schools in Great Yarmouth. The downside was that I lost regular contact with my many friends still at Rollesby School and, as a consequence, I became more and more isolated from them. The demands of daily travel to and from Great Yarmouth and progressively intrusive amounts of homework gave me little time during the week for mixing with other village children and contact became limited mainly to weekends and holidays. While most of my village friends remained constant, a few became antagonistic, implying that I had changed in becoming "a grammar school boy".

The grammar school, on the other hand, provided me with the opportunity to meet and make new friends from outside the village and from many different social backgrounds. Most of my new school companions were from middle-class homes and some displayed a great indifference towards working-class boys like me, particularly working-class boys from the countryside. No matter how hard I tried, I always felt that many of the teachers and my fellow students assumed that a working-class background limited my potential for achievement. When discussing my future career in the sixth form, I was positively discouraged from applying for a university place despite being in the top class throughout my grammar school career. Indeed in many ways I was disadvantaged by my home environment, for my culture was that of a working-class family, albeit a family well aware of the benefits to be derived from a good education. At the age of eleven, my reading was limited to a few children's classics and factual material mostly relating to geography and nature study; my knowledge of Shakespeare, the theatre and English literature in general was virtually zero. I enjoyed popular music but classical music was a mystery, and on the radio I listened mainly to Radio Luxembourg and the BBC Light programme, occasionally the Home Service but hardly ever to the Third programme. Without the basic knowledge possessed by many of my middle class contemporaries, I found myself struggling in many subject areas. It is not surprising that my greatest achievements were in science and mathematics rather than the arts, subjects where my practical rural upbringing was of the greatest value.

To say that I was bullied at grammar school would be a gross exaggeration, although being small and almost the youngest in my year I became a target for those who enjoyed dominating others. However, I quickly devised many strategies for avoiding confrontations: keeping to myself, restricting personal contacts to those boys from a background similar to my own, never expressing an opinion or reacting inappropriately to a tease or a jibe, and learning to endure a punch without crying. Although I enjoyed various aspects of grammar school life, I found it difficult initially to mix and make friends with many of my classmates, and they too were not forthcoming with their friendship. In the second year at grammar school, my apparent isolation gave rise to feelings of panic and anxiety, and on many mornings I would lock myself in our outside toilet refusing to come out until the school bus had left for Great Yarmouth. I am sure that the school secretary considered me to be a very sickly child, based on the number of notes she received from my mother apologising for my absence owing to a stomach upset. My salvation came in the form of sport. Encouraged by my parents and Uncle Cecil, I had developed a passion for both football and cricket and had practised my skills for hours against the toilet door and at the playing field. As an afterthought, and only to make up the numbers, at the end of my second year at grammar school I was selected to play in an under-14 cricket match between South House and North House, two highly competitive and rival grammar school houses whose members perceived this competition to be a matter of honour and of great importance. In true "Roy of the Rovers" style my luck was in and I was able to retrieve a lost game on behalf of South House by an exhibition of slogging in which I scored an unbeaten 43 and won the game by hitting a six over square leg. From that moment on, my skills and enthusiasm for football and cricket gave me a modicum of respect not only from my contemporaries at grammar school but also from my former classmates in Rollesby.

Although my move to the grammar school had divorced me from my village friends, it did enable me to mix with and feel at home in the company of adults and children from all social classes. My three closest friends came from very different social backgrounds yet I was comfortable in their company and their parents welcomed me into their homes. Tony, a farm worker's son, lived on the Back Road in Rollesby; he was my best friend from the age of five and remained a friend after I began my schooling in Yarmouth. Tim, whose parents owned a shop in Hemsby, I met at grammar school and, coming from similar rural backgrounds, we formed a strong friendship that lasted until university and beyond. My third friend, Richard, was a gentleman farmer's son and from a social class within the village that, in the 1940s and 1950s, would not normally encourage their children to develop friendships with the sons of bricklayers. Richard's father was himself the son of a millionaire clergyman and had been educated at Harrow and Cambridge University. My success in attaining the status of a grammar school boy enabled me to transcend such social barriers, and not only did Richard and I become close childhood friends but his parents also took an active interest in my education and insisted on being the first to buy books for my university course.

GREAT YARMOUTH GRAMMAR SCHOOL

In 1910, Yarmouth Grammar School, founded in the sixteenth century, was moved into purpose-built premises at its current location on the seaside end of Salisbury Road. Further extensions, erected in 1936 to cater for a growing number of pupils, completed the school buildings that were so familiar to me during the eight years of my secondary education from 1951 to 1959. The school, with a large grass playing field behind, abutted closely on to Salisbury Road between the railway line and the seafront. At the railway end the junior entrance, used by the lower school, opened out into the junior courtyard which was bounded on the right by the gymnasium with a firing range behind and on the left by the main school buildings. On the far side of the courtyard opposite the entrance was a long brick air-raid shelter, used at that time as a storeroom, a legacy of wartime when all the properties on Great Yarmouth's seafront were evacuated and prepared by the military to repel a possible invasion, and when the masters and boys of the Grammar School were temporarily moved to a safer location at Retford in Nottinghamshire. At the seaside end, the senior entrance opened into the senior courtyard, which was bounded on the left by the caretaker's house, the sixth form base and the woodwork shop, and to the right and in front by the main school buildings. The door into the school from the senior courtyard was underneath an impressive bell tower. A gap between these premises led to a long, cream-painted, single-storeyed building which housed the school kitchens and dining room. Behind these, the grass playing field boasted a well-tended cricket square and, at the far end well away from the school, a full size football pitch.

The entrances from both courtyards opened on to a long corridor that led past the junior and senior cloakrooms into a large central hall. To one side of this hall was a stage with an ornamental wooden lectern in the centre and on another adjacent side a large organ flanked either side by two doors, one leading to the staff room and the other to the headmaster's study. In the corner opposite the staff room was the school secretary's office. The teaching rooms were located in two two-storey blocks accessed from and either side of the main hall. The first, along the junior end of the building, contained teaching rooms downstairs for history, mathematics and biology; and upstairs for art, French, Latin and music. The second block, abutting on the senior courtyard, contained the library and rooms for mathematics and geography downstairs, and English and physics upstairs. Both wings were connected by a chemistry laboratory that was located above part of the main hall. The rooms were primarily allocated by subject and, consequently, the periods between teaching sessions saw much chaos as classes moved noisily from one room to another.

The school provided an education for approximately 300 pupils, small in comparison with many modern comprehensive schools but awesomely large and intimidating to an eleven year old used only to a small rural village school. Before the Second World War, Great Yarmouth Grammar was a fee-paying establishment with some "Free Scholars", their fees being paid by a governor's charity, or scholarships financed by either the Great Yarmouth or Norfolk Education Committees. As a consequence of the 1944 Education Act, all scholars were essentially "Free" by 1951 and the school provided the grammar element of secondary education for selected boys from Great Yarmouth and its surrounding villages. Occasionally girls from the High School would attend lessons in subjects for which there was no provision at their school. In September 1956, three such girls joined my sixth form class to study A level physics, an experience that most of us found extremely distracting as, even though they were not exceptionally attractive, we spent more time staring at their blouses than we spent listening to the teacher.

Grammar school boys were distinguished from other secondary pupils by their school uniform. This consisted of a navy blue blazer with the Great Yarmouth coat of arms in yellow and black on the breast pocket, grey flannel trousers (short trousers for the lower school and long trousers for fourteen year olds and over), grey shirts, red and black diagonally striped ties, grey socks, black shoes and a navy school cap with a coat of arms on the front. Sixth formers were allowed the luxury of white cotton shirts and were not required to wear caps. The staff too had a style of uniform. Graduates always wore gowns and the headmaster, a tall thin man with round horn-rimmed spectacles perched on the end of his prominent nose, wore a floor length gown and mortar board. At special events and Prize Day they would also wear their colourful university capes. The sports and art masters did not wear gowns as they were not graduates and were undoubtedly paid at a lower rate, which seemed to me to be most unfair as, to my mind, they were the best teachers. Most of the staff had taught at the school before the war when the scholars were mainly fee-paying students, and many made little attempt to hide their disappointment with the new free scholarship pupils, particularly those from a working-class background, who did not regard "the old school" as being central to their childhood days, pursuing interests outside those promoted by the school's curriculum and extramural activities. Despite one aberration, when Henry Neave was allowed to play the "Dam Buster's March" for a school assembly, there was certainly no place for Bill Haley, rock 'n' roll or any form of popular music or teenage culture at Great Yarmouth Grammar School. I can also remember the abject bewilderment on the senior games master's face when, having been presented with a choice, I elected to play cricket for my village in preference to playing for the school. Luckily, he took up a new position at another establishment very soon after, otherwise I expect that my opportunities in sport would have been considerably restricted. As it was, I was never picked again for the school's cricket team. His replacement, Mr Woodrow, was a football coach of national standing who initiated training sessions for fitness and football skills that I attended with enthusiasm, as well as expanding our sports opportunities to include tennis and basketball. Fortunately, no similar conflict arose with regard to football and I was able to play for both the school and village teams, which sometimes involved playing two games in one day, on Saturday morning for the school and in the afternoon for the village.

To my mind, although effective in achieving its goals, the teaching was uninspiring as learning was based mainly on following instructions, copying copious notes from the blackboard and undertaking exercises and tests to determine how much information we had remembered. One mathematics teacher promoted learning in his class by a method he called the Round Britain Quiz. Each boy in turn was asked to complete a mathematics task or calculation and, if unsuccessful, he was compelled to stand on his chair. Boys standing on their chairs would subsequently be given the opportunity to redeem themselves by correcting the mistakes of others and, if successful in this, allowed to sit down again. Those still standing on their chairs at the end of the lesson would be given extra mathematics homework. Despite this, we were an academic elite and I enjoyed the opportunities for learning provided by a grammar school education although I did not exhibit exceptional talent in any particular field, merely an acceptable competence over the whole curriculum. My favourite lessons were determined not by the subject matter but by my preference for the teacher at the front of the class. My enjoyment of history and mathematics was more to do with the fact that the masters were well-known local cricketers than any particular aptitude for the subjects.

The teaching I received during my time in the sixth form, however, was a different matter. The classes were small, particularly in mathematics and science subjects, allowing the teaching to be matched more accurately to the needs and skills of the learner. The choice of subjects for our A level courses was limited and as I wanted to study mathematics but avoid chemistry, I had no choice but to take mathematics, further mathematics and physics. I would have preferred art to physics but, unfortunately, that subject was not considered academically appropriate for a science orientated student and, in some masters' minds, only suitable as a potentially easier subject for less capable boys. Nevertheless, despite not being able to take it as an A level subject, I did manage to win the sixth form art prize. My aversion to chemistry was long standing and based on a pathological fear of being poisoned by noxious substances or gases, reinforced when one boy in my class discovered the potential laxative property of phenolphthalein and attempted to doctor the lunches of most of his classmates.

Relationships between staff and pupils were extremely formal. We were expected to stand up every time a member of staff entered a classroom and to call him "Sir". We were always called by our surnames; first names were never used, not even in the sixth form. One of our first duties was to learn by heart the verses of the school song which we were expected to sing at assembly and on any formal or public occasion. Discipline was strict and a prefectorial system was employed to support the teaching staff in implementing the school's rules and codes of behaviour. First year sixth formers were normally designated as House prefects, identified by a lapel badge in the colours of their House, and in this role administered the rules and organised activities associated with their respective Houses. Second and third year sixth formers were usually designated as school prefects and were responsible for general discipline and behaviour during school hours outside the classroom. These prefects were identified by a gold lapel badge. Enforcement was achieved through the threat of official and, occasionally, unofficial punishments. Usually a clout or a kick up the backside was sufficient to control boisterous and unruly pupils, and to eliminate unacceptable behaviour. In the classroom, many teachers had their own informal control techniques that included cuffing culprits around the ear; throwing chalk, the board rubber, and, occasionally, bunches of keys at disruptive pupils; detentions; and issuing lines or additional worksheets. Some had even more effective methods: the music teacher used a tuning fork to great effect and the biology teacher was adept at jabbing his thumbs into the kidneys of badly behaved boys.

When these methods failed, a formal discipline procedure was implemented. Each academic year, every pupil was issued with a personal yearbook that included a daily diary in which, at the end of the school day, we entered the details of the coming evening's homework. At the front of this book were spaces for a termly report on each subject studied, with our performance measured on a scale from 2 to 7: with 2 denoting an unacceptable performance and 7 excellence. At the back of the book were spaces for reporting incidents of bad behaviour, commonly referred to as "signatures". Staff or prefects reporting a boy for bad behaviour would write their signatures in the back of his yearbook while, at the same time, giving a detailed account of the misdemeanour in a punishment book held in the staff common room. Three signatures in a week for bad behaviour resulted in the loss of a merit half-day holiday awarded for each term by the mayor on behalf of the Great Yarmouth Education Committee during our annual Prize Day ceremony at the Town Hall. Persistent and frequent entries would result in three strokes of the cane administered effectively by the headmaster in his study. Signatures were also given for bad or unacceptable work and were treated more seriously than those given for bad behaviour. Three work signatures in a term could result in the cane.

For most of the time these various discipline procedures were very effective, particularly as they were fully supported by most of our parents. Had I erred at school and my parents found out, I would certainly have received further punishment at home. That this never happened was more down to deviousness than perfect behaviour, because if I did err I was always most careful that my parents never found out. My friend Tim, on the other hand, derived great satisfaction, and our admiration, from daring to do things that the rest of us would never risk. In the middle of an extremely boring fifth form mathematics lesson, I watched in horror as Tim raised the lid of his desk, leaned forward in his seat and closed the lid again with his head and upper body inside the desk. The unmistakable sound of a match being struck was quickly followed by clouds of blue cigarette smoke billowing from under the half-open lid. An eerie silence followed as one by one we became mesmerised by the spectacle of Tim smoking inside the desk while the mathematics teacher scribbled away on the board. After what seemed an age, the inevitable happened and Tim was led away by the ear to an inevitable assignation with the headmaster and his cane.

A year later, both Tim and I were sixth formers and prefects, and, as such, were assumed to have become sensible and responsible people. As new prefects, we were given responsibility for maintaining discipline at break times, for distributing the morning milk allowance, supervising dinner parades and table duties. At dinner time, one prefect sat at the head of every dining table, serving the meals for all the boys on that table and, supposedly by example, developing appropriate table manners. In the true spirit of prefects we were naturally careful to cater properly for ourselves before considering the needs of the other boys. At break times numerous crates of milk were spirited into the sixth form base where it was not unusual for the prefects to consume the contents of three or four of the third-of-a-pint bottles of milk. Not that we were denying the other pupils their right to a milk allocation as, particularly among the junior boys, many professed a dislike for the liquid and were happy that they were not forced to drink it. At dinner time we naturally served ourselves first, ensuring that our portions were appropriately large while the portions for the smaller boys were reduced accordingly to compensate. Contrary to popular opinion, most of us enjoyed school meals and I had no difficulty in consuming large helpings of mashed potato saturated in thick brown gravy, mounds of carrots, peas, chopped cabbage and orange-pink swede, with stews and meat pies containing cubes of meat, occasional lumps of inedible gristle and unidentifiable root vegetables. For pudding we enjoyed bowlfuls of rice, semolina and tapioca each enriched by a large central dollop of strawberry jam, prunes and custard, and large cubes of sponge covered in chocolate sauce that appeared to be more purple in colour than brown. At no time before or since have I been as healthy and well fed as during my time in the senior school at Great Yarmouth Grammar.

Although not the greatest linguist, I did enjoy French of which I learned most of my vocabulary through reading *Tintin* comic books. The French teacher was a round-faced man with a moustache and a fly-away hairstyle, famous for his facial contortions when attempting to pronounce the sounds of the French vowels, and who we affectionately called "Pip". Great Yarmouth's association and eventual twinning with the northern French town of Rambouillet gave rise to many opportunities for contacts with France and for practising our skills with French. In my third year, Pip organised a pen pal in France for every boy in my class and we were expected to correspond with them, in French, on a monthly basis. It soon became clear to me that my pen pal was a year or two older than myself, not at all proficient in his command of the English language and as unenthusiastic for this arrangement as myself. In his final correspondence, his letter consisted solely of one English word "Enjoy" and four French postcards depicting women in various states of undress. This correspondence became infamous among my classmates and the postcards were studied intently. That this was our final communication was down solely to my mother who, on discovering the well-thumbed cards in my bedroom and having elicited their

173

provenance, forbade me ever to correspond again with a Frenchman.

Another benefit from the imminent twinning was occasional staff exchanges with teachers from France. It was with great excitement that we greeted the news of the arrival of a mistress who, for the summer term, would be available to help us with our French. We were even more excited when, on meeting said mistress, she turned out to be an exceptionally good looking Frenchwoman in her early twenties. Lessons in oral French became a delight especially when, on fine summer days, she would take class outside, sitting on the grass, where we would laze in the sun, chew daisies, speak bad French and peer intently up her skirt.

As pupils at a school for boys, we were unused to the presence of females and, consequently, when a young woman teacher or visiting female students made an appearance on campus, their arrival was treated with so much excitement and curiosity as to become embarrassing for them. All the regular teaching staff was male; the only female that we saw on a daily basis was the headmaster's secretary, a lady of about forty years of age usually neatly dressed in a white blouse, tweed skirt, thick stockings and sensible shoes. Presumably as a device for promoting better behaviour towards young women by the older boys, the headmaster organised a special event — a sixth form party. In preparation for the party, we were instructed in party etiquette and told how to behave properly in the company of women. Formal invitation cards were distributed for us to send to our intended companions.

174

My selected partner was a farmer's daughter from Filby and, in due course, I received a reply accepting my invitation. On the evening of the party, I and the rest of the sixth form waited outside the senior school gates for our companions to arrive. Eventually a succession of cars deposited a bevy of attractive young women, suitably attired in colourful party gowns and dresses. All the boys were dressed in school uniform. As instructed, we linked arms with our partners and escorted them into the school to be introduced to the headmaster and the other members of staff who were attending to supervise the party. Despite some apprehension on my part, the evening turned out to be a most enjoyable occasion. A buffet was served in the library, and to drink we were provided with a non-alcoholic fruit punch. Following the buffet there was a dance in the hall as well as singing and a number of energetic party games. Clearly, in the staffroom the punch was a much stronger version, as, during one of the games that involved running from one end of the hall to the other while carrying one's female partner, a young member of staff tripped, sending his fiancée bouncing in a most undignified manner halfway across the floor. Perhaps this was not the example expected by the headmaster and was the reason why there was only one official party during my time in the sixth form at Great Yarmouth Grammar School.

As part of our essential character training, all senior school pupils were expected to join the school's army cadet unit, officially known as Number 1 Company, 2nd Cadet Battalion of the Royal Norfolk Regiment, and only those who claimed to be conscientious objectors or who belonged to a Boy Scout troop were exempted. As anyone claiming to be either was treated with derision and contempt, membership of the cadet unit by senior boys was virtually 100%. Every Friday, most senior boys, including myself, arrived at school dressed in army uniform, boots polished, belts and gaiters stiff with many applications of khaki Blanco, brasses shining and tunics neatly ironed, to be closely inspected at morning parade by our officer commanding, whom we nicknamed "Bushy" because of his thick ginger moustache. I did not particularly enjoy belonging to the army cadets, but the alternative four periods of English and mathematics was less attractive, and, in any case, I was neither a conscientious objector nor a Boy Scout. Some of the activities were interesting, although I could not see how long periods of marching and rifle drill contributed in any way to my character development. After five years in the cadets, my service record states that I was qualified as an instructor in map reading, weapons training and field craft, a first class shot with the .22 and .303 rifles, and proficient in the use of a Bren light machine gun.

Occasionally we would be taken out on manoeuvres in the dunes and marram grass of the North Denes sands. I remember well one exercise when Bushy selected an elite group from our company to form a defensive position in the dunes which the rest of us were instructed to attack. The exercise clearly required us to practise skills in crawling under cover, an action that would inevitably result in sand penetrating through every crevice in our tunics and into our underwear. Periodically the defenders would loose off a round of blank shot and Bushy would then point to one or other of the attackers indicating that they were technically dead and should stay where they were for the remainder of the exercise. Together with two colleagues of similar mind, I decided that our frontal attack was doomed to certain failure and adopted a more innovative approach where we merely walked off the beach, crossed over the road, walked unseen along the promenade and returned to the beach 50 or more yards behind the defenders. Unnoticed, we walked up behind this elite group and announced our presence by pushing the ends of our rifles between the cheeks of three defending backsides and demanding their immediate surrender. Bushy clearly did not appreciate our initiative and subjected us to a long ear-bashing in which he claimed that we — and me in particular — were not taking our service in the cadet force seriously enough. Throughout senior school Bushy and I experienced some problems with our interpersonal relationships, perhaps exacerbated by a mistake that I once made in my role as booking secretary for the Science Society. Bushy was also senior science master and enthusiastically attended all meetings of the Science Society. As booking secretary I had ordered a film whose subject was the production of rubber and its use in the home. Unfortunately the film also contained a section illustrating the use of rubber products in the bedroom which, although totally incomprehensible to the junior pupils, elicited ribald guffaws from many senior boys and some of the staff.

Apart from Friday morning parade, the only official duty that our cadet company performed during my time at the Grammar School was as a Guard of Honour to Prince Philip during his visit to Great Yarmouth in 1954. The headmaster had been informed that after performing his official morning tasks, which included opening the new Technical High School, the Prince would make a tour of the town passing the bottom of Salisbury Road before turning into Lawn Avenue and returning to the Town Hall. Accordingly, immediately after break the whole school staff and pupils were ushered to the bottom of Salisbury Road to find a suitable vantage point where they could cheer and salute the Prince as he passed. Our cadet unit was marched to the end of the road where we took up a position along Northgate Street in preparation for presenting arms to the passing convoy. The end result was disappointing as clearly the Prince's party was late for lunch at the Town Hall and the cavalcade had almost passed us by at full speed before the order to present arms had been given. As none of us knew which of the cars held our royal guest, few of us were at all certain which of the many blurred faces that passed speedily in front of us was indeed the Prince.

Owing to some ill-informed advice from a careers master, I had not applied to university during my second year in the sixth form, expecting, as I had been led to believe, that my A level results would not be good enough for university entrance. As it turned out, my results for mathematics were excellent and had I applied I would surely have begun a degree course in the autumn of 1958. My only option was to remain at Great Yarmouth Grammar for an additional year in the sixth form, which turned out not to be a wasted year but one that I enjoyed immensely, consolidating my knowledge in mathematics and physics and enjoying to the full the sporting opportunities available to me both at school and in Rollesby. It was made even more entertaining as I was joined for this third year by Tim, who had found himself in a similar predicament. Possibly in the hope of avoiding any further difficulties with me in the army cadets, Bushy promoted me to sergeant in command of the school's armoury where I spent most Friday mornings with my feet up, occasionally cleaning and issuing rifles and blank ammunition. My only serious misdemeanour occurred when I inadvertently pulled the trigger of a rifle before inspecting it. Unfortunately a cadet had left an unfired blank shot in the breach with the safety catch off. Luckily I had aimed the rifle through an open door before firing, by chance eliminating the possibility of injury from any discharge from the barrel, but the noise informed everyone of my mistake.

After a shaky first two years at the Grammar School, I must confess that I enjoyed the opportunities for learning that it provided and all the attendant ceremony of grammar school life: the assemblies and Prize Day at the Town Hall, the annual sports day at the Wellesley, the cross-country over the Caister marshes, the staff versus student cricket matches, and

179

the inter-House competitions. It may be true to say that in the 1950s, along with many other boys from a similar background, I did not totally fit the traditional model of a grammar school pupil, but most of us were eventually able to adapt to our new circumstances and draw great benefit from them. Grammar schools were also in a difficult transition period, having to adapt to the implications of the 1944 Education Act and the beginning of the general move towards comprehensive education.

CHAPTER
SIX

Health & Fitness

FAT AS BUTTER

Despite its momentous nature and the obvious benefits that it brought, I have no clear memories relating to the creation of the National Health Service. As a relatively fit and healthy family our medical needs were minimal. Perhaps as a consequence of a time when treatment was not free, my mother and grandmothers each had their own remedies for minor complaints and would consult a pharmacist first before troubling the doctor. My mother often recalled that during her pregnancy she saw the doctor on only two occasions: the first time when he confirmed that she was pregnant and the second, four months later, when the arrangements were made for my birth at home. I often wonder if the difficulty and trauma she experienced during her labour could have been avoided if better pre-natal care had been available at the time. Despite some reluctance on their part to use the services of our doctor, my parents used to rush me to his surgery at the slightest provocation. Luckily I was not a particularly sickly child, although I did endure a short period in hospital

181

during 1947 for a tonsillectomy. How this was financed before the establishment of a free National Health Service, I have no idea.

Perhaps as a result of a wartime diet, I was never an overweight child. An outdoor existence with plenty of exercise ensured that any excess sugar or fat in my diet was burned off well before it turned to flab. Mother, on the other hand, regarded being thin as unhealthy and tried her best to fatten me up, encouraged by our next-door neighbour, Mrs Holt, who frequently commented that I was "Pale and . . .". We never knew what came next as she never finished the phrase. Both mother and Mrs Holt considered that rosy cheeks and chubbiness were a measure of good health and something to be desired. For a while after the war, the Ministry of Food sought to supplement children's diets by a distribution of orange juice and cod liver oil. Mother and I often joined other mothers and their children queuing for our allowance at the back door of Colonel and Mrs Benn's farmhouse on the Back Road. Even after this distribution ceased, mother continued with the practice by feeding me daily cod liver or halibut oil capsules. While the contents were not particularly palatable, I did enjoy the taste of the chewy capsule coverings. I was also encouraged to take regular spoonfuls of a gooey brown malt extract called Virol. This was a delight and I cheerfully downed many spoonfuls at a time. Every evening Grandma Cole would take a bile bean and an Aspro tablet with her bedtime warm milk. In my late teens, I regularly stayed with her in North Market Road so that I could attend dances at the Floral Hall in Gorleston or the nearby Garibaldi Hotel. Although Grandma would be long gone to bed before my return, she always left a glass of milk, a bile bean and an Aspro for my supper, which I usually flushed down her outside toilet.

Although neither of my parents drank beer, wine or spirits on a regular basis, and frequently made disparaging comments about those who did, they considered alcohol to be beneficial to good health when taken in small amounts. From a very young age, I was regularly dosed with various alcoholic concoctions in an attempt to bring roses to my cheeks. Port with lemonade, brandy laced with sugar or sherry beaten together with raw eggs, were all regularly poured down my unwilling throat. The resulting rosiness was more the result of mild inebriation than any immediate improvement in my general health. Grandma Cole drank a bottle of Guinness on most days, just for her health, and Grandfather Miller consumed many bottles of a fortified tonic wine, called Wincarnis, in an attempt to purify his blood.

Both my parents regarded sugar and sweet things to be a quick energy source and a pick-me-up. If they felt tired, run down or even depressed, they would eat sweets or chocolate as an antidote. My friend Tony and I regularly played football for hours in the meadows off Martham Road, often until we both lay down on the ground exhausted. Mother would seek to revive our flagging energy with sandwiches containing jam, condensed milk, treacle, Fry's chocolate spread or even sugar. After an illness, I would be helped in my recovery by twisted orange rods of sticky barley sugar. Towards the end of the 1950s, energy drinks appeared and I became addicted to Lucozade, a strange tasting sweet drink that came in bottles with a yellow cellophane cover. I would drink large quantities of the stuff straight from the bottle, particularly if I was recovering from a cold or needed reviving at half time during a football match, on the understanding that this dubious yellow liquid would miraculously help to recover my failing energy.

Despite rationing during the war and immediately after, I cannot recollect that I was in any way deprived of sweets or other confectionery. They were certainly a treat and not unlimited in supply, but I was never without, undoubtedly because my mother and Grandmother Miller devoted most of their sugar ration to providing for my needs. The sweets that we bought from grandmother's shop were mainly unwrapped boiled sweets — pear drops, humbugs, peppermints and other hard fruit sweets — and toffee. Once sweet rationing finally ceased in 1953, the choice became immediately greater and the temptation was to make up for lost time by over-indulgence. Mother and I joined a long queue outside a confectioner's shop on Market Row in Great Yarmouth to enjoy for the first time the pleasure of buying unlimited quantities of sweets and chocolate. Both of my parents had a "sweet tooth" and began to consume confectionery in large quantities. Every Friday, they would buy sweets for the coming week, usually a collection of twenty-one bars, tubes or packs of different sorts, one for each of us for every night of the week: Cadbury's Dairy Milk or Fruit and Nut, Rolos, dark Bournville chocolate in its distinctive red pack, Mars bars, Kitkat, Rowntrees fruit gums and pastilles, Spangles, Fry's Peppermint Cream, Caramel and Crunchie bars, to mention but a few. Naturally I ate my quota well before the week had ended and spent the rest of the time begging pieces from my parents. For my parents, the ending of sugar rationing came when they were in their late thirties and less active than they had been. The consequence was that they both put on a large amount of weight that they found difficult to reduce in later life. Between us, my father and I could easily consume a full packet of chocolate digestives in one sitting, and frequently did.

HOME REMEDIES

For most of our minor ailments and accidents, mother had a remedy to hand, usually contained in bottles and tins stored inside the cabinet in the scullery. The doctor was called only for major problems when, more often than not, he made a home visit particularly if the patient was a child. Mother's remedies were a mixture of commercial medicines that she bought from the chemist and knowledge that she had learned from her own parents.

Many of our minor problems were related to our digestive systems. Stomach upsets, vomiting and diarrhoea were relatively common and undoubtedly

185

resulted from poor hygiene. Normally these were left to play themselves out, although for very severe bouts of diarrhoea and stomach-ache a bottle of Kaolin and Morphine was obtained from the doctor. Whether this runny clay mixture suspended in a brown liquid actually contained morphine is doubtful, but it was very effective and Mother frequently saved any unused amounts for use when needed at a later date. For simple indigestion I was given two teaspoons of Milk of Magnesia, an awful tasting thick milky substance that never failed to make me heave. My father suffered quite badly from indigestion and we both regularly chewed on tablets called Rennies, he for his stomach and me as I liked the taste. Grandma Cole had instilled in mother the importance of opening the bowels daily, a habit I had failed to acquire. There was never enough time for an active boy to waste straining on the toilet and, besides, like many young boys, I had a complex about doing my number twos — despite Mother's frequent reminder that the King and Queen did it too. Consequently, I was often constipated and had to suffer the indignity of a spoonful of Castor Oil or, even worse, Syrup of Figs. Eventually we reached a compromise with the effervescent fizz of Andrews Liver Salts or, sometimes, Eno's Fruit Salts, which seemed to have the same desired effect and were pleasant, even fun, to take. Occasionally, when our cats showed the telltale rice-like segments of intestinal worms on their tails, I was made to take a worming tablet. Despite looking like a chocolate sweet covered in blue and pink hundreds and thousands, it tasted unpleasant if chewed and I tried every trick I knew to spit it out without mother noticing.

Coughs and colds were mainly ignored and most of us continued to attend school and play outside, no matter what the weather, with green mucus hanging from our noses and our sleeves wet as a result of being used as a substitute for a handkerchief. For a bad sore throat, Mother made up a gargle consisting of a teaspoon of vinegar mixed into a tumbler of warm water. If I had a chesty cough, she applied Vic Vapour Rub to my chest at bedtime to ease my breathing. If the cold turned feverish then I was put to bed and the doctor called. Mother had a simple policy where fevers were concerned; she often said "You starve a fever and drown a cold", although I am not at all sure she had the saying correct. Her approach was to treat like with like and sweat out a fever. If I had a temperature extra blankets were added to my bed and two or more hot water bottles were inserted inside until the fever broke and the bed was soaked with my sweat.

Both my father and I suffered from an excess of ear wax which often gave rise to nagging earache. A teaspoon of olive oil was often poured down my ears in an attempt to loosen the offending wax. Occasionally I was taken to see the doctor who would clean out my ears with a large silver syringe filled with warm water. Father preferred to clean his ears out using one of Mother's hairgrips. Most evenings he excavated lumps of hard wax from inside his ears with the blunt end of the hairgrip, placing the evening's haul on to an old envelope for inspection before consigning it to the fire.

Once he bought his own syringe, a large black rubber ball with an inch-long nozzle that he filled with warm water. Every evening he squirted water down his ears in an attempt to clear out the wax. Occasionally he would insist on doing the same for Mother and me. My head would be held over the scullery sink while he squirted and I screamed, resulting in water everywhere but very little down my ears.

Being an active outdoors child, cuts and bruises were an everyday occurrence. As a result of wearing short trousers, my knees were regularly grazed and skinned, the wound often covered in mud and occasionally, being in the country, cow dung. My hands were continually pierced by thorns and splinters. Every evening, after my bedtime wash, Mother would treat the wounds of the day before covering them with bandages and plasters. Bruises were doused with witch hazel, and cuts and grazes were washed in a dilute solution of Dettol or a greenish-yellow liquid called TCP. Frequently, many of these wounds festered, particularly the embedded thorns and splinters, and then Mother would apply a bread poultice to draw out the pus. A piece of bread was soaked in boiling water and applied to the wound while still hot. The hot soggy poultice was then held in place by a bandage. The same treatment was served out to boils which were then quite common, usually on the back of the neck. A hot poultice applied to the back of the neck was not particularly pleasant, although it usually solved the problem. Burns were anointed with butter or Vaseline, nettle stings were rubbed with dock leaves and wasp stings were soaked in vinegar.

CHILDHOOD ILLS

For more serious illnesses, it was normal practice to retire to bed and call in the doctor. Our doctor was a round-faced, spectacle-wearing Irishman called Dr Rochford, who had a surgery on Repps Road in Martham. Despite a reputation for having a quick temper and for not tolerating malingerers, Dr Rochford was well respected and particularly kind to children. Mother always insisted that I called him "Sir" and only spoke if he asked a question. She was like a dog with two tails when, on one of his visits, he said to her that it was a delight to treat a child with manners.

Like many parents, mother considered it important that I should catch the normal childhood illnesses as early as possible, in the belief that they were less virulent in younger children than older children or adults. Measles, German measles, chickenpox, mumps and whooping cough were all still relatively common, while I can recall the consternation in the village when two children came down with scarlet fever. It was very common for parents to arrange contact between their children and those suffering a childhood complaint, in the hope that they would catch the disease and get it over with. Mother was particularly keen that I should catch mumps as she considered that having it as an adult would be a serious risk to my manhood. When our neighbour Mrs Holt's granddaughter, Pauline, caught mumps, I was duly dispatched to have tea with her in the hope that I would succumb to the disease. Fortunately, this ruse was unsuccessful and to this day I have never had mumps. I caught chickenpox when I was 32 years old and can confirm that it was a most unpleasant experience for an adult.

The only illnesses that I contracted during childhood were measles and whooping cough, both of which I had at a very young age and I have no clear memories of them. However, the legacy of whooping cough still lives with me today. The effort involved in the terrible cough that is a feature of the disease resulted in a deformity of my rib cage which, on the left-hand side, sinks inwards rather than curves outwards as it should. As a thin youngster, this deformity was very obvious and a cause of great embarrassment. At almost every medical I attended, the doctor or nurse would sound my chest and state the obvious: "I see that you have had whooping cough". At grammar school, while undressing for gym or games, my chest would be examined in detail by my classmates. After gym, we were expected to take a shower, a new experience for me and one that I did not particularly enjoy. I would attempt to complete my shower quickly so that I could cover up the source of my embarrassment as rapidly as possible. As a teenager, I was most concerned lest this deformity should make me less attractive to potential girlfriends and, while all my contemporaries were sunbathing and getting tanned, I would astutely avoid taking off my shirt, particularly if we were in the company of females.

I succumbed twice to influenza as a child, not the feverish cold that most of us call flu today but a full-blown virus that took a month or more to run its course. My worst experience was in January 1951 when I was away from school for nearly four weeks, particularly distressing for my parents as this was the year in which I was due to take my eleven-plus examination. My mother at one time feared the worst as I became delirious for a while and failed to recognise her. During the delirium, I apparently told her that I couldn't stay in bed as I had been selected to be a ballboy for an international football match at Wembley and would never be picked again if I failed to turn up. Dr Rochford visited regularly during the first week of the illness and during my recovery period insisted that I was taken to his surgery every other day for an injection which he said would help to pick me up. What was in these injections I have no idea, but they did the trick although Dr Rochford was not the most gentle injection giver, particularly if the previous patient had caused him grief. I do remember that one of my convalescence treats was a parcel of comics sent by Mrs Sally Pitchford, Mother's wartime friend from London. Most of the comics were American and were stories in pictures which, for the time, were very graphic in their depiction of violence, far different from my normal reading. Despite Mother's apprehension, these comics were perused in detail.

Yarmouth Hit by 'Flu Wave

. . . Schools have also suffered and on Tuesday the Chief Education Officer (Mr D.G. Farrow) said 24 teachers were sick with 'flu and colds and that there was an increase of 10 per cent in illness at both primary and secondary schools.

Yarmouth Mercury, 19 January 1951

Influenza Affects Attendance: More Norfolk schools closed

Some of the 30 Norfolk schools which were closed last week because of illness reopened yesterday but six more closed. The affected schools have been fairly evenly distributed throughout the county and range from small units of 20 or so pupils to larger ones of several hundred. In all about 2000 children in the county have had an enforced holiday from school. The chief cause of the trouble has been influenza and although the illness has been so rife among the pupils, the teachers in the main have escaped.

Eastern Daily Press, 23 January 1951

GOODBYE TONSILS

In the spring of 1947 I had my tonsils removed, an experience that, even in those days, was in no way a big deal and certainly one I shared with many of my contemporaries. However, to a six-year-old it was a most frightening ordeal, more frightening than anything that had happened to me during the war or since, and one that burned an indelible impression on my mind. Since starting school, I had suffered from one cold after another with continuous sore throats and uncontrollable nosebleeds. I can clearly remember sitting on a chair next to the living room window as Dr Rochford asked my mother to peer into my mouth while he shone a torch down my throat. "Tonsils and adenoids," he said with conviction. "Yes," agreed mother, although I am not totally sure she knew what she was supposed to be looking at. The outcome was that I was summoned shortly afterwards to the children's ward of the Great Yarmouth General Hospital, a long uninviting red-brick building on Dene Side, immediately behind St George's church at the top of King Street.

As I remember, it was early on a Thursday morning when we arrived at the children's ward where Mother was asked to undress me for bed. This she did as calmly as she could, as Mother hated hospitals and I am sure that she was more nervous and distressed than I. Five other young companions had joined us on the ward, having similarly been summoned, and they too were being undressed, their parents smiling nervously at the longer-term inhabitants of the other beds who watched the process with mild interest. Eventually all our parents suddenly disappeared, no doubt ushered out by the nursing staff, leaving me and my five new companions to tearfully acquaint ourselves with our

193

new surroundings. King Edward VII's children's ward was a large well-lit rectangular room with a high ceiling and windows on three sides, in which twelve children's beds were arranged in two formal lines of six against the walls either side of a central aisle. At one end of the aisle was a desk and chair where, periodically, a nurse would sit surveying the ward or working at her paperwork. At the other end was a large cathedral-like window that looked across an unseen courtyard to the window of an adult ward in the next building. Occasionally, kindly looking faces would peer across at us lying in our beds and wave, no doubt in an attempt to brighten our miserable existences. Some of us would even wave back as there was little else to do. The twelve beds had metal frames and wheels, with sides that could be raised to create a cot, thereby restraining us terrified beings who, had we the sense or the courage, would surely otherwise have made a valiant dash for freedom. I have always been fatalistic and even then, at the age of six, had resigned myself to accepting my fate as being inevitable and unavoidable. What made it difficult was that I had had no preparation for what was about to happen or, indeed, any idea about what was in store.

Later that morning, the six of us were bathed and clothed in nightshirts and dressing gowns. Eventually two porters arrived at the ward and sat us on a trolley, three facing one way and three the other alternately, on which they conveyed us, for what seemed an age, along corridors, across courtyards and eventually to a small room where we were seated unceremoniously on a row of chairs and left in the charge of a nurse. Another nurse entered our waiting room — at least I assumed she was a nurse although she was dressed differently from those on the ward in a green tunic with a shiny apron, a white mask hanging below her chin and a green skullcap. Looking round at us, she smiled and hand-in-hand escorted one of my companions through a door into another room where we could see a number of people waiting, dressed similarly in green gowns with masks over their faces. The door closed and we were left unnaturally quiet and fearful for what was about to happen. A short while later the same nurse reappeared and said, "Colin, it's your turn," then hand-in-hand we walked into a small, well-lit room with what I now know to be an operating table in the middle. A calm-voiced man asked me to climb up and lie down on the table, where I found myself peering up at six or more heads leaning over me. "As you can see we all have masks," he said, "so I think you should have one as well," at the same time placing something over my mouth and nose. "Now look back and see if you can see Mickey Mouse." What purpose this request served I still do not know, but immediately I was engulfed by a choking, evil-smelling vapour that seemed to be suffocating away my very existence. Try as I could I was unable to move as unseen hands held down my arms and legs, and my head was fixed in a vice-like grip. My cries of panic only served to make me breathe even more of this evil substance, presumably chloroform or ether. In reality it probably took only a few moments for me to become unconscious; to a child in panic it seemed a lifetime.

I have very little recollection of anything else before walking to find myself back in my cot. My throat burned, there was a taste of blood in my mouth and my dribble had stained the pillows pink. Periodically I would belch reminders of the anaesthetic but I have no recollection of being sick, although I am not sure what that would have done to my throat if I had been. We were a miserable crew, my companions and me, and I have a vague memory of much crying and moaning, and a fitful shock-induced sleep. The next morning we were all very much recovered from the trials of the day before, although my throat was still very sore and everything tasted of blood. We were allowed lots to drink although no food until, at lunchtime, we were offered the rare treat of an ice cream. Never before was ice cream such a delight, its smooth coolness giving a welcome relief to my burning throat.

To occupy us as we recovered, various toys and a pile of comics were distributed among the children in the ward. We had all reacted in our own individual way to the experience of the tonsillectomy, mostly whimpering submission and a satisfaction in the knowledge that the worst was over. However, one of my companions reacted somewhat differently from the rest of us, expressing his feelings in bouts of uncontrollable anger. Unfortunately he was the first to receive the pile of comics and I can see him now, sitting on his cot reading them slowly and carefully. After finishing each comic, he would stand on his bed and, with a look of immense satisfaction, tear every page into as many pieces as he could before hurling them at his neighbours. A nurse eventually arrived and restrained him, but not before most of the comics had been subjected to this destructive treatment. In the afternoon a doctor appeared who sounded our chests and looked carefully at our throats and mouths. One of the nurses said that his visit was to decide if we were fit enough to go home. Mr Angry was certainly more streetwise than the rest of us as he reduced us all to floods of tears by announcing that the doctor had declared him the only one well enough to go home; the rest of us had to wait until next week. Luckily my fears were quickly dispelled by the sight of my mother's smiling face appearing at the door. Asked why I had been crying, a nurse suggested that I had enjoyed myself so much that I did not want to go home, although nothing could have been further from the truth. According to Mother, after riding home in Grandfather's car I was put to bed where I slept for over twenty-four hours without waking.

JABS, NITS AND THE DENTIST

Whether or not a result of the formation of the National Health Service, there was certainly a focus on improving children's health during the 1940s and 1950s, and, in particular, providing greater protection against illness. Vaccinations, medical inspections at

197

school and easier access to dentistry all contributed to a general improvement in the health of young people.

Mother ensured that I was vaccinated against diphtheria and smallpox as a baby, encouraged no doubt by Grandmother Miller who had lost an infant child, Kenneth, during the last major diphtheria outbreak in the district. Mother, however, was both surprised and shocked by the drastic nature of the smallpox vaccination, a procedure carried out enthusiastically by the administering doctor that has left me with an unsightly 3-inch oval scar on my upper left arm. In the mid- to late 1950s the medical concern was poliomyelitis, more commonly called infantile paralysis as its effects were worse in children. The polio scare was worsened by images shown on newsreels at the cinema of children wearing callipers on their legs or having to be helped to breathe by a machine called an iron lung. Eventually all the boys at Yarmouth Grammar School were immunised against both poliomyelitis and tuberculosis. As I recall, the former involved eating a sugar cube impregnated with vaccine and the latter a course of injections.

At both primary and secondary school, we were regularly inspected by a nurse, commonly referred to as the nit-nurse. For the inspection we were required to strip down to our vest, pants and socks. The inspection itself usually involved measuring and recording our height and weight, taking our temperature, sounding our chest and inspecting our ears, eyes, throat, feet, hair and sexual organs. At Rollesby the inspection normally took place in the teachers' staff room, usually in the presence of a parent; at Yarmouth Grammar the gymnasium was requisitioned for the purpose. During my first year in the sixth form, I can remember waiting, undressed, in the gymnasium changing rooms with a number of other classmates for our turn to be inspected. A story was circulating that the inspection was being conducted by a glamorous young nurse and that it involved her asking us to cough as she held our testicles in her hand. Further, that on receiving this treatment, a boy in the second year sixth had become aroused, to which the nurse had responded unkindly by slapping him firmly on the end of his erect member and insisting that he controlled himself. In common with most of my waiting classmates, being gullible and inexperienced in such matters, I was terrified that the same embarrassment might happen to me. That the story was a fabrication and a prank became clear when the nurse turned out to be a matron-like figure in her fifties and the testicle inspection was carried out by a male doctor.

After one inspection at Rollesby, mother was issued with a special comb, a rectangular stiff white comb with small narrow teeth on two opposite sides. For a month or more after this inspection she would use it to comb my hair night and morning which caused many tantrums and wails of protest as my hair was regularly knotted. Mother explained that the comb was a special comb for removing sand from my hair. Clearly I was suffering from an infestation of head lice, a fact that would have caused mother great embarrassment as she regarded such infestations to occur only in dirty

199

children with dirty parents living in dirty homes. She never considered the fact that head lice themselves might prefer to live in clean surroundings.

At Rollesby we were also visited by the school dentist, who arrived towing a caravan that he parked in the school's playground. Inside the van were his dentist's chair and all the equipment he needed to carry out his work. Although my teeth were inspected I never had any treatment from the school dentist, unlike some of my other classmates who frequently returned to the classroom with red eyes and swollen cheeks. Mother was particularly keen on dental hygiene and insisted that I cleaned my teeth every morning and evening. She dreaded the thought of having to wear false teeth, and brushed her teeth conscientiously in the hope of avoiding that misfortune. To clean our teeth we used Gibbs dentifrice which came in a round tin with a castle on the lid, containing a hard, pink block which we rubbed with our toothbrush. Eventually we converted to using soft toothpaste from a tube, at various times "Tingling fresh" SR or Maclean's toothpaste — "Did you Maclean your teeth today?"

From the age of nine I was taken every six months to see a dentist at a dental practice near to St George's Park in Great Yarmouth. My first treatment was so traumatic that it took a long time before I was able to visit the dentist again without being terrified. The dentist decided to remove all my remaining rotten and loose milk teeth in one go and, consequently, an appointment was made at which I was anaesthetised to allow eleven teeth to be extracted. Again, I was held down, screaming, by six or more adults as a mask was placed over my mouth for the same chocking gas that I remembered from my tonsillectomy to invade my airways. Mother said that it took no more than a minute for all eleven teeth to be removed and only minutes after that for me to be conscious again. As a reward I was bought a green clockwork car from Woolworth's and taken to Grandma Cole's to recover. Unfortunately Grandma Cole decided that I would be revived by a bowl of warm oxtail soup. On the way back home, the oxtail soup and I parted company all over the front two downstairs seats of the number 5 bus to Norwich. Mother tried valiantly to catch my vomit in a punnet of raspberries which somehow tipped up in the process and added to the mess. Luckily the bus was not crowded and what few passengers there were moved tactfully to the rear seats.

SICKNESS AND DEATH

Despite an obvious detrimental effect on health, almost everybody smoked. Smoking was fashionable. All our role models in magazines and on the cinema screen were regularly shown with a cigarette in their hands. Smoking was the right of the labouring man and many spent most of their working days with a rolled up cigarette, often unlit, stuck firmly to their bottom lip. To a teenager, smoking was a grown-up activity and something to aspire to. Most of my family smoked, particularly members of the Cole family. Grandma Cole started smoking during the war, at the age of sixty, but made up for her late start by consuming ten or more Craven A cork-tipped cigarettes daily. My uncles, Arthur and Stanley Cole, smoked upwards of sixty Woodbines every day, the fingers and thumb of their right hands stained brown by nicotine. My other grandparents did not smoke and Grandmother Miller would not allow smoking in her house. Grandfather occasionally smoked a cigar at Christmas but he had to do this outside in the garden or in his office. Not that he enjoyed it as he was normally sick afterwards. Most of my aunts and uncles were smokers or ex-smokers, many, like Aunt Doris Miller, smoking untipped cigarettes, usually Players Full Strength or Senior Service.

My father smoked while he was in the army but gave up soon after he was demobbed. He discovered, as I was to discover later, that smoking and playing sport very rarely went together after the age of thirty. Playing sport was considered to be more important than smoking cigarettes and gave him sufficient motivation to stop. Like many ex-smokers he subsequently became vociferously anti-smoking. Out of necessity, Mother was a secret smoker, hiding her cigarettes in various places throughout the house and smoking only when alone. Unfortunately for her, I had accidentally discovered some of her hiding places and, whether she knew or not, my under-age smoking was subsidised by cigarettes taken from her hidden packets. I had my first cigarette at the age of fourteen, a Batchelor tipped cigarette given to me by a friend at school. One winter evening, on the pretext of visiting my grandmother, I smoked the cigarette while riding my bicycle from Rollesby to Martham and back, fascinated by the red glowing cigarette end in front of my face. Luckily there was no other road traffic as I must have ridden cross-eyed paying little attention to where I was going. From then on I was an addict, building up to about ten a day by the age of seventeen, most of that ten cadged from various aunts and uncles or "borrowed" from Mother's hidden caches. At eighteen, I bought my cigarettes from members of the American Air Force, usually at the Queen's Hotel at the top of Regent Road in Great Yarmouth. Most Americans were willing to sell cigarettes in exchange for English currency, enabling me to smoke Pall Mall, Marlboro, Camel and Lucky Strike more cheaply than any shop-bought English brands.

It is untrue to say we were not aware that smoking constituted a health risk. I was constantly warned by a retired doctor friend of mother's that smoking could lead to chest problems. He regularly complained about my habit of smoking in the half-time break at football matches. Many of my aunts and uncles who smoked had chesty coughs that they acknowledged were due to smoking, and Arthur and Stanley's Woodbines were christened "coffin nails", clearly identifying a link between cigarettes and premature death even if only as a joke. It is ironic that the only member of our two families to contract cancer during the 1950s was Grandmother Miller, a non-smoker. She was forced to retire from the post office when she contracted breast cancer in 1950 and underwent a particularly vicious mastectomy, from which she never fully recovered.

Death was a topic never broached by my parents and was clearly considered an inappropriate subject to discuss with a child. Until 1957 my only experience of death was the death of an animal. As a country boy, I had done my share of killing animals: rabbits at harvest, pheasants for the shoot, fish, mice and rats, not without an element of remorse on each occasion. I also inherited my father's airgun and became quite proficient at shooting sparrows. However, it was with the death of a dear pet that I experienced the pain associated with such an event, in particular Grandfather's dog, Rover, who had been a constant companion to Grandfather and myself on our various outings, and Whisky, a black and white cat, the first of our many cats at Martham Road and a personal favourite, who died from an infection when a sheep tick was inexpertly removed from his nose. I also saw how the death of an animal could affect others when Mother lost a pig. My friend Richard's parents kept pigs at their farm and offered Mother the runt of a litter that had been rejected by the sow. This she gladly accepted and attempted to hand rear it, keeping it in our sitting room inside the chicken incubator. The piglet became quite a pet, running around the sitting room and sitting on mother's lap to be bottle fed, until she gave it Carnation milk, having run out of cow's milk. For some reason, this did not suit the piglet's constitution and it died. Mother was inconsolable and cried for days.

In 1953, I experienced my first funeral when all the staff and pupils of Yarmouth Grammar School attended at Gorleston church for the funeral of the second master who had collapsed and died unexpectedly. It was a surreal experience as very few of us knew what to expect and were quite shocked to find that the dead body was actually brought into the church, even if contained inside a wooden coffin. I can clearly remember thinking, what if he is not really dead but asleep? What if he wakes up to find himself nailed down in a wooden box? Despite the fact that I hardly knew the man, I was quite disturbed by the experience. I had been too young to respond to the death of Grandfather Cole in 1942; consequently my first conscious experience of a family death was when Grandmother Miller died suddenly in May 1957, unfortunately on my mother's birthday. In the early hours of the morning, she suffered a massive stroke and, as she was clearly dying, Grandfather summoned the family. Despite being sixteen years of age, neither of my parents would tell me what was happening until after she had died. I was left sleeping in my room while they went to her bedside. They also insisted that I attended school on the day of her funeral, only joining the mourners afterwards. Whether or not the proximity and frequency of death in wartime had influenced their actions, I was certainly protected from the trauma of death to an extent not possible, or even attempted, by previous generations.

CHAPTER
SEVEN

Home Entertainment

CHILDREN'S TOYS

As a child, even as a teenager, I was never bored. There was always plenty to see and do at home, in the villages around Rollesby or in Great Yarmouth. I did not need computer games, videos or constant television to fill my time. When I was not content to play by myself, my parents and grandparents were always happy to play with me. I had many friends in the village and we were extremely imaginative in the games that we played. Every week, there was always an organised activity in a village institute or hall within cycling distance of home and, in winter as well as during the summer, Great Yarmouth had much to offer.

Compared with many of my contemporaries I was well blessed with toys, although compared with the children of today we were not so fortunate. During the war and immediately afterwards there was a shortage of toys, as materials and manufacturing had been directed towards the war effort. Consequently, many of our toys were everyday items, hand-me-downs or bought second-hand. At the post office, Grandfather provided me with a sandpit equipped with numerous enamel jugs, saucepans, spades and trowels to use in my sand play. As an infant, I was given a teddy bear and a panda which were my bedroom companions until they were eventually consigned to the garden shed when I was nine. Many of my better toys were bought at sales, particularly at the Thursday Acle sale, and included a blue pedal car which, as a small child, I pedalled aimlessly around the garden, a box of various Meccano pieces that gave me many hours of fun constructing cars, cranes and numerous other Heath Robinson machines, and a clockwork train set.

Unfortunately there was insufficient curved track remaining with the train set to make a complete circle and so it was necessary for me to be at one end of the track and Mother or Father at the other to field the train as it reached the end of the line, turn it round and send it back again. When I was ten, Uncle George brought me two pairs of boxing gloves that he had acquired from a Boys' Club in London. These I proudly took to the playing field where the older boys organised a boxing tournament in the sandpit. I was quite happy swinging away at most of my opponents, usually with little effect, until I was matched against a more street wise older boy. Our bout ended when he managed to land a right hook on the end of my chin. The end result was that my knees buckled, bells rang in my ears, my head buzzed and my eyes were full of flashing lights. I was so stunned that I actually forgot to cry. Needless to say, as soon as I had recovered, I gathered up my boxing gloves, staggered off home and threw them into my toy cupboard where they stayed, unused, until Mother eventually consigned them to the dustbin a year or two later.

As children, we were imaginative in compensating for a lack of expensive toys. My cousin Stephanie and I created a mini-theatre in the backyard of the post office made from some orange boxes and a pair of curtains that we found in a shed. We regularly wrote plays which we performed with home-made hand puppets to an invited audience of family and friends; we even produced programmes for the audience to read. Odd bits of wood, garden canes, tin cans, dustbin lids, old sheets and doormats, held together by nails, pins and binder twine, became the weapons, costumes and armour for children's armies recreating historic battles. Tony and I used an old sheet of corrugated iron as a sledge for sliding down the less hazardous side of a stone quarry in a wood behind Rollesby Hall. Discarded pram wheels were used with soapboxes to make carts which saw service at various times as tanks, transporters and racing cars, often competing in races down the hill on the Fleggburgh Road with little regard for any traffic that might come along.

During the 1940s, most of my toys were associated with war. I had a model of a First World War artillery piece which fired matchsticks for a distance of about 6 feet. Most evenings, my parents and our cat were shelled with matchsticks until, in self-defence, the gun and matches were confiscated. My absolute favourite toy was a clockwork American jeep with an Allied Forces star on its bonnet which, when fully wound, would go round in a circle a dozen or more times before it needed winding up again. I also had numerous warplanes including a large home-made wooden model of a Lancaster bomber. When he returned from Italy, my father brought me a tin soldier, a model of a German paratrooper, which he had confiscated from a German prisoner of war. For Christmas 1948, I was given a locally made wooden fort manned by thirty or more soldiers that mother had gathered together from various shops, sales and other sources — a motley crew consisting of a troop of Guardsmen standing to attention dressed in red tunics with busbies on their heads, a marching army band, ten or more cowboys (two on horseback), some Indians and a farmer with his wife, a pig and two sheep. For a while the fort was my pride and joy, and every night its defenders were shelled with matchsticks by my First World War artillery piece.

By the end of the 1940s, cowboys and Indians had become the fashion and, along with almost every other boy of my age, I owned a cap-firing six-gun which I kept in a genuine holster from the American West given to me by our vicar. The holster I attached to a gamekeeper's cartridge belt which I wore proudly around my waist, despite being far too large for the size of my toy pistol and too large for the size of my waist. Gangs of boys, and one or two girls, played long games of cowboys and Indians in the fields and woods along Martham Road and behind the Hall. The cowboys dressed usually in a cowboy hat, often a keepsake from a visit to a fairground, with a handkerchief tied around their necks. The Indians had pheasant feathers in their hair, occasionally stuck into a piece of elastic tied around their heads. Sometimes we cut supple branches from a tree to make bows which we strung with binder twine. For arrows we used reeds, pulled when no one was looking, from the thatch on various farm barns. Otherwise we used thin garden canes often with nails inserted into the tips. Every boy carried a knife, not as a weapon but as a useful tool to have in the countryside. I had a scout's sheath knife which I attached to the belt on my trousers. In the 1950s, the cap guns were replaced by water pistols and ping-pong ball firing bazookas. We regularly played cowboys and Indians with our water pistols around a Second World War pillbox in the corner of a field on Richard's farm, cowboys inside defending, Indians outside attacking. Refills of water were provided in old tin baths that we hauled to the pillbox on a soapbox cart. At the end of the day we often returned home wet through, especially after we discovered that a bicycle pump was an extremely effective water pistol.

In my early teens I collected Dinky toys, mainly racing cars, including models in the colours of Ferrari, Maserati and Alfa-Romeo. I even had a model of John Cobb's land-speed record-breaking Railton Special. Richard, too, collected racing cars and we regularly competed against each other, pushing our cars round a track that we constructed in the attic of his home. In the mid-1950s, Richard, Tony, Dick and I each had a Subbuteo football team and played against each other in a league that we organised among ourselves. After the age of sixteen, toys were put aside in favour of organised sporting activities, girls and rock 'n' roll music.

I also enjoyed playing various card and board games, mostly against my parents or other members of our family. Snakes and ladders and ludo eventually gave way to more thoughtful games such as draughts and chess. My parents owned a Monopoly set which they played at family parties when the children, myself included, had gone to bed. Everyone in the family, particularly the Miller family, played cards. By the age of ten, I could play many different card games at a reasonable standard. By myself I played patience, and a variation called clock patience; with others I played rummy, cribbage, whist and solo. My favourite game was knockout whist which we always played when members of the family got together, as the rules enabled any number of players to join in, although it was best played with four people. To start the game, as many cards as possible were dealt out to all the players, any left over remained on the table face down. Each player then estimated how many tricks they would win with the cards in their hand. The game was then played as normal whist, hearts as trumps on the first round, clubs, diamonds and spades in subsequent rounds. At the end of each round, players scored one point for every trick that they won, with a bonus of ten if their total tricks were the same as their prediction. In every subsequent round, one less card was dealt to each player until, in the last round, everyone only had a

211

single card to bid on. The winner was the person with the highest points total.

My grandparents were particularly fond of trying new games and I remember rowdy sessions of happy families, Lexicon (a forerunner of the word game Scrabble) and Pit, a card game based on the stock exchange which involved collecting shares in various commodities in as noisy a manner as possible. At Aunt Dolly's we always played beetle, a game that involved rolling a dice to win various parts of a beetle's anatomy. The winner was the first player who managed to collect a complete beetle. Tim introduced me to tuppenny-ha'penny football, a game for two players with two old pennies and a halfpenny played on any smooth surface, usually a table top. Two goals were drawn in chalk at either end of the surface and one penny was turned head upwards, the other tail upwards. These represented the two teams and the halfpenny was the ball. Each player in turn pushed his penny with a comb or a small ruler in an attempt to hit and move the ball or to take a defensive position in front of his goal. The aim of the game was to score by knocking the halfpenny through your opponent's goal. Our dining table hosted many 2½ penny football competitions, as well as table tennis and billiard tournaments between my father and me.

I also enjoyed various hobbies including my childhood favourite, stamp collecting. My collection was initially based on an album that my father gave me, a blue album containing stamps that he had collected during his childhood. Packets of foreign stamps were sold in Great Yarmouth's toyshops as well as at

Woolworth's, and I regularly bought a packet to add to my collection. Grandmother and, eventually, Uncle Cecil Miller would also cadge foreign stamps from cards and letters that they delivered in their role as postmistress and postmaster which they shared among my cousins and me. Uncle George Miller was a keen stamp collector and in his spare time ran a stamp approval business. When he eventually gave up this business, he gave me the remnants of his stock books and a large collection of foreign stamps. I was very proud of my collection which contained many thousands of stamps from all over the world, and I learned a great deal about the various countries from the pictures and designs on their stamps.

Grandfather had a bird's egg collection which he eventually gave to me. Although as children we were keen bird's-nesters, none of us collected the eggs, preferring to observe as the eggs hatched into chicks and, eventually, grown birds. Each of us had our own secret nests, the locations of which we jealously guarded from other children.

Richard and I were also keen model builders, spending hours making up Airfix kits of various aeroplanes, my best accomplishment being a large model of a Sabre jet-fighter. We also used shop-bought rubber moulds to make plaster of Paris models of animals and Disney characters, which we painted and gave as presents to our family and friends. For a time, the mantelpiece and windowsill of our front room was filled with models that I made for my mother until, eventually, the craze passed and the models disappeared. Another time, along with most of Rollesby's youngsters, I made lists of the numbers on car number plates, a particularly senseless activity. I spent long hours at the Horse & Groom crossroads meticulously recording in a notebook the registration number of every vehicle that travelled along the Main Road.

READING MATTER

My parents were not great readers, or more accurately, not great readers of books. Whether books were scarce because of austerity after wartime, or too expensive, or not something that gave them pleasure, I have no memory of them ever reading a novel. I can remember a pile of six or more books beside the front room fireplace, but these included a Bible, an English dictionary, a medical handbook and three books on building techniques, and were for occasional reference. They were, however, avid readers of newspapers. Every weekday, the *Daily Express* was delivered to our home; on Friday, the *Great Yarmouth Mercury*; on Saturday evening, the *Pink 'Un* sports paper; and on Sunday, the *Sunday Express* and the *Sunday Pictorial*. These were read thoroughly from front to back, from the headline news to the sports pages. Mother also had a regular order for two women's magazines, *Woman* and *Woman's Own*. Like my parents, I also read the newspaper from an early age and was quite well versed in current affairs and national sporting news, albeit derived from a potentially biased viewpoint. In addition to their newspapers, my Miller grandparents read two popular magazines, *Illustrated* and *Picture Post*, which they passed on to us when they had finished with them.

As most parents read to their younger children every night, I assume that Mother read to me. She said that I was particularly fond of *Gulliver's Travels* which she first read to me when I had measles — not an obvious choice for a young boy. However, once I could read for myself, my preferred reading was fact rather than fiction and my treasured books during the 1940s were a book on trains, a wartime aircraft recognition manual, a book on animals of the world, another about British birds and a geographic atlas. I spent many happy hours looking at the maps in the atlas, learning about the oceans and countries around the world, and memorising the names of the cities, rivers and mountains. By the time I began at grammar school, I had not read many of the children's classics. Those that I did own had been given to me as Christmas presents and included *Treasure Island, Lorna Doone, David Copperfield* and *Black Beauty*, the last two undoubtedly because of their association with Great Yarmouth. Once at grammar school, I was encouraged to read more and in order to help me I was registered as a reader at the public library in Great Yarmouth. Unfortunately for my education, I preferred borrowing Westerns to children's classics. I also borrowed books from my friend Richard, especially his story books about Richmal Crompton's

William and Enid Blyton's Famous Five and Secret Seven.

In my later teens, I still preferred fact to classical fiction and proved a great disappointment to my English teacher. English literature was one of my failures at school. The only time I showed any enthusiasm for the subject was when we were introduced to the Hornblower novels, which struck an immediate chord as I was by then a fanatical admirer of Lord Nelson — another Norfolk boy. For leisure reading I mainly enjoyed stories about Biggles by Captain W.E. Johns, and paperback books about military exploits in the Korean and Second World Wars. I far preferred reading my school mathematics and science books to studying the works of Shakespeare or Dickens. At home, beside my bed, I had a collection of *I-Spy* books, written by Big Chief I-Spy, Charles Warrell, which encouraged children to look about themselves and to learn from what they could see and do.

I also read comics; in the 1940s the *Beano, Dandy, Radio Fun* and *Film Fun*, the *Beano* especially with Dennis the Menace and the Bash Street Kids. In the *Daily Express*, I followed the exploits of Rupert Bear and every Christmas my parents gave me a *Rupert Bear Annual*, which I read again and again until the next Christmas. Like many other boys, in 1950 I became addicted to the *Eagle* comic and proudly wore my gold Eagle club member's badge on my jacket lapel. Every week I followed with interest the exploits of Dan Dare and his friend Digby, and their conflicts with the gruesome green Mekon, PC49, Harris Tweed and Luck of the Legion. The *Eagle*, edited by ex-teacher Marcus Morris, was also educational and informative, especially the innovative centrefold cut-away pictures of buildings and machines that I studied in minute detail. After 1950, the *Eagle Annual* replaced *Rupert Bear* as a regular Christmas gift.

Radio and TV

At home, apart from newspapers, our primary source of news and entertainment was the wireless. We had neither a television nor a record player until the late 1950s, and computers and video-players were unheard of. As far as I can recollect we had the same wireless for most of my time at Martham Road, a large, brown, box-shaped bakelite set that sat on a small table at the far side of our living room. To the front of the wireless, a large rectangular piece of patterned fabric covered the speaker, held in place by ornamental imitation fretwork. Below the speaker there was a dial with a movable pointer that lit up orange when the wireless was switched on and, under this, there were three knobs. The first was an on-off switch and volume control, the middle knob altered the position of the pointer along the dial — the wireless making strange squeaking noises as it moved — and the third changed the frequency between long, medium and short waves. The names of many European radio stations were written on the dial next to their transmitting frequencies, rather a waste as we were unable to receive most of them. The back of the set was covered by a piece of flexible board held in place by four screws. The working interior of the wireless could be clearly seen through four ventilation holes in the back of the set — a fascinating assembly of wires, coils and valves that glowed when the wireless was working.

For entertainment we normally listened to the BBC Home Service, the Light programme, and, if the reception permitted, Radio Luxembourg. My parents preferred listening to the popular programmes of the day: the news, most sporting events, quizzes, magazine programmes, comedy series and light dance-band music. Having enjoyed boxing in the army, my father was as enthusiastic about boxing as he was about football and I can remember him getting up in the early hours of the morning to listen to boxing broadcasts from the USA, particularly contests involving Freddie Mills and Randolph Turpin as they progressed to become light-heavyweight and middleweight world champions respectively in the late 1940s and early 1950s.

In the summer holiday, I listened endlessly to Test Match cricket, often scoring the match in a red exercise book. Every year we all listened fascinated to the commentary of the University Boat Race, supporting Oxford in preference to the more local Cambridge.

During winter evenings in front of the fire, we laughed together at comedy shows such as *ITMA, Much Binding in the Marsh, Life with the Lyons and*

Take it from Here, enjoyed chat shows such as *Have a Go,* with Wilfred Pickles and Violet Carson on the piano, *In Town Tonight* and Richard Dimbleby going *Down Your Way,* particularly when such programmes were broadcast from a local Norfolk village or town, and hummed away to the music of *Henry Hall's Guest Night.* During the day, if she was not busy, Mother listened to *Woman's Hour* and *Mrs Dale's Diary.* Sunday lunch was eaten with half an ear on *Two-way Family Favourites,* introduced by Jean Metcalfe and Cliff Michelmore, which was normally followed by *The Billy Cotton Band Show* and *Educating Archie.* How a ventriloquist managed to deliver a successful radio programme where the main character, Archie Andrews, was his ventriloquist's dummy was always a total mystery to me.

As a young child, I listened mainly to *Children's Hour,* and was especially captivated by stories about Larry the Lamb in Toytown. Despite Mother's disapproval, I was also addicted to the adventures of *Dick Barton,* special agent, until it was replaced in its 6.45p.m. slot by *The Archers* in the early 1950s. In my teens, my listening tastes began to differ from those of my parents. Luckily my father had bought a radio for my bedroom, a large modern-looking brown and cream set with a row of press-buttons for pre-selected stations, and I spent many evenings either on my bed or staring out of my bedroom window listening to my choice of programmes. Apart from *Top of the Form,* a schools' quiz programme that I never missed, and the zany *Goon Show,* at night I listened exclusively to Radio

219

Luxembourg as its programmes seemed to be teenager-orientated and the music mainly 1950s pop. Often I listened to Radio Luxembourg's late night music programmes, the volume turned down as low as possible and my ear pressed hard against the speaker, only to be frequently interrupted by my father at my bedroom door requesting me to "Turn off that blooming radio and get to sleep".

Despite most people's assertion that they had had television for the coronation in 1953, television reception in our part of Norfolk was hardly possible until the erection of the Tacolneston transmitter in 1956. Until that time, I had seen a television set only once before — that was on our visit to Uncle George Miller's house in Bexleyheath, Kent, for Christmas 1950. As I remember, his television set consisted of a floor-standing cabinet, about 3 feet high, containing a very small screen, so small that we all needed to sit fairly close around the set to see the picture in any detail. I can only remember watching one programme on this set, a Christmas Eve carol service broadcast from under Trafalgar Square's large Christmas tree.

Once Tacolneston came on line, Uncle Cecil Miller, by now resident at the post office, was the first in the family to buy his own set. In 1956, television was an exciting novelty, and we were all delighted to be invited every Sunday to tea and television at the post office. I usually arrived at 4.30p.m. to watch the children's programmes with my cousin, Stephanie. Even at the age of fifteen, watching children's television on a Sunday was acceptable as the programmes were usually short cowboy films featuring the Lone Ranger, the Range Rider or the Cisco Kid. During the interval between children's and adult programmes we had tea and listened to *Round the Horne* on the wireless. After tea, we all watched television again from 7.00p.m. until the end of *What's my Line?*, when we went home. *What's my Line?*, a quiz programme where a panel of four celebrities tried to guess the occupation of a contestant from a mime that they performed, was, for my parents, the highlight of the evening. To my mind it was boring and I could'nt wait to get back home to listen to Radio Luxembourg. The celebrity panel consisted regularly of David Nixon, Barbara Kelly, Isobel Barnet and the acerbic Gilbert Harding. Everybody waited expectantly to laugh at Gilbert Harding's rudeness towards the contestants, for me the only redeeming feature of the programme.

When Tacolneston became fully operational in 1957, we bought our first television set from Wolsey & Wolsey of Great Yarmouth, a Bush television with a 14-inch screen. Placed firmly on its own wheeled stand, our new television took pride of place against the wall on the far side of the living room, replacing the wireless as the focal point in the room. To receive the programmes, a large H-shaped aerial had been fixed on top of a long metal pole erected in the garden as the chimney was considered not strong enough to support it. The black and white pictures were not always distinct because the reception was often variable and susceptible to interference from passing traffic and electronic machinery, particularly the milking machines of Hall

221

Farm. Until 1959, it was only possible to receive BBC broadcasts and, consequently, there was no choice of programmes. Nevertheless, my parents were hooked and watching television became their main form of entertainment in the evenings. Whist drives, socials and other activities became a thing of the past. Not only my parents but also my friends became addicted to television. For a while our living room became regularly inhabited by many of my friends, until their parents too became television owners. Apart from some notable exceptions, I considered the available programmes to be less appealing than many of the social activities engaged in by an active male in his late teens. Consequently, television made little impact on my teenage lifestyle, but for my parents and some of my friends it constituted a major force for change.

PARTIES

Parties, particularly family parties, were a frequent occurrence. Any excuse was used as an opportunity for Mother or my two grandmothers to organise a party, whether to celebrate a special occasion, to meet with visiting relatives or friends, or just simply as a family get-together. With two large families to call on, most of them living locally, our parties were well attended and could become rather boisterous.

As with most children, my favourite party time was Christmas, a celebration that always seemed ages in coming, yet was over all too quickly. Special events at both Rollesby Primary and Great Yarmouth Grammar schools, the tree in Yarmouth's market place, the lights and decorations in the shops, Father Christmas's Grotto at Arnold's, carols and the Nativity play at Rollesby church, Christmas stories on the wireless, all added to my mounting excitement. Preparations at home were not over-elaborate. Mother would usually make her own Christmas cake and spend the last few days before Christmas baking and getting all the kitchen arrangements finalised. I made my own Christmas cards which I sent to close relatives and friends, or, more accurately, I coloured in blank cards that had the outlines of various Christmas scenes printed on them. My father and I decorated the front room with streamers that we cut from rolles of crepe paper, first crimping their edges with Mother's crimping scissors and then twisting and hanging them with drawing pins from the light fitting to various points on the picture rail. To supplement the trimmings, and after much huffing and puffing blowing them up, we added tied up bundles of balloons which, eventually, mysteriously became untied to be used as footballs, or, batted around the front room, frequently knocked over ornaments, glasses and crockery. We always had a small Christmas tree in the front room bay window which we decorated with tinsel, candle-holders and Mother's collection of seemingly ancient Christmas tree ornaments. Each Christmas these got fewer in number as our cats treated them as playthings and knocked them off the tree. The small coloured candles in the holders were never lit for fear of fire. By the end of Christmas, the floor in the bay window was covered in pine needles. To complete the decorations, branches of holly, brought from the post office garden or the Field, were stuffed behind the pictures on the walls and the mirror over the fireplace. Cards stood in lines along the mantelpiece, the piano top and the bay window sill, regularly falling over in a draught every time the back door was opened or shut. In our house, only the front room was decorated for Christmas.

Our Christmas was always a three-day celebration starting in the afternoon of Christmas Eve when Uncle George and Aunt Eve arrived by car from London, and Grandmother Miller's sister, Great-aunt Elsie from Wisbech, was met off the train at Martham. All three stayed with my grandparents at the post office, or Hall Cottages when they moved after Grandmother retired as postmistress. Before tea, I rushed excitedly to my grandparents' home to meet the visitors and to join in with the card game that was always under way. After tea, they visited relatives and friends in Rollesby, including a visit to our house, where they became moderately tiddly and very talkative after consuming numerous glasses of sherry.

As a young child, Christmas Eve was made even more exciting with the prospect of a visit from Father Christmas. As an older child I became more blasé in the knowledge that he was fictitious, although I continued to hang up a pillow case well into my teens. Mother told me later that, as a small boy, I was allowed to inspect my stocking when she went to bed at

10.30p.m., pretending that it was Christmas morning and that Father Christmas "had been". Apparently this ruse always worked as, after inspecting its contents, I slept soundly until fairly late in the morning. Not that its contents were very special: usually there was an apple, a walnut, a sugar mouse and some sweets, possibly a comic, some crayons and a colouring book, but always beside it was the *Rupert Bear Annual* or its eventual replacement, the *Eagle Annual.* On Christmas morning, I took my stocking into my parents' bedroom and crawled into the bottom of their bed, where I was given their present to me and those from my Cole relatives.

Except for one year, when my grandmother was recovering from her cancer operation, Christmas Day was always spent at my Rollesby grandparents' house in the company of my Miller aunts, uncles and cousins, often fifteen or more in number. The party started at eleven in the morning with "the Sack", a tradition whereby all the family presents were placed inside one or two mailbags and drawn out one by one to be distributed by my grandmother. After all the presents had been handed out, opened and carefully inspected by everyone, the mess was cleared away and the table set for lunch. Often, to accommodate the numbers, two or more tables were placed end to end. Christmas lunch was always turkey, reared at Great-aunt Nellie's farm in Fleggburgh, with the usual trimmings, including the brussels sprouts that I hated, followed by Christmas pudding and brandy sauce. The pudding had to be eaten with care as included in its contents were a number of silver threepenny pieces and good luck charms. Those finding one in their portion were rewarded with a prize. We were certainly lucky that nobody ever swallowed or choked on any of these treasured and annually used silver items.

After lunch, the men retired to another room and spent the afternoon sleeping, and playing crib or poker dice. The women washed up, chatted and began preparing tea, while the children were left to play with their presents or to annoy the men. Christmas tea was taken at 5p.m. and was as much a feast as was the lunch: sandwiches of ham, tongue, salmon and pressed beef were followed by jelly and blancmange, eaten with brown bread, then jam tarts, mince pies, chocolate log and various kinds of fancy cakes, finished off with a compulsory slice of Christmas cake. After a sufficient period to clear up and recover, the games began. Grandmother Miller was marvellous at organising and inventing games and we were all expected to join in. Reluctance on the part of some disappeared once the Christmas drinks began to take effect, always sherry, port or whisky, soft drinks for the children, but rarely ever beer or cider. In those days no one had heard of lager.

The games were many and varied, getting sillier and louder as the evening progressed, and as the sherry, port and whisky bottles emptied. Usually we started with a version of pass-the-parcel, each unwrapping revealing a forfeit requiring the victim to sing a song or tell a joke. Spin-the-wheel was a favourite with me and my cousins. A pointer was fixed to a board and was spun round like one hand of a clock. Around the board were placed prizes or money. Everybody took turns to spin the pointer, trying to spin it so that it would stop when aiming at a prize, which then became theirs. The game continued until all the prizes were won. At other times we hunted for rubber bands hidden around the house, played lotto — the 1940s and 1950s version of bingo, a game of chance popular with the forces during the war — betted on a card game called Newmarket, sang songs and played riotous games of charades. Grandmother Miller was good at inventing participation games based on a storyline which everyone was expected to experience, usually suffering in the process. Grandmother and her assistants, often in fancy dress, would set up a scene in another room while we waited to become, one-by-one, her latest victim. As these stories were normally scary, we children usually helped Grandmother or watched in amazement, as it was the adults who were to be the victims. One story that I remember involved a torch shining through a sheet held vertically in a darkened room. After various initiation rites, the victim was told to follow the sun with their nose until they reached the sea. Obediently, every victim followed the torch to the edge of the sheet where they were smacked in the face with a sponge soaked in cold water. Another story required a blindfolded victim to kiss the high priest; they were actually guided to kiss Grandmother's fleshy bent arm. The blindfold was immediately removed so that the victim could see me pretending to pull up my trousers. Great-aunt Elsie was thoroughly convinced that she had been made to kiss my bottom, and spent at least an hour washing her face and rinsing out her mouth, while everyone else collapsed in hysterical laughter. The evening ended at about 11.00p.m. with cheese, biscuits, celery and tea.

On Boxing Day, the party moved to our house where we entertained not only all the Millers but also many of Mother's family from Great Yarmouth. Grandma Cole always came and stayed for a few days, sleeping in my bed, while other visiting aunts and uncles occasionally stayed over, especially Aunt Edie and Uncle Frank Hammond who had no car. I would be relegated to sleep on the front room sofa. Not that this was a hardship as the sofa was comfortable and the room was warm, much warmer than my unheated bedroom in the depth of winter. The front room fire spluttered constantly and gave out a comforting glow for most of the night.

Our party followed a similar pattern to that of Christmas Day, with some variations. Mother's tea was famous for her home-made cakes and custard trifle. Mother was an expert cake baker and her Christmas table was laden with currant buns, angel cakes, Bakewell tarts, gingerbreads, Norfolk shortcakes, vanilla slices, mince pies, jam tarts in which the jam had been cooked to toffee, jam sponges and macaroons, and in the centre on a tall glass stand, her home-made Christmas cake. Throughout the year, we were never without a cake or bun to eat as a snack as Mother really enjoyed baking. After tea, we again played games, but the evening always included a sing-song. Aunt Eve was an accomplished pianist and could play most of the favourite songs of the day, which we all sang at the tops of our voices. We also provided actions to accompany some of the songs, bobbing up and down while singing "Sons of the sea", waving our our arms about to "I saw the old homestead" and shaking parts of our bodies to the "Hokey-Cokey". Occasionally pairs danced around the room as she played waltz music on our often out-of-tune front room piano. Uncle Billy Parnell was a fine harmonica player, and when he came to the party he took his turn at entertaining the gathering. In my late teens I learned to play the ukulele-banjo and the guitar, and I too was expected to do my bit, giving adequate renditions of the songs of George Formby and Lonnie Donegan. The party was repeated yet again on New Year's Eve at Aunt Doris and Uncle Cecil's house, despite the fact that Uncle Cecil, used to early morning starts as a postmaster, usually slept through most of the evening, including the musical interlude. When Grandmother Miller died in 1957, Aunt Doris took over Christmas Day duties.

The next party after Christmas and New Year was usually held on 14 February, Valentine's Day, when we all went to Grandmother Miller's house for tea. After tea we waited for Jimmy Valentine to call, a tradition restricted apparently to East Anglia where presents were left on the doorstep for those inside, heralded by a loud knocking on the door. When we children asked who had left them, we were always told "Jimmy Valentine". Other parties were organised throughout the year, particularly when relatives came on a visit;

George and Eve Miller from London to Rollesby, and Arthur and Stanley Cole with their families from Birmingham to Great Yarmouth. At Rollesby, summer parties were usually held outside with tea taken in the open air on long trestle tables and afterwards we played games of bowls, clock golf or badminton on the lawn.

I only ever had one birthday party, a party to celebrate my eighth birthday. Mother suggested that I might like to invite four or five children from school to come for tea. Unfortunately my concept of four or five was suspect and seventeen children arrived, luckily with one or two parents to help. From conversations with other parents, Mother had become aware of my generosity and had prepared accordingly, although seventeen was even more than she had expected. From a child's point of view, the party was excellent. I received seventeen small gifts from my guests, and we ate everything on the table and more. From Mother's point of view it was a headache as, despite valiant attempts to organise party games, the house was full of children barely under control and the noise was deafening. At 7.30p.m. my guests were collected and peace returned. The only damage was a rip in the front room sofa, caused when it was being used as a trampoline. My father was sensible; he worked overtime until it was all over. However, from then on, birthday parties were never mentioned.

CHAPTER
EIGHT

Sport & Leisure

VILLAGE ACTIVITIES

Despite being a relatively isolated rural community, there was always plenty to entertain everyone in either Rollesby or the neighbouring villages a short bike ride away, in winter as well as summer. Rollesby itself had numerous sports and social clubs: the darts and bowls clubs at the Horse & Groom public house, the Old Peoples' and Ladies' Social Clubs held in the hut, and, particularly during the 1950s, the highly successful cricket and football clubs based at King George's playing field. Although Rollesby was without a purpose-built village hall, all the adjoining villages had active institutes where regular whist drives, film shows and dances were held.

From about the age of ten, being a fairly proficient card player, I accompanied my parents and grandparents to local whist drives, mainly at Ormesby, Fleggburgh and Martham. Most of the whist drives were organised to raise funds for village clubs, national charities or special events.

Grandmother Miller was a keen supporter of St Dunstan's — a charity for the blind — and organised regular fund-raising whist drives on their behalf at Little Ormesby village hall. Most whist drives were very well supported and it was not uncommon for a hundred or more players to be in attendance. Men and women of all ages took part — young and old, expert and novice, some playing to win, others treating the game as a social occasion and frequently infuriating the better players by their casual attitude. One of the most popular whist drives in our area was the annual Christmas Drive at Martham Institute, a long, low, wooden building near to the green on the Winterton Road. Most of the prizes were donated, but at the Martham Christmas Drive the donations were very generous, the winner usually receiving a turkey. There was always a draw with many prizes — few of the hundred or more players went home with nothing. As my father was a keen local footballer, I can remember attending a drive in Caister in aid of a young footballer who had been seriously injured in a football match. The attendance was so great that the organisers had difficulty accommodating them.

248 at Whist Drive

The stage, balcony and ante-room were all brought into use at Caister Community Hall on Monday evening to accommodate the capacity crowd of 248 players at the Whist Drive in aid of Mr George Seabroke, a member of Caister Football Club, who broke his leg during a Christmas week game. Mr J. H. Brown was MC and three players tied with a top score of 180, and the first prize ultimately went to Mrs E. Benton of Caister.

"Village News: Caister",
Yarmouth Mercury, 23 February 1951

Many local institutes held monthly film shows and I regularly attended performances at Great Ormesby and Martham. Film shows at the Martham Institute were held on a Thursday evening, when Tony and I would walk the 1½ miles, winter and summer, rain or shine, to join an excited audience waiting for the show to begin. At one end of the function room, nearest the door, was the projector, at the other a square white screen, and in between were about twenty rows of chairs with a central gangway. The front rows were reserved for the very young who fidgeted and shouted out incessantly throughout the performance, occasionally silenced by a reprimand from their parents sitting behind them. The middle rows were usually designated for adults and the back two rows were filled with courting couples waiting for the lights to go out. The show began with cartoons, which were greeted with cheers and laughter, followed by the main film which usually ran for 1½ hours, provided that the film did not break or the projector bulb fuse. Both happened with some regularity and, consequently, the performance normally overran its allotted time. The only film that I saw at Martham that has left a lasting imprint on my memory was about Scott of the Antarctic. I have no memories of any films that I saw at Ormesby, possibly because I only began attending their shows in my late teens when I usually sat in one of the back two rows entwined around a female companion.

Every Friday or Saturday evening, it was always possible to attend a dance or social at one of our neighbouring village halls or institutes. Dances were mainly targeted at the grown-ups in the community, although they were particularly well attended by younger unmarried adults as they provided an excellent opportunity for meeting members of the opposite sex. My parents were very good dancers and had taught me the moves for most dances in our living room. From the age of fifteen, I attended a dance almost every week, enjoying both the twirls and intricacies of the different dances and the excuse to hold a female in my arms. Unfortunately, at the age of fifteen, that female was more likely to be my mother, an aunt, a novice girl dancer who had little respect for my toes, or an older woman who had taken sympathy on a young boy on his own, or occasionally, an older woman who enjoyed holding on to a younger male.

Our dances were still old-fashioned ballroom dances where we performed the waltz, foxtrot and quickstep, interspersed with novelty dances such as the cha-cha, the valeta, the Gay Gordons and the St Bernard's Waltz. Rock 'n' roll and jive had made little impact on village dances, only becoming an alternative to the quickstep in the very late 1950s. However, I was very good at jiving and became a popular partner for aspiring boppers, although I regretted the lack of opportunity for holding on to my more attractive partners. The music for our dances was normally provided by small local bands, made up, more often than not, from village musicians. In our area, the most successful local band of the 1950s was Eddie Bates and his Accordion Band, a group of musicians from Rollesby and the surrounding villages. Occasionally, when no live band was available, the music was provided by dance-band gramophone records played on a radiogram, a much quieter forerunner of the disco. The treat of the evening was the Excuse-me Waltz, where males and females could take over from another to dance with a selected victim by tapping their partner on the shoulder and saying "Excuse me". There was always a queue to dance with the best-looking female in the room, and I found that no sooner had I taken over as the partner of this fortunate lady than someone else was tapping on my shoulder and saying "Excuse me". By eighteen, I was competing with other eighteen-year-olds to dance with the best-looking females in all dances, not just the Excuse-me Waltz. At eighteen, I preferred to be blessed with an attractive partner for the last waltz of the evening, a smoochy finale to the proceedings.

Socials, or social evenings, were similar to dances but designed to provide entertainment for the whole family, from the youngest child to the oldest grandparent. Most of the evening would be taken up with dancing interspersed with guest entertainers or party games. Many of the games involved kissing and were keenly contested by the teenage element, in particular a game called Twilight. Men and women were divided into two teams and each team member was given a number. The game then involved one member from a team spinning a disc, usually a wooden chair seat or a drinks tray, and calling out a number. The member of the opposite team with that number had to catch the spinning disc before it fell to the ground. If the disc was successfully fielded, then the catcher would spin it again and call out a number belonging to the first team. If he or she failed then the spinner would allocate a forfeit — the type of forfeit obviously depended on whoever it was for. Forfeits for good-looking males or females frequently involved kissing somebody.

Other games involved two or more teams in novelty races. Teams formed lines, alternately male and female, and the race involved either passing a balloon from one end of the line to the other as quickly as possible without using one's hands, or passing a matchbox down the line from nose to nose, or even an orange held underneath the chin from chin to chin. One memorable game for mixed teams involved passing a key attached to a long piece of string along the line, on the way passing down each man's trousers and out through the bottom of their trouser leg, then down through the neck and out at the bottom of the next woman's dress. Once each team's key had reached the end of the line, alternately down a trouser and down a dress, the competition was to pull the key back to the start in the quickest possible time, with the inevitable risk to each participant's modesty. Frequently, the key caught on an item of underwear and needed releasing, the contortions involved in this process exhorting great hilarity from the watchers. Most of the ladies in the team concentrated hard on holding down their skirts or holding up their necklines as the string got tighter, while most of the males were concentrating hard on the prospect of a glimpse of female flesh that males did not normally glimpse. In addition to the games, refreshments were sold, usually tea, soft drinks and cakes, and there was the inevitable prize draw. Occasionally a bar was provided selling alcoholic drinks, but not always. When there was no bar, many of the men would be conspicuous by their absence in the early part of the evening. Towards the end of the dance, many young couples were also conspicuous by their absence, preferring to spend the last few minutes outside in the dark.

In the summer it was possible to dance every night of the week at the Eel's Foot Inn, just over the bridge into Little Ormesby. This Broad-side public house was a popular stopover for evening coach tours from Great Yarmouth, and visitors to the inn were musically entertained in an old green corrugated iron boathouse next to the jetty which had been converted into a dance hall. Most evenings an organ player, and at weekends a dance band, serenaded visiting coach parties and other drinkers with a sing-song or music to dance to. Along with many other local teenagers, I was a regular early evening visitor to the Eel's Foot, improving my dancing skills at a time when I should have been doing my school homework.

Every August, the annual Horticultural Show and church fete was held on the playing field, a well-attended event that most of us looked forward to and participated in with some degree of enthusiasm. Each year, the fete was officially opened by a village dignitary or, occasionally, a guest celebrity from Great Yarmouth who gave an opening speech while standing on the back of a farm trailer. Part of the field closest to the entrance gate was used as a car park although, in the 1940s and 1950s, most people arrived on foot or on bicycles which were left stacked against the fence, often two or three deep. As a churchwarden's wife, my grandmother was heavily involved with organising the fete and usually spent most of the afternoon overseeing the sale of teas and cakes in the hut. As well as refreshments, entries for the garden produce, painting and handicraft competitions were also laid out on tables erected inside the hut.

Between the hut and the ladies' toilet two lines of stalls were usually sited, where visitors were encouraged to buy various items or to try their luck at a competition or two. There was always a white elephant stall selling unwanted household items and an extremely popular stall selling home-made cakes and jam. Prizes were awarded for the man and woman with the highest score at darts or skittles; a play-off took

238

place at the end of the fete if there was a tie. Visitors were encouraged to buy tickets for a prize draw, to guess the name of a doll or to state how many dried peas there were in a glass jar. Apple bobbing in a bath of cold water, attempting to throw ping-pong balls into a metal bucket or throwing hoops over a stick challenged everyone's skill. My favourite game involved rolling a penny down a chute on to a grid covered in squares. An amount of money was indicated in each square and if your penny landed completely inside without cutting or touching any side, then the amount stated was given as a prize. Unfortunately, the squares were so small that this very rarely happened.

Throughout the afternoon, various competitions and events took place on the rest of the field. The early part of the afternoon was usually given over to competitions for children — competitions to find the most beautiful baby, the best fancy dress, the most original head-dress or the best decorated bicycle. As the prizes were usually money prizes, these competitions were keenly contested. I can only remember ever winning a prize once, in a fancy dress competition when I went dressed as Professor Jimmy Edwards of *Whacko*. After the competitions came various races for different age groups including egg-and-spoon, sack, and three-legged, as well as conventional running races. One year there were even cycle-speedway races. The day normally ended with an adult event, usually a ladies-versus-men cricket match where the men had to bat and bowl left handed. In the evening, a social was held in the school or at the Little Ormesby Village Hall.

In 1953, the fete was held in June to celebrate the coronation, at which I, along with all the children in the village, was given a commemorative mug.

Rollesby's celebrations

Despite a heavy shower, the sports programme at Rollesby was carried through by the committee and its chairman (Mr S.I. Gaze). The celebrations were opened by Mrs Gascoign and prayers and the National Anthem were led by the Rector (the Rev. H. Gascoign). This was followed by a fancy dress parade for children and adults. Messrs Evans, Barber and Carter were among the prize-winners.

After tea, Lieut-Col and Mrs I.B.H. Benn were thanked for the souvenir mugs which they presented to all the children. Refreshments were provided throughout the evening which was taken up with a social at which the MC was Mr R. Attew. Music for dancing, games and songs was provided by Messrs W. Allard and H. Haynes.

Yarmouth Mercury, 5 June 1953

In 1957 I joined the Martham branch of the Young Conservatives, not that I was in any way committed to Conservative politics. I became a Young Conservative as my friend Tim was the local branch secretary and because membership gave free access to a tennis court in Martham. Apart from football and cricket, sports facilities in rural areas were limited and any means for gaining access to those that were available was acceptable. I was not a brilliant tennis player. My serve was fast but rarely landed in court. My father and Grandmother Miller had been good tennis players and played in competitions before the war when Rollesby had its own tennis courts close by the church. Grandmother had given me her old tennis racket to play with, a revolutionary racket for the time with the frame made from lightweight aluminium strung with wire strings. In all honesty I must admit that I became a Young Conservative because of my liking for Martham's vicar's daughter who played tennis in exceedingly revealing costumes.

THE FOOTBALL AND CRICKET CLUBS

In my late teens, along with most of Norfolk, I became an enthusiastic supporter of Norwich City Football Club — the Canaries — following in detail the accounts of their exploits in the *Pink 'Un* and the daily newspapers. However, on Saturdays I chose to play football for Rollesby and my school rather than join the thousands of supporters travelling to Carrow Road, although I did accompany Uncle Cecil to many of City's midweek home games. The excitement was most intense during the 1958–9 season, when Norwich, then a third division side, reached the semi-final of the FA Cup eventually losing to Luton Town 1-0 in a replay, having beaten the mighty Manchester United 3-0 on the way. I can clearly remember that disastrous Wednesday afternoon, listening at home to the match on the radio having missed school on the pretext of a stomach bug. It must have seemed as if there was an epidemic as nearly half the school was absent that day! Mother had tears in her eyes when the final whistle sounded and Norwich lost, having had much the better of the game.

Yarmouth support for the Canaries

Another big exodus of Norwich City supporters from Yarmouth and district is due to take place tomorrow when the Canaries, in the semi-final of the F.A. cup for the first time in their history, play Luton Town, First Division Cup favourites, at Tottenham's White Hart Lane ground.

City's chance of being the first Division 3 club to reach the Final have continued to be the big talking point and semi-final tickets have changed hands at inflated prices at Yarmouth as in many other places. Up to £1 was being offered this week for a 2s 6d ground ticket. Many people were ready to pay more for the chance of seeing Norwich City make East Anglian sporting history by appearing in the semi-final.

One of nearly a score of special trains out of Norfolk for the match will run from South Town station and hundreds more supporters from East Norfolk will go by coach and car."

Yarmouth Mercury, 13 March 1959

Like all boys, I followed closely the fortunes of the English International side and the major teams in the first division, particularly Arsenal. I was also a great admirer of Stanley Matthews and can remember listening with my parents to the 1953 Cup Final when Matthews' club, Blackpool, came from behind to beat Bolton 4-3 in an exciting game, another highlight in the year of the coronation and one that featured regularly in many cinema newsreels. For a short time in 1958, along with many of my generation, I became a Manchester United sympathiser following the tragic crash of their team's aircraft in Munich.

As both my father and Uncle Cecil were keen sportsmen, it is not surprising that I have clear memories of Rollesby's football and cricket clubs. As a young man, my father was an accomplished footballer, captaining the East Flegg Boys at the age of 13 and playing in distinguished company for Gorleston Juniors until the age of 18. In Birmingham, he played for Hearts Old Boys in the West Midlands League and was approached by Aston Villa with a view to playing professionally. Unfortunately for him, the war interrupted his progress and by the time he was demobbed in 1947, he was too old for anything other than local football. On his return home, apart from one season with Yarmouth Town Reserves, he played all his football for Rollesby until he eventually hung up his boots in 1956 at the age of 40. Uncle Cecil's sport was cricket in which he excelled as a spin bowler, his exploits earning him the nickname "Crafty", and in 1930 he was a founder member of the Rollesby Cricket Club. Cricket was his passion and during the summer all his spare time was spent mowing and marking out the pitch, organising the teams, writing reports and doing most of the other administrative tasks involved in match preparation. Luckily he was supported by his wife, Aunt Doris, who was equally enthusiastic about cricket and happy to prepare teas for home matches and act as official scorer at every game.

During the war, very little football or cricket was played locally as most of the young men of the village were away on war service. Once the war ended, both clubs were quickly reformed, the football club joining the reconstituted Flegg League for the 1946–7 soccer season, transferring to the Great Yarmouth and District League in September 1947. The cricket club resumed playing friendly matches in 1946 and eventually joined the local Beck Cricket League in the summer of 1950. During the 1940s and 1950s, both clubs played their matches at King George's playing field, using the hut as a changing room. The football season ran from September to the end of April, allowing cricket matches to be played from the beginning of May until the end of August, a mutually convenient arrangement that no longer exists. However, the fact that both teams used the same playing field did disadvantage the cricket club, because on a relatively small ground it was not possible to assign a designated space for exclusive use as a cricket square.

Mother loved watching football, so every Saturday during the soccer season we accompanied my father to his matches, both at home and away, come rain or shine. During the early 1950s, Rollesby had a large and enthusiastic following of possibly up to fifty or more regular supporters who gathered along the touchline to chat and gossip, as well as to give encouragement to the players. Mother always joined a group of players' wives and mothers close to the halfway line, while I joined the many children who were usually playing a game of their own behind the Main Road end goalposts. When we tired of playing, we often acted as ball boys behind one or other of the goals, fighting among ourselves for the honour of retrieving balls kicked into touch. While the game was in progress, four or five of us regularly lined up behind the goal net imitating the actions of the goalkeeper, diving or jumping as he dived or jumped pretending to save an opponent's shot. An attacking forward or a nervous penalty taker would be confronted not only by a defending goalkeeper but also by a line of grubby juveniles crouched ready behind the goal. After the match, my father and I returned home to wash off the mud from our legs and knees in our old tin bath, as there were no showers or hot water in the hut.

During the 1950-1 and 1951-2 seasons, Rollesby Football Club appeared in successive finals of the Norfolk Junior Cup, a prestigious countywide competition with the final played at Carrow Road, the home ground of Norwich City Football Club. This was a commendable achievement especially as all of the players and the trainer, with his sponge and pail, were from Rollesby, a village with only 500 inhabitants. A fund-raising effort among the team's local supporters enabled the club to purchase a new strip for the 1951 final consisting of white shirts with black collars and cuffs, black shorts and black and white hooped socks, earning Rollesby the nickname of "The Lilywhites". I can remember clearly the excitement engendered by the team's success in the competition and the expectation as we set off for one of the finals at Carrow Road. Three coaches from Bensley's of Martham arrived at the playing field to transport an excited band of one hundred or more supporters to Norwich. Mother had made a number of black and white rosettes which she distributed among the passengers on our coach. Everyone wore black and white rosettes, hats and scarves, or had banners exhorting "Up the Lilywhites" and "Come on Rollesby". I had been given a small wooden rattle which I twirled incessantly, undoubtedly driving everyone insane. Unfortunately, Rollesby's luck deserted them in each of the finals as they lost both, beaten by Costessey 5-2 in 1951 and Hevington 2-1 in 1952.

Beaten in Primary Cup Final.
Rollesby's bid fails

After sharing four goals with Costessey, their Norwich Business League opponents, with less than half an hour to go, Rollesby lost 5-2 in the final of the Norfolk Primary Cup at Carrow Road on Saturday evening. Rollesby are the second Yarmouth and District League club to fail in successive years.

Smith put Rollesby ahead early in the game but although they had the better of the play in the first half they failed to prevent Costessey equalising and then taking the lead. Rollesby got on terms again through Smith and were shaping promisingly when a badly timed back pass by one of their defenders gave Cannell, Costessey's left-winger, the chance to recover the lead.

Costessey, whose attack had plenty of punch in the middle, then went on to score two more goals. For Rollesby, R. Miller at centre-half was always prominent.

Yarmouth Mercury, 27 April 1951

With my father as my role model, I too developed some ability at football progressing through Rollesby's reserve team to become a regular first team player by the age of 18. At Yarmouth Grammar, I played senior football for South House and for the school, earning my full football colours in 1958. By the time I began playing for Rollesby Football Club, my father had assumed the role of reserve team captain, passing on his skills to a new generation of footballers. For a short time it was a pleasure for us both to be playing in the same team. Football occupied much of my sports time at Yarmouth Grammar, and regular matches against other schools were organised for Wednesday afternoons and Saturday mornings. The match that we all enjoyed the most was our annual visit to Wymondham College, a mixed boarding grammar school near Norwich, not especially for the football but for the fact that after the match we were given tea by the sixth form girls.

A big kick

Rollesby first team on Saturday were away to Ravens and, despite the last minute inclusion of four reserves, were beaten only 6-3. The reserves at home, despite the withdrawal of players to complete the first team, beat Caister Reserves 3-1, scorers being S. Evans, R. Miller and B. Harrison. Miller's goal was scored with a kick from the Rollesby goal area.

Yarmouth Mercury, 15 January 1954

In football, my father was a difficult act to follow, which might be the reason why I marginally preferred to play cricket. He also played cricket for Rollesby and was an opening fast bowler until he retired from the game after the 1956 summer season. As a batsman, he lacked technique but was exciting to watch as his sole intention was to hit every ball for six. Consequently, he was never long at the crease but, if he did manage to last more than a few balls, runs would come in abundance. One unforgettable moment occurred when, during one of his purple patches, he hit the ball high into the air, over the bushes and into the men's toilet in the far corner of the playing field. After falling through the open top of the toilet, the ball could be heard rattling round and round inside this corrugated iron structure. Seconds later, everyone collapsed in laughter at the sight of a red-faced man stumbling out of the toilet, shaking his fist and yelling obscenities, his trousers around his ankles and the ball clutched in his other hand. Recovering some of his composure, he then proceeded to hurl the offending ball as far as he could into the adjacent corn field before returning to complete his business in the toilet. Despite Uncle Cecil's careful tuition in the finer arts of cricket, my father's cavalier attitude must have had an effect as there was nothing more satisfying to me than watching a cricket ball that I had just hit soar over the boundary for six. Despite it being a team game, I also enjoyed cricket because individual performances often brought about the most unlikely of outcomes.

As a youth, I had my share of match turning performances, for example, when I scored 65 out of a total of 72 runs to help Rollesby Youth beat a confident Caister Youth side. At Yarmouth Grammar, I captained South House seniors in the 1959 House cricket final against North House, an end of term match tradition-ally watched by the whole school. Batting first on an uneven Beaconsfield pitch, under my command, South House were dismissed for a meagre 21 runs before rain stopped play. After lunch, the rain cleared and the match resumed without any school spectators, as the result seemed to be inevitable and hardly worth the walk to Beaconsfield. They actually missed a treat as the damp pitch well suited the bowling of Derek Bacon and me, and we restricted North House to a total of 17 all out to become house champions — although it was hard to convince an unbelieving school of this fact.

I was 17 when I scored my first half-century for Rollesby Cricket Club's first team, all the more satisfying as it was against our fiercest rivals, Martham, and at Martham's ground. Put into bat on a wet pitch, Rollesby were struggling on 25 for 5 when rain stopped play. At the cessation, I had just joined Mickey Cooper at the crease, where I was surrounded at every ball by a ring of glowering fielders. Naturally, with the break for rain, Rollesby saw an opportunity to save the situation by pushing for the game to be abandoned. Martham, on the other hand, scented a quick victory and insisted on holding out for the rain to stop. After an early tea, with the rain still falling, most of Rollesby's players gave up and went home. Luckily Mickey and I had stayed on, as the rain eventually stopped and the Martham captain insisted that we resumed our innings, although everyone except us two and Uncle Cecil had left. Mickey and I were given strict instructions to "Just stay there", as Uncle Cecil set off in his car to recall the rest of our team. This we did, blocking every ball and ignoring the taunts of the Martham players. By the time Mickey was out, Uncle Cecil had returned and joined me at the crease, where we saw Rollesby through to a total of 105 for 6 before another downpour brought an end to the game, my score of 54 not out being my first fifty in adult league cricket.

In the 1940s and 1950s, Rollesby played their home cricket matches at the playing field, which they shared with the football club. When the football season ended, a cricket square was established on part of the football pitch. Despite intensive heavy rolling, watering and mowing, it was not possible to eradicate all of the humps and bumps created in a season of competitive football. Consequently, during matches the batting pitch was covered by two strips of coconut matting, which had the effect of creating a consistent if slow batting surface and eliminating the possibility of an erratic and potentially dangerous bounce. Held in place by a dozen or more iron pins, this matting provided an adequate solution to a difficult problem. However, occasionally a wayward ball would hit one of the pins, ricocheting in an unpredictable manner and causing fielders and batsmen alike to scatter in an attempt to avoid injury or, as sometimes happened, deflecting the ball on to the stumps, much to the batsman's disgust. Without expensive gang mowers it was also difficult to maintain the outfield. The area occupied by the football pitch was usually devoid of grass, which left a bare uneven surface that often resulted in injuries to the fielders, as the ball frequently hit a bump and bounced

251

up as it was being collected, flattening noses, blacking eyes or running on to the boundary, much to the fielders' embarrassment. The rest of the outfield, the part that Uncle Cecil was unable to cut with his small petrol mower, grew so long that balls were frequently lost in the undergrowth, giving the batsmen an opportunity to score extra runs as the fielders frantically searched for it. I remember Mickey Cooper again taking a magnificent diving catch in this outfield, only to disappear in the long grass, his arm with the ball securely clasped in his hand appearing a few seconds later like a lighthouse out of a sea of green.

Our pitch was no different from those of many other teams in the district. During the war they had either been left unattended or dug up for food production, and, as a consequence, were in a poor condition throughout the 1940s and 1950s. Some, like the one at Seacroft Holiday Camp, the home pitch for Hemsby Cricket Club, had installed a concrete pitch as their answer to an uneven surface. Unfortunately, at Hemsby the concrete had sunk in the middle and the ball ended up on the stumps no matter where it was aimed by the bowler. Changing rooms were a luxury — I can clearly remember changing for one game in a cow shed, complete with fresh manure on the floor. A few local sides were lucky enough to have a designated square roped off in the parkland of their local manor house. However, in such cases the outfield was frequently a meadow where the grass was kept short by grazing cattle and cowpats were an ever present hazard. On many occasions, I retrieved a cricket ball from the middle of a cowpat, taking care not to spend time cleaning it if there was any chance of a run out. Apart from our whites, none of us owned any personal cricket equipment; the bats, pads and gloves that we wore belonged to the club and were contained in a large brown cricket bag. It was always a lottery as to what bat was available and whether the pads matched. Rollesby possessed only two abdominal protectors for preventing injury to a batsman's private parts. It was a common sight to see outgoing batsmen ferret inside their trousers to produce a protector for the new incoming batsman to use. I was not at all happy with this exchange and normally elected to bat without a protector. Besides, as I did not wear a strap to hold the protector, when I wore one it rarely stayed in place inside my pants and regularly slid down and out of the bottom of my trouser leg. I frequently maintained that batting without a protector improved my batting, as I needed to concentrate hard at all times. I was particularly lucky when the inevitable happened, as it was a slow bowler that rattled my private parts and took my breath away. Fearing what might have happened had it been a fast bowler, the next week I bought my own personal protector and never again batted without the security of wearing one.

My personal association with Rollesby Cricket Club had begun at about the age of ten when, encouraged by Aunt Doris and Uncle Cecil, I was put in charge of the scoreboard. On the occasions when visiting teams did not bring a scorer, I scored the opposition's score book under Aunt Doris's guidance. Being always available, it was inevitable that I would eventually be called on to field as a substitute when a player was injured, or to make up the numbers if the team was short. Consequently, I made my first appearance for Rollesby Cricket Club, albeit briefly, in 1953 at the age of 13. From then on I was hooked and played for Rollesby during a very successful period in the late 1950s when they became Beck League champions and won the Yarmouth Weekend League four times in succession. In my final season before university in 1959, the club moved from the playing field to their own exclusive cricket ground in the parkland of Rollesby Hall.

GREAT YARMOUTH

We were extremely lucky to have Great Yarmouth virtually on our doorstep as, apart from possessing the normal all year round leisure amenities of a large town such as cinemas, dance halls, sports arenas, restaurants and theatres, it also provided us with an opportunity to use the additional summertime entertainment facilities associated with a popular seaside resort of the 1950s.

Despite being neither a strong swimmer nor an enthusiastic sunbather, when visiting Great Yarmouth during the summer months I regularly spent an hour or two exploring the sights of Regent Road and Marine Parade between the Britannia Pier and the Pleasure Beach, or walking the shoreline searching for shells or flat stones to bounce on the incoming waves, sometimes with my mother, other times by myself. I can clearly remember the excitement when the first stretch of beach between the Britannia and Wellington Piers was cleared of mines after the war, and the crowds of men, women and children that arrived to sit on deckchairs or blankets to stare at the sea. By the late 1940s, most of the debris of war had been removed and Great Yarmouth was again fully functional as a holiday resort for working people, predominantly from the Midlands.

I enjoyed all the familiar beachside spectacles and facilities. The water gardens where I would run and play hide-and-seek with my mother around the paths and bridges that weaved through the ornamental canals, the two piers with their amusement arcades and end of pier theatres in which popular artists and comedians of the time appeared in summertime variety shows. Behind the theatres at the end of each pier, I often watched as fishermen tried their luck in the rough North Sea, occasionally interrupted by an exhibition of high diving by swimmers who launched themselves from various ladders and poles. Along the beachside promenade, wooden teashops with roofed over bench seats provided a convenient shelter in the event of rain, while the younger visitors were entertained by the Punch and Judy Show and the sand sculptures near to the Britannia Pier. On a fine summer's day, I spent many happy hours watching the antics of the holidaymakers playing bowls, tennis and crazy golf, sunbathing or cavorting around on the beach. I was always fascinated, and frequently disappointed, by the way that many female sunbathers could change from their everyday clothes into a bathing costume while covered only by a small beach towel without accidentally exposing any naked flesh. I had a few special places that as a teenager I visited whenever I could: a specific one-penny-a-go pinball machine that through weeks of practice I had learned how to play and could double my money almost every time I used it, an amusement arcade near to the Hippodrome where there was a juke box that always had the latest rock 'n' roll records, and Vetesee's ice cream parlour at the top of Regent Road selling great swirls of soft ice cream on top of a cone or inside two wafers, as well as Knickerbocker Glories and other fruit and ice cream creations.

Summer was a busy time for both my parents. My father was fully occupied at work in the building trade as well as tending the Field most evenings and at weekends, while mother's casual work was also at its peak. Consequently we did not have many opportunities as a family to avail ourselves of Great Yarmouth's holiday entertainment. We usually managed at least one visit to a variety show at the Britannia or Wellington pier, at various times enjoying contemporary entertainers such as Ronnie Ronalde, an extraordinary whistler, singer and yodeller, famous for his birdsong imitations, comedians Jimmy Jewell and Ben Warriss, and singer comedian Stan Stennett, who had me in stitches with his song about three cowboys Art, Bart and Fargo. I must have driven everyone mad by continually repeating these three names with a long emphasis on the "F" of Fargo. I enjoyed the comedy and novelty acts involved in these shows but derived little pleasure from listening to the male tenor and female soprano singers belting out strangled versions of popular arias from little known operas, often sung in a foreign language. For a fourteenth birthday treat I was taken to the Hippodrome, a permanent venue for a circus style entertainment, famous for the fact that half-way through the performance the ring flooded with water and transformed to provide a water-based spectacle complete with swimmers, fountains and performing seals. Sometimes I accompanied mother to the Marina, an open-air venue where, during the daytime, holidaymakers sat on rows of canvas chairs to listen to band music or to watch talent and bathing beauty contests.

It is probably true to say that, as a family, we used the entertainment facilities of Great Yarmouth more often in the winter than in the summer. During the off-season months, from September to May, Sunday afternoon car excursions regularly finished with a drive along the Great Yarmouth seafront from the North Denes to the South Denes, normally parking close to the harbour's mouth from where we watched the waves breaking on to the shore or against the sea wall, sometimes in spectacular fashion, or to follow the progress of distant ships through grandfather's binoculars. From the late 1940s, a small kiosk at the entrance to Wellington pier opened on Sundays throughout the year selling snacks and ice creams. On the coldest and stormiest winter days we often sat in the car looking at the view while eating choc ices. In September and October, we always drove along the river to marvel at the North Sea herring fleet during its annual visit to Great Yarmouth,

257

the trawlers moored all the way from the harbour's mouth to the Town Hall quay, usually three or four deep.

THE EASTER FAIR

Great Yarmouth's annual fair was held in the market place over the first Friday and Saturday after Easter, an event anticipated with great excitement by most of the children and teenagers within a 10-mile radius. For two days before the start of the festivities, convoys of gigantic lorries, each towing one or more trailers filled with the paraphernalia of the fairground, headed towards Yarmouth from all over the county, some of them fresh from the Easter Fair that had been held the previous weekend at Norwich cattle market. I often rushed up to the Horse & Groom crossroads to watch as a convoy of fairground vehicles rumbled noisily through the village, staring at the weather-beaten drives and wondering what it would be like to be one of the grubby children crammed inside the cabs or hanging out of its windows. We also knew that soon we were likely to be visited by women selling pegs or bundles of lucky heather. Mother always swore by these home-made pegs and bought some every year, although I think that she was also intimidated by the women and afraid that she might be cursed with bad luck if she bought nothing from them.

Every year without fail I joined the crowds flocking to enjoy the attractions of the fair usually, and for differing reasons, on a Friday. As a young child, I explored the stalls and attractions of the fairground with my mother, but as a teenager I toured the fairground with my male friends in search of excitement and girls. The fair occupied most of the market place and the two plains in front of Lacon's Brewery and the bomb-damaged St Nicholas's church. Only the permanent stalls remained at the top end of the market place, notably the fish and chip, confectionery and seafood stalls that did a roaring trade with the visiting fair goers. The main attractions were lined up along the centre of the market place. Usually one or two large roundabouts, waltzers, a cakewalk, dodgems and, in the centre, the Mat, a tower that dominated the middle of the fairground around which a smooth metal slide spiralled from top to bottom and down which children descended sitting on a small mat. On either side of these were sideshows where contestants tried their luck at hitting targets with darts or rifles, shied at coconuts or attempted to ring prizes with hoops, usually without success. Those that did succeed walked away with a coconut, a cuddly toy or a goldfish in a plastic bag filled with water. Scattered through the fairground were smaller rides for children, powered by an attendant turning a wheel. At the church end of the fair were ranks of swing boats and large highly decorated caravans, the living quarters of the fairground folk. In some of the caravans, elderly women read palms and predicted fortunes for sixpence a go. Novelty booths covered the Brewery Plain; one year the main attraction was a boxing booth where any challenger could try to box for three rounds with a resident fighter, if successful to be rewarded by a share of the entrance money. Naively I paid my entrance fee only to watch one challenger beaten to a bloody mess by the resident fighter and carried out of the ring after two rounds with no reward to justify the pain. Behind the stalls huge generators hummed continuously as they produced the electricity to drive the larger rides and illuminate the hundreds of coloured light bulbs that covered every roundabout and stall, linked by miles of thick black cables that snaked across the fairground, often tripping up unobservant visitors.

Mother insisted that I should not waste all my money at the fair, even if what I held in my purse or my pocket had been given to me for that purpose. As a child, before going to the fair, I was always taken to Woolworth's where I was made to buy a toy or a book so that I had something to take home with me at the end of the day. Even as a teenager and without Mother's influence behind me, this habit persisted and I always bought something I wanted, a record or an item of clothing, before spending any money at the fair. In truth, I spent very little at the fair, preferring to watch the antics of others and to save the remainder in my money box. As a teenager, I naturally spent more but then only as a means to an end. My first purchase was always a soft ball attached to the end of an elastic string. With my friends, we then moved to a high vantage point on one of the adult roundabouts from where we proceeded to bombard passing females with these balls in the hope of effecting an introduction, normally unsuccessfully, the usual response being a V-sign or an encouragement to "bugger off".

Fun and jollity at the Fair

For the children and very many grown-ups in Yarmouth there was only one road on Friday and Saturday — the road to the fair. People flocked from near and far and the question everyone asked was "are you going to the fair?"

Yarmouth fair was in town and every child was rushing and worrying to get there as fast as he or she could move. Money boxes were emptied, savings were drawn and house-keeping money was raided and all thoughts of saving were forgotten in the glamour of coloured lights, gaily coloured hats, monstrous balloons, yelling showmen and gay laughter of several thousand voices . . .

. . . A notable change at this year's fair was the number of coconut shies for until recently coconuts have been unobtainable . . .

. . . by 11 o'clock on Friday morning the larger part of the fair was in motion. Stall holders were inviting people to "Roll up" and try their luck amid the noise from loudspeakers and the crack of rifles from their shooting galleries. People doing their morning shopping felt the atmosphere of the fair creeping on them . . .

Yarmouth Mercury, 21 April 1950

The Cinema

Before we had television, going to the cinema was a regular event, normally once or even twice a week. During the 1940s and for most of the 1950s, Great Yarmouth had five cinemas to cater for the popularity of "the pictures": the Regal, Regent, Aquarium, Empire and Windmill, all conveniently spaced down Regent Road and opposite the seafront along Marine Parade between the two main piers. During the 1950s, the Windmill mostly showed cartoons and became a theatre performing live variety shows during the summer season. Each cinema had only one screen but could accommodate many hundreds of picture goers seated in the main auditorium or a large first floor balcony, called the upper circle. Each cinema's entrance was similarly designed with a short flight of concrete stairs topped with glass double-doors leading into a reception foyer. On one side of the foyer was a ticket kiosk and on the other, a refreshment counter selling drinks, confectionary, ice cream, popcorn and film magazines. To either side of the entrance doors were display cabinets containing information, posters and photographs about current and forthcoming films. From the foyer, central doors opened into the ground floor auditorium and, to either side, stairs led to the upper circle.

During the week, cinemas normally opened at midday, or 3.30p.m. on a Sunday, and the programmes started half an hour later. Most programmes began with adverts, trailers for forthcoming films, newsreels covering the main news stories of the time and, occasionally, a cartoon. These were followed by a "B picture", a cheaply produced short film that was more often than not a dramatisation of a real-life police investigation, and then the main feature film, usually with a ten minute interval before and after. At the Regal, customers were often entertained during intervals by music played on a brightly illuminated organ that seemed to rise up in front of the screen from under the floor. Usherettes also appeared in each gangway selling soft drinks and ice cream from a tray. A programme lasted between 3 and 3½ hours and was repeated three times during the day, twice on Sunday, the last show ending around 10.30p.m. Programmes were regularly changed, twice or even three times over the course of a week, one programme on Monday, Tuesday and Wednesday, the next on Thursday, Friday, Saturday and Sunday, or, periodically, a third separate Sunday only showing, catering for the different tastes of the cinema goers. We were not particularly excessive in our cinema going, unlike some, including my Yarmouth based Aunt Edie and Uncle Frank Hammond, who went to the pictures three or even four times every week.

Ticket prices varied: the upper circle seats were the most expensive, while those downstairs at the front were the cheapest. Tickets were not allocated to any particular seats, only to an area of the cinema; nor were customers prevented from entering or leaving at any time, many arriving even while a film was playing, others remaining in their seats to see the main film twice through. Our concentration was frequently broken by the squeaking of seats, people standing up and sitting down again as new customers attempted to locate a seat in their designated area in the darkness as a film was in progress, accompanied by grumbles and muttering from those around them. At busy times, customers were guided to empty seats by usherettes equipped with a torch. For the most popular films it was normal for queues to form outside as people waited for seats to become available or for a convenient interval. The usherettes regularly informed a uniformed commissionaire standing in the foyer about the location and availability of seats. The commissionaire, who was usually an ex-serviceman proudly displaying his service medals on his uniform and with responsibility for organising the waiting queues and for maintaining an orderly admission, passed on this information in parade ground manner by barking out details such as "queuing only for the one-and-nines, two pairs in the two-and-sixes, no waiting for the two-and-threes". The usherettes would also use their torches to ensure that there was no inappropriate behaviour in the cinema, particularly between the couples who occupied the rear seats.

Before my father returned home from army service, Mother and I went to the pictures every Wednesday and Saturday after she had finished her shopping in Great Yarmouth, the first programme conveniently ending in time for the 4.15p.m. bus home to Rollesby. My memories are of comedies and lavish American musicals, with Old Mother Riley and George Formby coming readily to mind. When my father came home in 1947, Saturdays were devoted to cricket and football although Mother continued to visit the cinema every Wednesday afternoon. Occasionally during my early teens, we went to the cinema as a family on a Friday night, mostly to see dramas about wartime heroics or popular comedies, especially those featuring Bob Hope and Bing Crosby, Norman Wisdom and James Robertson Justice in the *Doctor* film series. In 1954, we joined the long queues outside the Aquarium to see *The Robe* in the newly installed wide-screen Cinemascope. We also each donned a pair of red and green glasses at the Regent to watch *The Charge at Feather River* in 3D, ducking with the rest of the audience to avoid arrows, spears and a striking rattlesnake. My parents stopped going to the cinema on a regular basis in 1957 when they bought their first television set, although I continued to enjoy film going, particularly when I had a companion on my arm.

At the age of ten, I became an ABC minor and every week at 10a.m. I attended a Saturday morning film club for children at the Regent Cinema while mother did her shopping, my tin ABC minor's badge clipped firmly to my jacket lapel. For an entrance fee of sixpence I, along with a hundred or more noisy companions, was entertained to a two-hour film programme consisting of cartoons, a serial featuring a children's hero — at various times Tarzan, Hopalong Cassidy or Buck Rogers — and a one-hour adventure film. Before the start of the programme an MC, usually the manager of the cinema, would take the stage in front of the screen to organise games, to extend birthday congratulations and to lead the singing of the ABC minors' song. Despite his entreaties and threats of expulsion, these activities were always accompanied by whistles, shouts and requests to "start the blooming films", a semblance of order returning only when the lights dimmed and the first film commenced accompanied by cheers from the whole auditorium.

By the age of fifteen, I was too old for the ABC minors, and preferred to join the older village teenagers who, on winter Sundays, caught the early afternoon bus to Great Yarmouth to spend the rest of the day at the pictures. Gangs of teenage boys and girls would giggle and make eyes at each other on the bus, occasionally pairing off, but more often than not remaining in their single sex groupings and enjoying the outing as a crowd rather than as independent doubles. Normally, the trip involved attending the 4p.m. performance at one of the cinemas and meeting up afterwards at 7.30 for a fish and chip supper before catching the 9.05 bus home. I can remember clearly my first trip with the Sunday gang. My companions had decided to see an adult only classified film at the Regent in the hope that it might be "smutty" or include some "blood and guts". Being only fifteen, I was concerned that I would not be allowed in to see the film or, worse still, that its contents might be too extreme for my sensibilities. At fifteen I was still rather naive about some matters and excess horror gave me nightmares. Consequently, I broke off from the group and went on my own to the Empire where, to my surprise, I was admitted to see an A-classified film starring Debbie Reynolds entitled *Susan Slept Here*, which I enjoyed immensely. The adult film had been a disaster for my intended companions, meeting neither of their hoped-for criteria, and I managed to regain some respect on the return bus journey by recounting the story of my film, albeit as a distortion of the truth, giving my account an X-, rather than an A-rated slant.

SPORTING EVENTS

Of all the entertainments that Great Yarmouth could provide, my parents preferred sporting events. We frequently sat in the stands at the Wellesley Road ground to watch the Yarmouth football team play in the Eastern Counties League or to support their brief campaigns in the preliminary rounds of the FA Cup. My father's absolute favourite was horse racing and he regularly finished work at lunchtime so that he could attend a race meeting at the Great Yarmouth racecourse. Every day without fail he studied form in the racing pages of the *Daily Express*, whose tipster, the Scout, he always followed. Immediately after lunch on a Saturday, he walked to the Horse & Groom where he was able to place a bet with a shady looking gentleman who toured the villages in a car collecting wagers. As my tenth birthday treat, we all stayed in Great Yarmouth at Aunt Edie and Uncle Frank's house in Tottenham Road so that I could be taken to the Bank

Holiday horse race meeting in the afternoon and to the dog racing at the Caister Road Stadium in the evening. This turned out to be a real, if unexpected, treat as Uncle Frank, who was an excellent cake maker, had made me a birthday cake decorated as a basket containing chocolate eggs, and most of my selections at both the horse and dog race meetings won. To keep me involved, mother had placed a sixpenny wager on each of my selections and we went home with a pocket full of money while the rest of the party had glum faces — beginner's luck, no doubt.

In 1948, the Caister Road Stadium became the home venue for Great Yarmouth's speedway team. I attended a number of times with my Aunt Doris from Rollesby, who was a fanatical speedway follower. I was not particularly enthused by this noisy spectacle but enjoyed immensely collecting badges in the colours of the different teams and photographs of the various team members. Every time Aunt Doris went to the speedway, I tried to be at her house when she returned in the hope that she had brought back a badge or photograph to add to my collection. For a while speedway was extremely popular and some of the riders, like Billy Bales, became part of local folklore. If ever I was in a hurry, mother would always ask, "Who do you think you are, Billy Bales?" Eventually, as interest waned, speedway was replaced by stock car racing, a spectacle that I found far more entertaining. On many Tuesday evenings during my late teens, I stood on the terraces at the Caister Road Stadium watching the races, being excited by the many and often spectacular collisions, singing loudly to the latest pop songs blaring out from the speakers around the venue and sizing up the female talent that always attended in abundance. I have one abiding memory from 1956 of standing alone at the Caister end of the stadium singing almost tearfully to the Frankie Lymon hit "Why do fools fall in love?", at the end of one teenage relationship.

For a while, in the early 1950s, my parents were regular spectators at the outdoor roller skating rink in the gardens next to the Wellington Pier. Among the members of Great Yarmouth's roller skating club were a number of national individual and pairs skating champions, including Frank Martin, Jocelyn Taylor, Howarth Hargreaves and Sheila Wilkinson. Under their direction, the club mounted shows of skating under the title "Skaterscades" which we attended on a regular basis. These included exhibitions of roller dancing, team and individual skating displays and comedy items with clowns on skates. Inspired by these spectacles, I bought a pair of roller skates which were attached by leather straps to the underside of my shoes. My achievements were limited as I never mastered the art of turning or stopping, and frequently my legs would move in opposite directions with the inevitable result. In no time at all, my attempt to become a national skating champion was abandoned and the skates were consigned to the rear of my toy cupboard.

CHAPTER
NINE

Manners, Beliefs & Teenage Culture

MANNERS

In many respects at 19 years of age I was a man, a thinking independent human being and a product of my upbringing; in other respects I still maintained the naivety of a child. My time at grammar school had given me the strategies to survive in any social environment, despite the insecurities inherent in coming from a working-class background. Yet growing up in a small self-contained village community where everybody and everything had its place and purpose and where differences, even privilege, were accepted as a fact of life, meant that I was totally unprepared for university and urban living where everybody and everything had an opposition and change was an objective. I cannot say that I held any strong beliefs about anything, and saw positive aspects in all and even the most extreme viewpoints. I frequently allowed those whom I thought more knowledgeable and capable than I to make my

270

choices for me, and often the views I expressed were those that I felt were acceptable to my teachers, parents or peers rather than any that I adhered to with conviction. I remember that as part of my general studies in the sixth form, I was asked to prepare a talk on the characteristics of communism. The research for the talk I found extremely interesting and it raised many questions in my mind, although it did not in any way convert me to a belief in communism. The talk that I gave, however, was the talk that I naively thought that I was expected to give. In the late 1950s, communist Russia was generally seen as a threat to world peace and the politics of communism a threat to democratic society. My family were strongly anti-communist, particularly Grandfather who advocated that Russia should have been next after Hitler's Germany. As I recall, the conclusion to my talk was that a communist was a person who had nothing of his own but was willing to share in another person's wealth. I was quite surprised to find that this was not the conclusion that was expected from me by the young teacher who set the question.

Undoubtedly my parents had the most influence on my personal development, particularly my mother. Mother had a motto or wise saying for almost every eventuality. Indeed Mother lived her life guided by mottos and these were engrained into my psyche. An often recited favourite was that "manners maketh man". According to Mother, a gentleman was someone with perfect manners and, consequently, she

271

always emphasised the importance of good manners, possibly in the hope that the converse was also true and that with the acquisition of good manners I might become a gentleman. Nevertheless, it soon became clear to me that, at every level of society, people did respond positively to good manners and, together with a friendly smiling disposition, they were a means of establishing good interpersonal relationships and helped to achieve desired goals. Both my parents were insistent on proper table manners and I was constantly reminded not to bolt my food, to close my mouth when eating and never to talk when my meal was on the table. I was never allowed to use my fork as a spoon. All my food had to be eaten off the back of my fork, even peas, and even those hard bullet-like processed peas that came in tins and tasted nothing like the squashy fresh peas brought back from the Field. Normally we ate our main meal of the day together at the table and never on our knees, even when we eventually acquired a television set, although then we frequently ate with one eye on the screen.

Most of the manners instilled in me by my mother were essentially the dos and don'ts of behaviour in society. Children should be seen and not heard, and should only talk in adult company if asked a question. Females, particularly adult women, were to be treated with respect. I should always open the door for a lady, give up my seat on a bus or in a room if no seat was available for a lady to sit on, and never call a married woman by her first name

272

but always refer to her as Mrs So-and-so. Some people warranted special deference. The doctor, vicar, the village policeman and school teacher, usually male, were always to be called "sir", and I was expected to touch or lift my cap on meeting any of the important or "better off" members of our village society. Certain behaviours were regarded as unacceptable — only the lowest-of-the-low used swear words, women who smoked in the street were common and those who kissed or showed affection in public were "loose". I cannot ever recollect either of my parents swearing. I can recollect receiving a backhander for using the word "blooming".

Another of mother's frequent sayings was "spare the rod and spoil the child", not that either of my parents used a rod, cane or slipper to discipline bad behaviour. Indeed I was rarely smacked and when I was it was on the back of my legs, and I have no doubt that it was well deserved. Nor have I any recollection that my friends or cousins were treated any more harshly. Nevertheless, discipline at home was strict. I was kept under a tight rein and taught never to question my elders and betters. Father was the disciplinarian and had an authoritative manner, undoubtedly as a result of being a sergeant in the army. What he said went; if he said "no" he meant no and never changed his mind. I never had the courage to question any of his decisions or criticisms of my behaviour, even in my late teens. On the other hand, Mother I regarded as a soft touch, a loving person who would frequently succumb to gentle persuasion. Only once can I ever remember her losing her temper with me when I was a small child, so unlike the mother I was used to that I ran away and hid under the hedge behind the outside toilet. I must have stayed there for at least half an hour before my red-eyed mother appeared, back to her old self again, to give me a reassuring cuddle. Although this event was never repeated, it taught me to be a bit more careful and never to push things too far. Usually Mother would try to exert discipline by a combination of psychological blackmail and appealing to a higher authority. "If you really love your mother", "I don't know what your father is going to say", or "The policeman will come and lock you up" were all phrases often used in her attempts to stop me being naughty or to persuade me to do something I didn't want to do. As a result, I was nervous at the sight of a policeman's uniform and always felt guilty at the appearance of our local constable, even if I had done nothing wrong.

VILLAGE SOCIETY

Within our village population there were many different social and professional groupings that formed a well-defined hierarchy, from the landowners, wealthy farmers and others at the top to the agricultural labourer at the bottom. It was an accepted fact of life that some people lived in big houses and warranted special respect while others were crammed into council houses and tied cottages. Yet, on the whole, there was little obvious antagonism or resentment between these different groups and each had their duties and responsibilities to the community which most accepted and performed to the best of their ability. Undoubtedly, some of those at the top of the hierarchy were rather pompous and self-opinionated, while others worked hard on behalf of the community and were well respected and even loved. For those at the bottom, life was not easy, but most, like my parents, were content and worked hard to achieve the goals that they set for themselves. I am sure that, as ordinary working parents, it was not easy for them to support a child in fulltime education until the age of nineteen.

Although most villagers kept to their own social group for their regular leisure activities, everyone played their part in everyday village activities: as parish councillors, school governors, playing field committee members and in organising annual and special events such as the village fete, school treats and the cricket and football club dinners. While the better off were normally elected as presidents and chairmen of the various village societies and clubs, they not only showed their commitment by opening fetes, presenting prizes and giving speeches at the annual dinners but also in financial sponsorship, without which many clubs would have been unable to function.

As a teenager, I found that many factors inhibited my ability to mix with other young people from a different social background. As a result of my friendship with Richard, I was introduced to a young woman, the daughter of a local industrialist, whose company I enjoyed immensely. One Saturday I accidentally met her in Yarmouth on a shopping expedition when we spent a pleasant hour or so chatting over coffee. She then asked me to join her for lunch, an offer I could not refuse, although, being an emergent gentleman, it was inevitable that I should pay the bill. She then invited me back to her house for the afternoon, which turned out to be an immense Victorian country mansion surrounded by acres of parkland, where we talked and listened to the Chris Barber jazz record that I had bought that morning. Eventually, she asked where I intended to take her for the evening, at which request I had to excuse myself by declaring that I was otherwise engaged, as the cost of the lunch had used up all my week's entertainment allowance. It became immediately clear to me that, no matter how attractive the person, I did not have the means to compete for daughters of wealthy industrialists.

In common with most of the rural electorate my parents professed a preference for the Conservative Party in general elections, although I am sure that, if true, this was a traditional rather than a reasoned choice. It was always an unchallenged belief among most of the village residents, reinforced by Rollesby's elite, that the Conservatives would better represent landed and rural interests than any other party. Most of the farm labourers and allied workers in the village followed the example of their employers and voted Conservative. On the other hand, the Coles, an urban family with many family members working in industry, were more inclined to vote for the Labour or Liberal candidates. I once asked Mother why she voted Conservative when she had been brought up to follow Labour politics. Her reply, given with a wink and a smile, was that you could never be sure how anyone actually cast their vote in a secret ballot.

RELIGION

Despite grandfather's commitment to the Church of England and my early career as a choirboy, after the age of eleven I rarely attended any form of religious service. Not that I was an atheist; I did maintain a belief in some kind of powerful God-like life force and thought that the universe, and my existence as part of it, had some purpose. However, as a teenager I found church services dull and irrelevant, and many of the assumptions made in church doctrine difficult to believe. My parents were similarly unenthusiastic. The fact that I was baptised two weeks after my birth was an expedient of wartime and not in any way evidence of devotion. Undoubtedly mother was hedging her bets in case the war took a turn for the worse and I failed to survive.

Of my closest friends, Tony was the most devout: a lifelong Methodist who attended services every Sunday without fail. Occasionally I was persuaded to accompany him to special meetings, usually at a chapel close to the beach in Winterton. These I found more joyful and far better attended than the more sombre Church of England services. However, I was still uninspired by the message promoted in these meetings and joined the majority of my other friends in lethargic agnosticism. Tony, however, became even more attached to the evangelical message of Methodism and attended Billy Graham's crusade meetings in London, where he was inspired to stand on stage with the minister and proclaim his faith.

Strangely, it was religion that caused me to have my first and, perhaps, only disagreement with my grandfather. At eighteen I began my first long-term relationship with a girl I had met on the school bus. Both sets of parents acknowledged that we were old enough to begin such a relationship, and we spent a lot of time in each other's home and in the company of both families. My companion travelled every day to the St Louis High School at Great Yarmouth, a Roman Catholic school for girls. One Saturday when I was playing cricket at Rollesby, Grandfather arrived to watch and, when I was alone, took me aside for what turned out to be a serious conversation. "I do hope that you are not getting too involved with that girl," I remember him saying. "Whatever happens," he continued, "you can't marry her, you mustn't marry her. She is a Catholic." At eighteen the prospect of marriage was far from my thoughts, although my first experience of religious prejudice did stir me strongly and noisily to defend my right to make my own choices. As is the case with most teenage romances, my girlfriend and I eventually parted, but not because of any religious differences. Yet Grandfather was quite happy to present the local Methodist community with a large ornate Bible for use in their chapel near Rollesby Bridge.

Oluwole Siwoku

Some have suggested that the 1940s and 1950s were a time when a majority of the white population of Britain was racially prejudiced. I cannot say that I have any memories that would in any way confirm this opinion although, at that time, my experience of people from other races was very limited. Other than during the holiday season, it was rare for me to meet with anyone from outside Norfolk, let alone from another country or another continent. Living in a relatively isolated and self-contained village, I certainly regarded all strangers from anywhere, home or abroad, with curiosity and, sometimes, suspicion. Like my peers, I would stare at and interrogate any newcomers to our school, taking some time before accepting them as part of the community. Other than those from adjoining villages, incomers to Rollesby were never fully accepted as local no matter how long they were resident. We often held stereotypical notions about peoples from other countries and I was no exception in that regard. I marvelled at and took pride in the large regions of pink on my atlas of the world, yet was oblivious to the fact that that pink might in some people's eyes represent subjugation rather than, as I commonly believed, liberation from political, religious and social deprivation. It was always my belief that the inhabitants of these regions were happy to be part of the pink empire.

My personal experience of individuals from another race was limited to only two people, a Chinese doctor living in Great Yarmouth and an African teacher from Nigeria, both caring and intelligent men who undoubtedly greatly influenced my formative thinking. The doctor was almost revered by my mother and aunts as he had attended to my cousin, Deanna, after she had accidentally tipped a pan of boiling water over her face. His regular visits, medical skills and kind, confident manner contributed to a full recovery devoid of any obvious scarring. My only personal contact with a black person during the whole of my time in Rollesby was with Mr Oluwole Siwoku, a Nigerian teacher working at Rollesby School.

It was in the spring of 1956 that Mr Siwoku came to Rollesby. All the village children were excited on being told that a black African teacher was to spend a few weeks teaching classes at Rollesby School. Although I was by then studying at Great Yarmouth Grammar

School, I was equally excited as he was to lodge with my grandparents at Hall Cottages during this school attachment. I am not sure what I expected. My perception of a black African was derived solely from literature, the cinema and school projects on the Zulu wars and the British exploration of Africa. Some younger children even believed he would arrive dressed in a leopard's skin, capped with ostrich feathers and carrying a spear. When I eventually met him, Oluwole Siwoku turned out to be a short thin man with horn-rimmed glasses, dressed in a dark suit, grey pullover, white shirt and tie, and well polished black shoes. For transport he had brought with him a battered old bicycle that he rode sedately, his trousers held well away from the chain by a pair of cycle clips. When he spoke, he spoke in perfect BBC English and clearly found some difficulty in understanding our Broadland Norfolk dialect. His manners were impeccable and gentlemanly, and he quickly established a good relationship with my grandmother who had clearly been apprehensive about his visit. He also had endless patience with inquisitive children and in the evenings spent long periods looking through my stamp collection and explaining for me the motifs on the African stamps, particularly those from his home country, Nigeria. As promised, when he returned home to Africa he sent me a large parcel of stamps and numerous booklets about Nigeria.

At the time of his visit, the craze among those of us that gathered on the veranda of the hut was for long-distance running. In the lighter spring evenings a dozen or more children of all ages often set off from the playing field on a run around the village, usually along the Main Road, into Court Road passing the Courthouse and joining the Fleggburgh Road at Old Maid's Corner. Then, passing by the church, on to the Horse & Groom crossroads where we turned back along the Main Road to the playing field, a distance of about 2 miles. Many of the less capable runners frequently used the convenient footpaths to shorten the length of their race, not always letting the others know that they had done so. It was inevitable that Mr Siwoku would be invited to join one of our runs, which he did dressed in his suit and pullover, with a pair of white plimsolls on his feet and his trouser legs held at calf-height by his cycle clips. Our belief in the legendary running skills of the African, particularly the Zulu, as told to us in our history lessons, was shaken by the fact that he took over an hour to complete the course and arrived back at the playing field sweating profusely, followed in Pied Piper fashion by a horde of cheering under-elevens.

Nigerian teacher has fortnight at Rollesby School

Mr Oluwole Siwoku, one of the Nigerian teachers visiting Norfolk, left Rollesby School on Monday after a fortnight teaching practice and study of rural education. "He made himself very popular, both with the staff and the pupils," said the Head Teacher (Miss A.T. King).

Mr Siwoku comes from Abeokuta and was on the staff of Urhobo College, Warri, Nigeria. While at Rollesby he made a survey of the area and visited a farm, Yarmouth Waterworks Company's premises at Ormesby and the excavation on the site of the Roman settlement at Caister.

He studied all aspects of the work at Rollesby School and also paid visits to the woodwork centre at Martham School (where senior boys from Rollesby spend one session a week), to Caister Senior school (where pupils move on reaching the age of 14) and to Yarmouth Grammar School (where success in the Common Entrance Examination can take successful candidates). While in the village he stayed with Mr and Mrs W.J. Miller.

Mr Siwoku and his Nigerian colleagues will spend a further fortnight at Morley Hall, Wymondham.

Yarmouth Mercury, 11 May 1956

GIRLFRIENDS

I was fifteen before I acquired my first real girlfriend. I had certainly had crushes on many girls before then, but I had never been courageous or lucky enough to turn longing into reality. I had held hands with many girls at primary school and played postman's knock at parties but I had never had a real girlfriend. Naturally I had discussed the matter with my friends Tony and Richard, both of whom professed to be experienced in this regard and described to me in detail the intimate minutiae of their relationships. It was Tony who decided that the time had come for me to have a girlfriend and a strategy for the selection of a suitable conquest was devised. The first decision to be made was who: who did I fancy, was she available, would she be willing? After some consideration, a fifteen-year-old-girl who lived near to the school was identified as my intended target. As far as we knew she had no current boyfriend and Tony vouched for the fact that she was willing, as he claimed to have "snogged" her six months or so earlier.

Bonfire Night, 5 November, was selected as the date for the conquest. That year the village bonfire celebration was held on a field adjoining the playing field behind the school. As usual, the proceedings began at about 6.30 in the evening when the bonfire was lit and groups of parents set off rockets, Catherine wheels, Roman candles and other fireworks throwing cascades of green, red and gold sparks high into the air.

Sparklers on the end of wires were lit and given to the younger children to hold and make weird patterns against the night sky. Most of the older teenagers watched intently from a distance despite professing their lack of interest. Guided by Tony, I joined this watching group and manoeuvred myself closer to my target. Most of the teenage boys held in their pockets a number of exploding fireworks — penny bangers variously called Little Imps, Mighty Atoms, Cannons, Squibs and Jumping Jacks — which they lit with the intention of scaring the girls. Whether they were scared or not, the girls understood the game and when one of these bangers exploded, usually close behind them, they would let out the expected scream and grab hold of the best-looking boy in their vicinity. I was both relieved and surprised when my target responded to a particularly loud bang, no doubt organised by Tony, by grabbing hold of me tight around the waist and burying her head into my shoulder. I was further surprised that she continued to hold on to me well after any apparent danger had long passed. Eventually, linked together in this manner we made our way to the veranda of the hut where we joined other pairs of teenagers who also had been similarly induced to lock themselves together. That she had become a real girlfriend was confirmed when she agreed to let me walk her home. At her garden gate, we engaged in what I naively considered to be a passionate embrace and parted, agreeing to meet on the veranda of the hut the next evening. As I left, Tony, who had been shadowing me throughout the proceedings, emerged out of the darkness and congratulated me on an efficiently executed first conquest. The romance, if indeed it ever was one, lasted only for a brief period before my newly acquired girlfriend tired of my innocence and moved on to someone more experienced than I was in these matters.

Nevertheless, 5 November 1955 marked my transition from a boy to an emergent adult, the day when I finally put away my toys and childish thoughts to concentrate on the pursuit of females. I became totally addicted to kissing girls and would kiss anyone willing to engage in this activity with me anywhere and everywhere — on the back seat of the school bus, the veranda of the hut, in the back row of the cinema and behind many village halls on dance nights. It was inevitable that my parents would eventually hear of my activities and I can remember receiving a long lecture from my father about my responsibilities to study and that I was far too young to think of girlfriends. Not that I was particularly good at kissing, my technique definitely lacked finesse. A friend once asked if I had experienced French kissing, to which I answered yes, although I had no idea what he was talking about. My first experience of such kissing occurred on the back seat of the number 5 bus, returning home from a Sunday at the cinema. When I attempted to kiss my partner for that day, a young lady from Potter Heigham, I discovered a gaping void where her lips should have been and a rampant tongue attempting to knock out my back teeth. At sixteen, I found this assault on my tonsils somewhat terrifying although I proudly reported the incident to all my friends.

SEXUAL RELATIONSHIPS

In most issues relating to sex, I was dangerously ignorant. Luckily, before university and despite my best efforts, other than kissing and mild petting, my practical experience of sex was nil as my theoretical knowledge was extremely inaccurate and unsafe, derived as it was from teenage gossip and some minimal information acquired from lessons at school. I merely understood from my contemporary males that sex was the ultimate goal of all boy–girl relationships and to do "it" was the final triumph. What "it" was, what "it" entailed and what its consequences were, few of us were at all sure and "it" remained a mystery for me until well after I had moved to Leicester.

We were all well aware that boys and girls were different, and the fact that our parents took great care to try and conceal those differences guaranteed that they were well known to all of us. Most of us had only the vaguest idea why those differences existed and our parents were not forthcoming in developing our understanding. Each time I tried to initiate a conversation on the subject with my mother she would round on me and proclaim "That's dirty talk". Indeed, neither of my parents had any meaningful conversation with me regarding procreation or the problems associated with romance and sex. Having caught sight of a diagram in my biology notebook one evening, Mother exclaimed "Well, at least I won't have to tell you about the facts of life". What the renal system of a rabbit had to do with the facts of life I was not at all sure, but true to her word, apart from a warning never to bring a pregnant girl back to her home, she never did. Other than identifying those girls in the village he thought too worldly-wise for me to associate with, a list that included almost every female between sixteen and twenty, my father left all discussions on these matters to Mother.

Official sex instruction at school was limited to a lecture in biology class on the topic of human reproduction given to the third year grammar school students and repeated in the fourth year, which was based on a film strip consisting of about twenty pictures and diagrams. The first picture was of a man and a woman with a boy and a girl, naked. Despite careful scrutiny, the picture was taken at such a distance that no one could see their intimate parts in any detail. The sex bit was dispensed with diagrammatically in the next two frames and added very little to my knowledge, the remainder of the film strip concentrating on gestation and birth. Most of my actual sex instruction was delivered by older school colleagues and included many myths as well as some useful knowledge, although for an inexperienced youth it was difficult to judge which was which. Pictures of nakedness were not commonplace and any that appeared were studied in detail. One sixth form pupil, a member of a local photographic society, had acquired a picture of a naked woman taken in a life class. Using his society's photographic enlarger, he had produced a number of magnified photographs of certain parts of this woman's body which he proudly circulated among most of the senior school, although, during the enlargement process, they had become misty and indistinct to the extent that we were not at all sure what we were looking at.

What information I had about birth control was acquired informally from my peers; for parents or teachers to discuss such issues was unusual. I cannot remember any boy saying that he had received any instruction on this matter from his parents. By a process akin to osmosis, I became aware that to have sex without running the risk of a pregnancy required the use of a condom. In the 1950s, these devices were not called condoms but "rubber Johnnies" or "French letters", why I am still unsure. Neither was I totally sure what a Johnny looked like or how it was used. I was told that they could always be bought from the barber where they were normally kept inside a closed cabinet on the wall. Every time thereafter, as I sat waiting my turn in the barber's shop, I watched carefully to see if I could observe a Johnny being sold. My first real sight of a Johnny occurred on the coach returning from a Sunday cricket match. After a stop at a public house everyone began singing, happily under the influence of a few drinks. From the back seat, a blown up light-brown translucent balloon appeared which everybody proceeded to bat to and fro, up and down the coach's aisle. My uncle, clearly more knowledgeable than most of the other passengers, his face like thunder, grabbed hold of the balloon and hurled it out of the driver's window. "Why did he do that?" I asked. "'Cos it was a blown up Johnny," was the reply from the back seat.

However, I had no need for Johnnies as pragmatism, ignorance and fear proved to be very effective as deterrents to early sex. Pragmatism, as any opportunity for engaging in intimate activities was seriously limited. In our small and often overcrowded houses, even if not deliberately chaperoned, unmarried couples were rarely left alone for any length of time. Outside the house, in summer it was almost impossible to conduct any activity without the danger of being observed, and in winter the weather and a lack of street lighting proved inhibiting factors. Most teenagers were without the convenience of a car and sex on a bicycle was not a practical possibility. At home, my movements were restricted by certain house rules laid down and strictly enforced by my parents. On an ordinary weekday evening up to the age of seventeen I was expected to be in the house by nine and in bed by ten. Not that this was unreasonable as my parents were themselves in bed by ten in preparation for an early start the next morning. I could negotiate for an extension to attend an organised function such as a whist drive or a film show, but I was expected to return home immediately that activity finished, usually between ten and half past. Even the public house licensing hours were such that closing time was variously at ten or half past. Until the age of seventeen I was expected to come away from weekend dances and socials at 10.30; thereafter I could stay out much longer providing that I gave a definite and reasonable time for returning home. On one notable occasion, I abandoned my cycle for a lift on my friend Roger's motor scooter to a party in Horning. Unfortunately I had told my parents that I would be home by 11.30 but on the return journey Roger's scooter developed a problem. I eventually arrived home at one in the morning to find both my parents marching up and down Martham Road, and received a terrible telling-off from both of them before being allowed to go to bed. To their minds, by staying out so late I must have been up to no good and engine malfunction was not an acceptable excuse. I was eighteen years old at the time.

Ignorance and fear were other inhibiting factors. We were particularly fearful of getting caught, frightened by our personal ignorance and terrified of causing a pregnancy. I remember cycling home with one young lady who, when we stopped near to her house, was concerned that we might be discovered together despite the fact that nothing untoward was happening. Apparently, on a previous occasion she had been discovered in the company of a boy by the local policeman who had threatened to tell her father if he caught her in a similar situation again. The consequences of an accidental pregnancy for a single woman were horrific: for some a hasty marriage or, for those who decided to remain single, to be treated no better than lepers. When I was seventeen years old I

291

regularly met two young women of a similar age at local dances who had suffered the misfortune of unmarried pregnancies. Despite being delightful companions, they were completely ostracised by many of their contemporaries and former friends. Their loss was my gain as my two friends were great fun to be with and excellent dancers.

TEENAGE CULTURE

Clearly, the mid-1950s witnessed great changes in my life. I was no longer a child but a young man. I had put away my toys and taken up new pursuits. On reflection, it seems now that the change was not just in me, not just a natural stage in my growing up, but a general movement throughout the younger generation. Strongly influenced by trends from America, and probably assisted by the advent of television, greater wealth and big business, young people seemed no longer willing to accept growing into clones of their parents but instead developed fashions, beliefs and a culture of their own.

One area where we began to differ from our parents was in hairstyles. Up to the age of fifteen, my hairstyle was the same as my father's, a short back and sides. Every fortnight, early on a Friday evening or on a Saturday morning, depending on his work, my father and I would drive in his car to Frank Short's hairdressing salon, near Bracey's Pond on Martham Green, for a haircut. He chose Frank Short's in preference to Smith's salon in Rollesby as Frank Short was a family friend before the war. Our haricuts were similar, clipped short almost to the skin up to an inch above the ears, the top thinned with scissors and comb, then plastered with a handful of Brylcreem and combed to each side with a perfectly straight off-centre parting. Occasionally we had our hair washed and sometimes my father requested that his hair was singed with a flaming taper, for what reason I have no idea. At sixteen, much to his disgust, I wore my hair longer, still plastered thick with Brylcreem, with both sides swept to the back meeting at a line and the top curled over in a style called a Tony Curtis. I spent many an hour preening my hair in front of the living room mirror, my comb greasy and my hair stiff with Brylcreem. Frequently, the pillow on my bed was black and shiny, impregnated by this hair additive. For a while I adopted another style popular with the American forces called a crew cut, where my hair was short all over and the top cut flat like stubble on a mown cornfield. Mother preferred this style as it did not involve using hair cream and made her washday easier. However, I quickly abandoned the style when the barber suggested that to improve the look I should wet my hair before going to bed and sleep with it covered in a hairnet. As far as I was concerned, no self-respecting young male would ever adopt a hairstyle that involved wearing a hairnet.

At sixteen, I also hankered after more colourful and fashionable clothes. Until then, my casual wear had been my old grey school trousers, jacket, shirt and pullover, and, for more formal social events, the blue suit that my grandmother had bought me, despite its old-fashioned look and turn-ups that gathered dust and fluff. Influenced by the casual wear of the off-duty American servicemen in Great Yarmouth and the outrageous dress of the infamous Teddy Boys, I gradually began to adopt teenage styles: flamboyant sweaters, blue jeans, slip-on shoes, luminous green and pink socks, and narrow trouser bottoms with no turn-ups. At eighteen, I was addicted to traditional jazz and attended sessions dressed in a long black sweater, brown corduroy trousers, suede shoes and a duffle coat. I also cadged striped collarless shirts from my grandfather, adding stiff white collars attached to the shirt with studs, but no tie.

At weekends my habit was to meet up with friends in a coffee bar. When not otherwise engaged, on Saturday mornings I would travel to Yarmouth with my mother and gather with my sixth-form friends at Purdy's coffee bar, near the market. This was not a teenage-orientated coffee bar as was fashionable in London, nor a centre for the developing culture of youth with jukeboxes and musical groups playing rock 'n' roll and skiffle, but a more sedate establishment providing refreshments for tired shoppers. Situated above Purdy's bakery shop with a side entrance into the first floor of Palmer's department store, Purdy's coffee bar could seat about thirty persons around tables on fixed bench seats in five or more cubicles. Despite its old-fashioned style, it sold "frothy" Espresso coffee in shallow glass cups and became the regular Saturday morning meeting place for a dozen or more grammar school sixth formers who spent an hour or two discussing issues of the day while consuming a single cup of lukewarm coffee, much to the annoyance of many older shoppers who could not find a seat.

After coffee, most of us visited various music shops listening to and, occasionally, buying the current popular records of the day. Before 1956, I was not particularly interested in popular music. My childish tastes were limited to novelty songs such as "Sparky's Magic Piano", "The Runaway Train" and "Three Billy Goats Gruff", while my parents listened to big band music and crooners such as Bing Crosby and Frank Sinatra. In 1956 everything changed and, like most teenagers at the time, I became converted to the music of rock 'n' roll — especially as it was music to dance to, a lively energetic style of dancing primarily for young people. Thereafter, influenced by my peers, films, television and radio, particularly Radio Luxembourg, I listened avidly to the pop music of the time as well as, eventually, to the equally popular skiffle and traditional jazz.

Boom in sales of gramophone records

Yarmouth, in common with the rest of the country, is experiencing a great boom in the sales of gramophone records. Dealers in the town report that their sales are almost double those of twelve months ago.

At a leading department store where the sale of records was introduced only a year ago, the popularity of records has increased considerably. Hundreds of copies of such discs as Eddie Calvert playing "Cherry Pink Mambo" and Slim Whitman's modern version of "Rose Marie" have been sold. "Indeed, so fast has Frankie Laine's 'Cool Water' been selling that we cannot keep up with the demand", commented one salesgirl. She added that nearly all the records sold were of popular tunes. "We sell very little classical music", she said. Most shops find their best customers are teenagers and it is through them that the high sales of popular records are gained.

Yarmouth Mercury, 7 October 1955

ROCK 'N' ROLL IS HERE TO STAY

Much of the initial thrust to the promotion of rock 'n' roll was provided through the cinema, particularly in a number of films targeted at teenagers and featuring rock 'n' roll music, one of the first being the film *Rock Around the Clock* starring Bill Haley and his Comets. I can clearly remember the excitement among my friends in the autumn of 1956 when *Rock Around the Clock* was booked to be shown at the Regal Cinema on Regent Road in Great Yarmouth. We had all read in newspapers about the riots that had accompanied the showing of this film in London and elsewhere, and that teenagers had danced to the music in the aisles of various cinemas. It was, therefore, with a feeling of excitement and anticipation that a number of my school friends and I joined the long queue of young people outside the Regal Cinema, not sure what to expect. We were not disappointed as, despite the best efforts of the usherettes and the cinema management to control the teenage audience, screams and shouts greeted the appearance of the various musical stars on the screen and many couples attempted to dance to the music on the stairs and in the gangways. As a consequence of this film, Bill Haley, with his kiss curl, became an unlikely teenage hero and introduced into our vocabulary the parting phrase "See you later, alligator", to which the response was, "In a while, crocodile". *Rock Around the Clock* was immediately followed by a number of films of the same genre, popularising the music and establishing the musical reputation of many rock 'n' roll stars. Elvis Presley made his first appearance in the film *Love me Tender* which I saw at the Aquarium Cinema, a civil war drama rather than a rock 'n' roll film at which the screaming of the six girls in the front row together with their

297

attempts to jive to Elvis's slow ballad singing seemed to be somewhat incongruous and a little bit silly.

Jiving in the cinema when Rock 'n' roll film is shown

Teenage couples jived in the upper circle of the Regal Theatre on Monday evening when the rock 'n' roll musical, *Rock Around the Clock*, opened a week's run at the cinema. Throughout the film they had clapped and stamped to the rhythm and the noise often drowned the sound track.

After the last performance on Monday, a crowd of about 100 teenagers sang rock 'n' roll hits and jived in front of the theatre. They blocked the pavement and spilled out into Regent Road and slowed down the traffic. After about ten minutes the crowd was broken up by the police and dispersed into St. George's Park and the market place, singing and shouting.

Yarmouth Mercury, 23 November 1956

In 1957 I bought my first record player, a beige and red Dansette electric single play model with three speeds to accommodate 78, 45 and 33 rpm records, which I acquired second-hand for £2. The plastic playing arm contained a rotating cartridge with two needles, one for 78 rpm records and the other for 45s and 33s. Up to that time I had no means of playing records. My

Rollesby grandparents had an old-fashioned wind-up gramophone which used steel needles to play their collection of 78 rpm records, mostly of dance music from the 1930s. However, by the early 1950s it had obviously lost its appeal as it had been consigned to an outside shed together with their collection of records, relegated to become a plaything for the grandchildren. Richard was the first of my friends to own a modern electric record player and we spent many hours in the kitchen of his home listening to his record collection which included pieces such as "Coronation Scot" and "The Westminster Waltz". However, in 1956 our tastes were changed completely when he bought a long-play record entitled simply "Elvis Presley" that contained most of Elvis's early hits. We must have driven his parents mad by playing this record time after time and providing an out-of-tune vocal accompaniment to all of the tracks.

The first record that I bought to play on my newly acquired record player was a song called "Love is Strange" by Mickey and Sylvia. Thereafter, records were added at a rate of about one every fortnight, mostly popular skiffle or rock 'n' roll records especially those recorded by Lonnie Donegan, the Everly Brothers or Buddy Holly and the Crickets. These I bought from Wolsey & Wolsey on King Street where, with many of my grammar school friends, I spent many an hour reviewing the latest top twenty records in two personal listening booths designated for that purpose. Occasionally we were asked to leave by the shop manager when it became clear that we were using this

299

facility to while away the time listening to records with little intention of making a purchase.

As well as the cinema, radio and television also played an important part in popularising rock 'n' roll music through programmes targeted specifically at the young, in particular popular music programmes transmitted by Radio Luxembourg. Every Sunday without fail, I would listen in my bedroom to the week's top twenty records played on Luxembourg's late-night music programme between ten and midnight, the light turned off and my ear pressed hard against the speaker so as not to alert my parents as they slept in the next bedroom. Not that I managed to hear all twenty as the reception was variable and I regularly fell asleep well before the week's number one was played. From 1958, the highlight of my week was BBC television's Saturday evening popular music programme called 6–5 *Special*, the first of its kind, a 1950s forerunner to *Top of the Pops*. Introduced by Pete Murray, Josephine Douglas and ex-boxer Freddie Mills, and with its resident band, Don Lang and his Frantic Five, this early-evening show featured popular songs of the day and gave exposure to many young artists such as Tommy Steele, Marty Wilde and Lonnie Donegan.

Inspired by my rediscovered interest in music, Grandmother Miller gave me a small ukulele-banjo and a collection of song books. Not that I was able to overcome my total inability to make sense of musical notation, far from it, but, luckily for me, above the musical score were small diagrams giving the relevant ukulele fingering for the chords used in each song. Over a period of time I became quite proficient at playing the ukulele and, as mentioned earlier, often entertained family and friends to renditions of George Formby hits and my own variations of songs from Grandmother's song books. As I was unable to read the musical notation, I was never sure if my interpretations of those songs with which I was unfamiliar were true to the original. In 1958 I bought my first guitar and spent many hours following practice exercises from my Bert Weedon guitar tuition book. Luckily for me, although the guitar had six strings, chord fingerings on the top four strings were exactly the same as for the ukelele-banjo; I just had to learn what to do with the other two strings. I was quickly able to strum accompaniments to most of the current pop songs, facilitated by the fact that most involved the same simple sequence of four chords. However, my singing was not as accomplished as was my guitar playing. Eventually I joined four other emergent musicians and formed a skiffle group complete with guitar, drums, tea-chest bass and washboard but, despite our enthusiasm and effort, we were never considered suitably proficient to be asked to perform in public.

Rock 'n' roll and eventually jazz, as distinct from skiffle, were dance music and I loved dancing no matter whether traditional ballroom or jive. As well as those held in our local village halls, I regularly attended dances at the Floral Hall in Gorleston, staying over at Grandma Cole's house on Northgate Street in Great Yarmouth. With one or two school friends, my courage strengthened by a pint or two of Lacon's beer, I would survey the talent on the dance floor from the safety of our male only table. Together, my friends and I would join the long lines of young people dancing the cha-cha, manoeuvring ourselves into a position for engaging in conversation with females that we had previously targeted. My targets were always the best dancers and, if my luck was in, I would enjoy jiving wildly with my chosen companion causing chaos among those more traditional dancers attempting to quickstep to the upbeat music, or holding her tight against my body during a waltz or slow foxtrot. Rarely did I ever manage to follow up on these liaisons as it was imperative that I caught the last bus back to the mandatory bile bean, Aspro and glass of milk at Grandma Cole's house.

Epilogue

These are some of my earliest memories; memories of my childhood, the excitement of being a teenager and of everyday and family life in the small Broadland village of Rollesby. I have tried to describe my recollections as honestly and accurately as I can but, undoubtedly, there will be errors as memories can often deceive. I have also found that words are at times inadequate for describing in detail the memories that often remain as pictures in my head. Nevertheless, for those of my readers who were themselves children in the 1940s and 1950s, I can only hope that my words have reignited happy memories of their own childhood. For the rest of my readers, I hope that my recollections have given a glimpse of the everyday life of an ordinary working family fifty or more years ago, a time not so long in the past but in many respects very different from today.

Also available in ISIS Large Print:

A Romany in the Fields

G. Bramwell Evens

Preferring to "loiter in green meadows" discussing the balance of nature with John the Gamekeeper and learning tricks from Jerry the Poacher, Romany dons his brown tweed suit and sets off on a journey through the seasons of the countryside. Along the way, we learn about the bravery of mother hares and how moles store worms, and watch lambs have their first taste of milk. We also see how the countryside changes from one season to another, from crisp snow to the rich colours of autumn.

ISBN 0-7531-9316-7 (hb)
ISBN 0-7531-9317-5 (pb)

Walking In My Sleep

Jane Chichester

Untroubled by any formal education or adult supervision, Jane fills her days with her animals, imaginary companions and the eccentric people who live or work on the farm. She observes her glamorous parents' parties with a critical eye, but they are not part of her life.

When war breaks out, this peaceful existence is shattered by the arrival of a family of female cousins who move in for the duration. They bring with them a governess and, therefore, discipline, timetables and regular meals. This enchanting book, sometimes sad and sometimes hilarious, tells how she comes to terms with an invasion, which she sees as bad as any going on across the Channel.

ISBN 0-7531-9322-1 (hb)
ISBN 0-7531-9323-X (pb)

A Midhurst Lad

Ronald E. Boxall

Although poverty and illness marred his young life, the author's sense of mischief and humour shine through this charming childhood autobiography.

Born into the Boxall family in 1924, Ronald was brought up in Duck Lane, Midhurst, at that time an address synonymous with hardship. The tale of "the average life of an average boy born of poor parents, who lived under slum conditions, yet dwelt in the centre of a tiny and pretty town set in a near paradise of pastoral and sylvan delights". Ronald tells his story with natural wit and clarity, sharing his memories of a bygone age.

ISBN 0-7531-9320-5 (hb)
ISBN 0-7531-9321-3 (pb)

Down the Cobbled Stones

John Lea

A Cheshire farmer born and bred, John Lea was the youngest of a family of four, born on a small tenanted farm in Mid-Cheshire in 1935.

His childhood memories are of the tough times in the 1920s and 1930s as his father fought to keep the farm alive. There are tales of horses, water mills and the "Smithy", the exciting and profitable war years and above all his love of his life and the countryside in which he made his home.

John was struck down by polio at the age of twenty, and left severely disabled as a resul. After a slow recovery, he eventually married and set about building the life that he had always dreamt of.

ISBN 0-7531-9300-0 **(hb)**
ISBN 0-7531-9301-9 **(pb)**